C-791   CAREER EXAMINATION SERIES

This is your
PASSBOOK for...

Senior Sewage Treatment Worker

Test Preparation Study Guide
Questions & Answers

COPYRIGHT NOTICE

This book is SOLELY intended for, is sold ONLY to, and its use is RESTRICTED to individual, bona fide applicants or candidates who qualify by virtue of having seriously filed applications for appropriate license, certificate, professional and/or promotional advancement, higher school matriculation, scholarship, or other legitimate requirements of education and/or governmental authorities.

This book is NOT intended for use, class instruction, tutoring, training, duplication, copying, reprinting, excerption, or adaptation, etc., by:

1) Other publishers
2) Proprietors and/or Instructors of "Coaching" and/or Preparatory Courses
3) Personnel and/or Training Divisions of commercial, industrial, and governmental organizations
4) Schools, colleges, or universities and/or their departments and staffs, including teachers and other personnel
5) Testing Agencies or Bureaus
6) Study groups which seek by the purchase of a single volume to copy and/or duplicate and/or adapt this material for use by the group as a whole without having purchased individual volumes for each of the members of the group
7) Et al.

Such persons would be in violation of appropriate Federal and State statutes.

PROVISION OF LICENSING AGREEMENTS – Recognized educational, commercial, industrial, and governmental institutions and organizations, and others legitimately engaged in educational pursuits, including training, testing, and measurement activities, may address request for a licensing agreement to the copyright owners, who will determine whether, and under what conditions, including fees and charges, the materials in this book may be used them. In other words, a licensing facility exists for the legitimate use of the material in this book on other than an individual basis. However, it is asseverated and affirmed here that the material in this book CANNOT be used without the receipt of the express permission of such a licensing agreement from the Publishers. Inquiries re licensing should be addressed to the company, attention rights and permissions department.

All rights reserved, including the right of reproduction in whole or in part, in any form or by any means, electronic or mechanical, including photocopying, recording, or by any information storage and retrieval system, without permission in writing from the Publisher.

Copyright © 2024 by
National Learning Corporation

212 Michael Drive, Syosset, NY 11791
(516) 921-8888 • www.passbooks.com
E-mail: info@passbooks.com

PUBLISHED IN THE UNITED STATES OF AMERICA

PASSBOOK® SERIES

THE *PASSBOOK® SERIES* has been created to prepare applicants and candidates for the ultimate academic battlefield – the examination room.

At some time in our lives, each and every one of us may be required to take an examination – for validation, matriculation, admission, qualification, registration, certification, or licensure.

Based on the assumption that every applicant or candidate has met the basic formal educational standards, has taken the required number of courses, and read the necessary texts, the *PASSBOOK® SERIES* furnishes the one special preparation which may assure passing with confidence, instead of failing with insecurity. Examination questions – together with answers – are furnished as the basic vehicle for study so that the mysteries of the examination and its compounding difficulties may be eliminated or diminished by a sure method.

This book is meant to help you pass your examination provided that you qualify and are serious in your objective.

The entire field is reviewed through the huge store of content information which is succinctly presented through a provocative and challenging approach – the question-and-answer method.

A climate of success is established by furnishing the correct answers at the end of each test.

You soon learn to recognize types of questions, forms of questions, and patterns of questioning. You may even begin to anticipate expected outcomes.

You perceive that many questions are repeated or adapted so that you can gain acute insights, which may enable you to score many sure points.

You learn how to confront new questions, or types of questions, and to attack them confidently and work out the correct answers.

You note objectives and emphases, and recognize pitfalls and dangers, so that you may make positive educational adjustments.

Moreover, you are kept fully informed in relation to new concepts, methods, practices, and directions in the field.

You discover that you are actually taking the examination all the time: you are preparing for the examination by "taking" an examination, not by reading extraneous and/or supererogatory textbooks.

In short, this PASSBOOK®, used directedly, should be an important factor in helping you to pass your test.

SENIOR SEWAGE TREATMENT WORKER

DUTIES
Senior Sewage Treatment Workers assist and supervise subordinates who perform the following duties when necessary: operate, maintain and repair machinery, equipment and structures in wastewater treatment plants, pumping stations, intercepting sewers, sludge treatment and disposal facilities and associated equipment and facilities; take samples and test sewage. All Senior Sewage Treatment Workers perform related work.

EXAMPLES OF TYPICAL TASKS
Supervises and assists in the maintenance and repairs of pumps, sewage screens, blowers, compressors, air filters, and other equipment and auxiliaries found in a sewage treatment plant. Supervises the work of other employees. Prepares reports.

TESTS
The written test will be of the multiple-choice type and may include questions on supervisory ability including training; knowledge of sewage treatment plants, operations, processes, and equipment; knowledge of maintenance and repairs to sewage treatment plants and equipment; reports and record keeping; basic arithmetic; safety; basic technical reading comprehension; interpretation of sewage treatment plant instrument readings and other related areas.

HOW TO TAKE A TEST

I. YOU MUST PASS AN EXAMINATION

A. *WHAT EVERY CANDIDATE SHOULD KNOW*

Examination applicants often ask us for help in preparing for the written test. What can I study in advance? What kinds of questions will be asked? How will the test be given? How will the papers be graded?

As an applicant for a civil service examination, you may be wondering about some of these things. Our purpose here is to suggest effective methods of advance study and to describe civil service examinations.

Your chances for success on this examination can be increased if you know how to prepare. Those "pre-examination jitters" can be reduced if you know what to expect. You can even experience an adventure in good citizenship if you know why civil service exams are given.

B. *WHY ARE CIVIL SERVICE EXAMINATIONS GIVEN?*

Civil service examinations are important to you in two ways. As a citizen, you want public jobs filled by employees who know how to do their work. As a job seeker, you want a fair chance to compete for that job on an equal footing with other candidates. The best-known means of accomplishing this two-fold goal is the competitive examination.

Exams are widely publicized throughout the nation. They may be administered for jobs in federal, state, city, municipal, town or village governments or agencies.

Any citizen may apply, with some limitations, such as the age or residence of applicants. Your experience and education may be reviewed to see whether you meet the requirements for the particular examination. When these requirements exist, they are reasonable and applied consistently to all applicants. Thus, a competitive examination may cause you some uneasiness now, but it is your privilege and safeguard.

C. *HOW ARE CIVIL SERVICE EXAMS DEVELOPED?*

Examinations are carefully written by trained technicians who are specialists in the field known as "psychological measurement," in consultation with recognized authorities in the field of work that the test will cover. These experts recommend the subject matter areas or skills to be tested; only those knowledges or skills important to your success on the job are included. The most reliable books and source materials available are used as references. Together, the experts and technicians judge the difficulty level of the questions.

Test technicians know how to phrase questions so that the problem is clearly stated. Their ethics do not permit "trick" or "catch" questions. Questions may have been tried out on sample groups, or subjected to statistical analysis, to determine their usefulness.

Written tests are often used in combination with performance tests, ratings of training and experience, and oral interviews. All of these measures combine to form the best-known means of finding the right person for the right job.

II. HOW TO PASS THE WRITTEN TEST

A. NATURE OF THE EXAMINATION

To prepare intelligently for civil service examinations, you should know how they differ from school examinations you have taken. In school you were assigned certain definite pages to read or subjects to cover. The examination questions were quite detailed and usually emphasized memory. Civil service exams, on the other hand, try to discover your present ability to perform the duties of a position, plus your potentiality to learn these duties. In other words, a civil service exam attempts to predict how successful you will be. Questions cover such a broad area that they cannot be as minute and detailed as school exam questions.

In the public service similar kinds of work, or positions, are grouped together in one "class." This process is known as *position-classification*. All the positions in a class are paid according to the salary range for that class. One class title covers all of these positions, and they are all tested by the same examination.

B. FOUR BASIC STEPS

1) Study the announcement

How, then, can you know what subjects to study? Our best answer is: "Learn as much as possible about the class of positions for which you've applied." The exam will test the knowledge, skills and abilities needed to do the work.

Your most valuable source of information about the position you want is the official exam announcement. This announcement lists the training and experience qualifications. Check these standards and apply only if you come reasonably close to meeting them.

The brief description of the position in the examination announcement offers some clues to the subjects which will be tested. Think about the job itself. Review the duties in your mind. Can you perform them, or are there some in which you are rusty? Fill in the blank spots in your preparation.

Many jurisdictions preview the written test in the exam announcement by including a section called "Knowledge and Abilities Required," "Scope of the Examination," or some similar heading. Here you will find out specifically what fields will be tested.

2) Review your own background

Once you learn in general what the position is all about, and what you need to know to do the work, ask yourself which subjects you already know fairly well and which need improvement. You may wonder whether to concentrate on improving your strong areas or on building some background in your fields of weakness. When the announcement has specified "some knowledge" or "considerable knowledge," or has used adjectives like "beginning principles of…" or "advanced … methods," you can get a clue as to the number and difficulty of questions to be asked in any given field. More questions, and hence broader coverage, would be included for those subjects which are more important in the work. Now weigh your strengths and weaknesses against the job requirements and prepare accordingly.

3) Determine the level of the position

Another way to tell how intensively you should prepare is to understand the level of the job for which you are applying. Is it the entering level? In other words, is this the position in which beginners in a field of work are hired? Or is it an intermediate or advanced level? Sometimes this is indicated by such words as "Junior" or "Senior" in the class title. Other jurisdictions use Roman numerals to designate the level – Clerk I, Clerk II, for example. The word "Supervisor" sometimes appears in the title. If the level is not indicated by the title, check the description of duties. Will you be working under very close supervision, or will you have responsibility for independent decisions in this work?

4) Choose appropriate study materials

Now that you know the subjects to be examined and the relative amount of each subject to be covered, you can choose suitable study materials. For beginning level jobs, or even advanced ones, if you have a pronounced weakness in some aspect of your training, read a modern, standard textbook in that field. Be sure it is up to date and has general coverage. Such books are normally available at your library, and the librarian will be glad to help you locate one. For entry-level positions, questions of appropriate difficulty are chosen – neither highly advanced questions, nor those too simple. Such questions require careful thought but not advanced training.

If the position for which you are applying is technical or advanced, you will read more advanced, specialized material. If you are already familiar with the basic principles of your field, elementary textbooks would waste your time. Concentrate on advanced textbooks and technical periodicals. Think through the concepts and review difficult problems in your field.

These are all general sources. You can get more ideas on your own initiative, following these leads. For example, training manuals and publications of the government agency which employs workers in your field can be useful, particularly for technical and professional positions. A letter or visit to the government department involved may result in more specific study suggestions, and certainly will provide you with a more definite idea of the exact nature of the position you are seeking.

III. KINDS OF TESTS

Tests are used for purposes other than measuring knowledge and ability to perform specified duties. For some positions, it is equally important to test ability to make adjustments to new situations or to profit from training. In others, basic mental abilities not dependent on information are essential. Questions which test these things may not appear as pertinent to the duties of the position as those which test for knowledge and information. Yet they are often highly important parts of a fair examination. For very general questions, it is almost impossible to help you direct your study efforts. What we can do is to point out some of the more common of these general abilities needed in public service positions and describe some typical questions.

1) General information

Broad, general information has been found useful for predicting job success in some kinds of work. This is tested in a variety of ways, from vocabulary lists to questions about current events. Basic background in some field of work, such as sociology or economics, may be sampled in a group of questions. Often these are principles which have become familiar to most persons through exposure rather than through formal training. It is difficult to advise you how to study for these questions; being alert to the world around you is our best suggestion.

2) Verbal ability

An example of an ability needed in many positions is verbal or language ability. Verbal ability is, in brief, the ability to use and understand words. Vocabulary and grammar tests are typical measures of this ability. Reading comprehension or paragraph interpretation questions are common in many kinds of civil service tests. You are given a paragraph of written material and asked to find its central meaning.

3) Numerical ability

Number skills can be tested by the familiar arithmetic problem, by checking paired lists of numbers to see which are alike and which are different, or by interpreting charts and graphs. In the latter test, a graph may be printed in the test booklet which you are asked to use as the basis for answering questions.

4) Observation

A popular test for law-enforcement positions is the observation test. A picture is shown to you for several minutes, then taken away. Questions about the picture test your ability to observe both details and larger elements.

5) Following directions

In many positions in the public service, the employee must be able to carry out written instructions dependably and accurately. You may be given a chart with several columns, each column listing a variety of information. The questions require you to carry out directions involving the information given in the chart.

6) Skills and aptitudes

Performance tests effectively measure some manual skills and aptitudes. When the skill is one in which you are trained, such as typing or shorthand, you can practice. These tests are often very much like those given in business school or high school courses. For many of the other skills and aptitudes, however, no short-time preparation can be made. Skills and abilities natural to you or that you have developed throughout your lifetime are being tested.

Many of the general questions just described provide all the data needed to answer the questions and ask you to use your reasoning ability to find the answers. Your best preparation for these tests, as well as for tests of facts and ideas, is to be at your physical and mental best. You, no doubt, have your own methods of getting into an exam-taking mood and keeping "in shape." The next section lists some ideas on this subject.

IV. KINDS OF QUESTIONS

Only rarely is the "essay" question, which you answer in narrative form, used in civil service tests. Civil service tests are usually of the short-answer type. Full instructions for answering these questions will be given to you at the examination. But in case this is your first experience with short-answer questions and separate answer sheets, here is what you need to know:

1) Multiple-choice Questions

Most popular of the short-answer questions is the "multiple choice" or "best answer" question. It can be used, for example, to test for factual knowledge, ability to solve problems or judgment in meeting situations found at work.

A multiple-choice question is normally one of three types—

- It can begin with an incomplete statement followed by several possible endings. You are to find the one ending which *best* completes the statement, although some of the others may not be entirely wrong.
- It can also be a complete statement in the form of a question which is answered by choosing one of the statements listed.

- It can be in the form of a problem – again you select the best answer.

Here is an example of a multiple-choice question with a discussion which should give you some clues as to the method for choosing the right answer:

When an employee has a complaint about his assignment, the action which will *best* help him overcome his difficulty is to
- A. discuss his difficulty with his coworkers
- B. take the problem to the head of the organization
- C. take the problem to the person who gave him the assignment
- D. say nothing to anyone about his complaint

In answering this question, you should study each of the choices to find which is best. Consider choice "A" – Certainly an employee may discuss his complaint with fellow employees, but no change or improvement can result, and the complaint remains unresolved. Choice "B" is a poor choice since the head of the organization probably does not know what assignment you have been given, and taking your problem to him is known as "going over the head" of the supervisor. The supervisor, or person who made the assignment, is the person who can clarify it or correct any injustice. Choice "C" is, therefore, correct. To say nothing, as in choice "D," is unwise. Supervisors have and interest in knowing the problems employees are facing, and the employee is seeking a solution to his problem.

2) True/False Questions

The "true/false" or "right/wrong" form of question is sometimes used. Here a complete statement is given. Your job is to decide whether the statement is right or wrong.

SAMPLE: A roaming cell-phone call to a nearby city costs less than a non-roaming call to a distant city.

This statement is wrong, or false, since roaming calls are more expensive.

This is not a complete list of all possible question forms, although most of the others are variations of these common types. You will always get complete directions for answering questions. Be sure you understand *how* to mark your answers – ask questions until you do.

V. RECORDING YOUR ANSWERS

Computer terminals are used more and more today for many different kinds of exams.

For an examination with very few applicants, you may be told to record your answers in the test booklet itself. Separate answer sheets are much more common. If this separate answer sheet is to be scored by machine – and this is often the case – it is highly important that you mark your answers correctly in order to get credit.

An electronic scoring machine is often used in civil service offices because of the speed with which papers can be scored. Machine-scored answer sheets must be marked with a pencil, which will be given to you. This pencil has a high graphite content which responds to the electronic scoring machine. As a matter of fact, stray dots may register as answers, so do not let your pencil rest on the answer sheet while you are pondering the correct answer. Also, if your pencil lead breaks or is otherwise defective, ask for another.

Since the answer sheet will be dropped in a slot in the scoring machine, be careful not to bend the corners or get the paper crumpled.

The answer sheet normally has five vertical columns of numbers, with 30 numbers to a column. These numbers correspond to the question numbers in your test booklet. After each number, going across the page are four or five pairs of dotted lines. These short dotted lines have small letters or numbers above them. The first two pairs may also have a "T" or "F" above the letters. This indicates that the first two pairs only are to be used if the questions are of the true-false type. If the questions are multiple choice, disregard the "T" and "F" and pay attention only to the small letters or numbers.

Answer your questions in the manner of the sample that follows:

32. The largest city in the United States is
    A. Washington, D.C.
    B. New York City
    C. Chicago
    D. Detroit
    E. San Francisco

1) Choose the answer you think is best. (New York City is the largest, so "B" is correct.)
2) Find the row of dotted lines numbered the same as the question you are answering. (Find row number 32)
3) Find the pair of dotted lines corresponding to the answer. (Find the pair of lines under the mark "B.")
4) Make a solid black mark between the dotted lines.

VI. BEFORE THE TEST

Common sense will help you find procedures to follow to get ready for an examination. Too many of us, however, overlook these sensible measures. Indeed, nervousness and fatigue have been found to be the most serious reasons why applicants fail to do their best on civil service tests. Here is a list of reminders:

- Begin your preparation early – Don't wait until the last minute to go scurrying around for books and materials or to find out what the position is all about.
- Prepare continuously – An hour a night for a week is better than an all-night cram session. This has been definitely established. What is more, a night a week for a month will return better dividends than crowding your study into a shorter period of time.
- Locate the place of the exam – You have been sent a notice telling you when and where to report for the examination. If the location is in a different town or otherwise unfamiliar to you, it would be well to inquire the best route and learn something about the building.
- Relax the night before the test – Allow your mind to rest. Do not study at all that night. Plan some mild recreation or diversion; then go to bed early and get a good night's sleep.
- Get up early enough to make a leisurely trip to the place for the test – This way unforeseen events, traffic snarls, unfamiliar buildings, etc. will not upset you.
- Dress comfortably – A written test is not a fashion show. You will be known by number and not by name, so wear something comfortable.

- Leave excess paraphernalia at home – Shopping bags and odd bundles will get in your way. You need bring only the items mentioned in the official notice you received; usually everything you need is provided. Do not bring reference books to the exam. They will only confuse those last minutes and be taken away from you when in the test room.
- Arrive somewhat ahead of time – If because of transportation schedules you must get there very early, bring a newspaper or magazine to take your mind off yourself while waiting.
- Locate the examination room – When you have found the proper room, you will be directed to the seat or part of the room where you will sit. Sometimes you are given a sheet of instructions to read while you are waiting. Do not fill out any forms until you are told to do so; just read them and be prepared.
- Relax and prepare to listen to the instructions
- If you have any physical problem that may keep you from doing your best, be sure to tell the test administrator. If you are sick or in poor health, you really cannot do your best on the exam. You can come back and take the test some other time.

VII. AT THE TEST

The day of the test is here and you have the test booklet in your hand. The temptation to get going is very strong. Caution! There is more to success than knowing the right answers. You must know how to identify your papers and understand variations in the type of short-answer question used in this particular examination. Follow these suggestions for maximum results from your efforts:

1) Cooperate with the monitor

The test administrator has a duty to create a situation in which you can be as much at ease as possible. He will give instructions, tell you when to begin, check to see that you are marking your answer sheet correctly, and so on. He is not there to guard you, although he will see that your competitors do not take unfair advantage. He wants to help you do your best.

2) Listen to all instructions

Don't jump the gun! Wait until you understand all directions. In most civil service tests you get more time than you need to answer the questions. So don't be in a hurry. Read each word of instructions until you clearly understand the meaning. Study the examples, listen to all announcements and follow directions. Ask questions if you do not understand what to do.

3) Identify your papers

Civil service exams are usually identified by number only. You will be assigned a number; you must not put your name on your test papers. Be sure to copy your number correctly. Since more than one exam may be given, copy your exact examination title.

4) Plan your time

Unless you are told that a test is a "speed" or "rate of work" test, speed itself is usually not important. Time enough to answer all the questions will be provided, but this does not mean that you have all day. An overall time limit has been set. Divide the total time (in minutes) by the number of questions to determine the approximate time you have for each question.

5) Do not linger over difficult questions

If you come across a difficult question, mark it with a paper clip (useful to have along) and come back to it when you have been through the booklet. One caution if you do this – be sure to skip a number on your answer sheet as well. Check often to be sure that you have not lost your place and that you are marking in the row numbered the same as the question you are answering.

6) Read the questions

Be sure you know what the question asks! Many capable people are unsuccessful because they failed to *read* the questions correctly.

7) Answer all questions

Unless you have been instructed that a penalty will be deducted for incorrect answers, it is better to guess than to omit a question.

8) Speed tests

It is often better NOT to guess on speed tests. It has been found that on timed tests people are tempted to spend the last few seconds before time is called in marking answers at random – without even reading them – in the hope of picking up a few extra points. To discourage this practice, the instructions may warn you that your score will be "corrected" for guessing. That is, a penalty will be applied. The incorrect answers will be deducted from the correct ones, or some other penalty formula will be used.

9) Review your answers

If you finish before time is called, go back to the questions you guessed or omitted to give them further thought. Review other answers if you have time.

10) Return your test materials

If you are ready to leave before others have finished or time is called, take ALL your materials to the monitor and leave quietly. Never take any test material with you. The monitor can discover whose papers are not complete, and taking a test booklet may be grounds for disqualification.

VIII. EXAMINATION TECHNIQUES

1) Read the general instructions carefully. These are usually printed on the first page of the exam booklet. As a rule, these instructions refer to the timing of the examination; the fact that you should not start work until the signal and must stop work at a signal, etc. If there are any *special* instructions, such as a choice of questions to be answered, make sure that you note this instruction carefully.

2) When you are ready to start work on the examination, that is as soon as the signal has been given, read the instructions to each question booklet, underline any key words or phrases, such as *least, best, outline, describe* and the like. In this way you will tend to answer as requested rather than discover on reviewing your paper that you *listed without describing*, that you selected the *worst* choice rather than the *best* choice, etc.

3) If the examination is of the objective or multiple-choice type – that is, each question will also give a series of possible answers: A, B, C or D, and you are called upon to select the best answer and write the letter next to that answer on your answer paper – it is advisable to start answering each question in turn. There may be anywhere from 50 to 100 such questions in the three or four hours allotted and you can see how much time would be taken if you read through all the questions before beginning to answer any. Furthermore, if you come across a question or group of questions which you know would be difficult to answer, it would undoubtedly affect your handling of all the other questions.

4) If the examination is of the essay type and contains but a few questions, it is a moot point as to whether you should read all the questions before starting to answer any one. Of course, if you are given a choice – say five out of seven and the like – then it is essential to read all the questions so you can eliminate the two that are most difficult. If, however, you are asked to answer all the questions, there may be danger in trying to answer the easiest one first because you may find that you will spend too much time on it. The best technique is to answer the first question, then proceed to the second, etc.

5) Time your answers. Before the exam begins, write down the time it started, then add the time allowed for the examination and write down the time it must be completed, then divide the time available somewhat as follows:
    - If 3-1/2 hours are allowed, that would be 210 minutes. If you have 80 objective-type questions, that would be an average of 2-1/2 minutes per question. Allow yourself no more than 2 minutes per question, or a total of 160 minutes, which will permit about 50 minutes to review.
    - If for the time allotment of 210 minutes there are 7 essay questions to answer, that would average about 30 minutes a question. Give yourself only 25 minutes per question so that you have about 35 minutes to review.

6) The most important instruction is to *read each question* and make sure you know what is wanted. The second most important instruction is to *time yourself properly* so that you answer every question. The third most important instruction is to *answer every question*. Guess if you have to but include something for each question. Remember that you will receive no credit for a blank and will probably receive some credit if you write something in answer to an essay question. If you guess a letter – say "B" for a multiple-choice question – you may have guessed right. If you leave a blank as an answer to a multiple-choice question, the examiners may respect your feelings but it will not add a point to your score. Some exams may penalize you for wrong answers, so in such cases *only*, you may not want to guess unless you have some basis for your answer.

7) Suggestions
    a. Objective-type questions
        1. Examine the question booklet for proper sequence of pages and questions
        2. Read all instructions carefully
        3. Skip any question which seems too difficult; return to it after all other questions have been answered
        4. Apportion your time properly; do not spend too much time on any single question or group of questions

5. Note and underline key words – *all, most, fewest, least, best, worst, same, opposite*, etc.
6. Pay particular attention to negatives
7. Note unusual option, e.g., unduly long, short, complex, different or similar in content to the body of the question
8. Observe the use of "hedging" words – *probably, may, most likely*, etc.
9. Make sure that your answer is put next to the same number as the question
10. Do not second-guess unless you have good reason to believe the second answer is definitely more correct
11. Cross out original answer if you decide another answer is more accurate; do not erase until you are ready to hand your paper in
12. Answer all questions; guess unless instructed otherwise
13. Leave time for review

b. Essay questions
1. Read each question carefully
2. Determine exactly what is wanted. Underline key words or phrases.
3. Decide on outline or paragraph answer
4. Include many different points and elements unless asked to develop any one or two points or elements
5. Show impartiality by giving pros and cons unless directed to select one side only
6. Make and write down any assumptions you find necessary to answer the questions
7. Watch your English, grammar, punctuation and choice of words
8. Time your answers; don't crowd material

8) Answering the essay question

Most essay questions can be answered by framing the specific response around several key words or ideas. Here are a few such key words or ideas:

M's: manpower, materials, methods, money, management
P's: purpose, program, policy, plan, procedure, practice, problems, pitfalls, personnel, public relations

a. Six basic steps in handling problems:
1. Preliminary plan and background development
2. Collect information, data and facts
3. Analyze and interpret information, data and facts
4. Analyze and develop solutions as well as make recommendations
5. Prepare report and sell recommendations
6. Install recommendations and follow up effectiveness

b. Pitfalls to avoid
1. *Taking things for granted* – A statement of the situation does not necessarily imply that each of the elements is necessarily true; for example, a complaint may be invalid and biased so that all that can be taken for granted is that a complaint has been registered

2. *Considering only one side of a situation* – Wherever possible, indicate several alternatives and then point out the reasons you selected the best one
3. *Failing to indicate follow up* – Whenever your answer indicates action on your part, make certain that you will take proper follow-up action to see how successful your recommendations, procedures or actions turn out to be
4. *Taking too long in answering any single question* – Remember to time your answers properly

IX. AFTER THE TEST

Scoring procedures differ in detail among civil service jurisdictions although the general principles are the same. Whether the papers are hand-scored or graded by machine we have described, they are nearly always graded by number. That is, the person who marks the paper knows only the number – never the name – of the applicant. Not until all the papers have been graded will they be matched with names. If other tests, such as training and experience or oral interview ratings have been given, scores will be combined. Different parts of the examination usually have different weights. For example, the written test might count 60 percent of the final grade, and a rating of training and experience 40 percent. In many jurisdictions, veterans will have a certain number of points added to their grades.

After the final grade has been determined, the names are placed in grade order and an eligible list is established. There are various methods for resolving ties between those who get the same final grade – probably the most common is to place first the name of the person whose application was received first. Job offers are made from the eligible list in the order the names appear on it. You will be notified of your grade and your rank as soon as all these computations have been made. This will be done as rapidly as possible.

People who are found to meet the requirements in the announcement are called "eligibles." Their names are put on a list of eligible candidates. An eligible's chances of getting a job depend on how high he stands on this list and how fast agencies are filling jobs from the list.

When a job is to be filled from a list of eligibles, the agency asks for the names of people on the list of eligibles for that job. When the civil service commission receives this request, it sends to the agency the names of the three people highest on this list. Or, if the job to be filled has specialized requirements, the office sends the agency the names of the top three persons who meet these requirements from the general list.

The appointing officer makes a choice from among the three people whose names were sent to him. If the selected person accepts the appointment, the names of the others are put back on the list to be considered for future openings.

That is the rule in hiring from all kinds of eligible lists, whether they are for typist, carpenter, chemist, or something else. For every vacancy, the appointing officer has his choice of any one of the top three eligibles on the list. This explains why the person whose name is on top of the list sometimes does not get an appointment when some of the persons lower on the list do. If the appointing officer chooses the second or third eligible, the No. 1 eligible does not get a job at once, but stays on the list until he is appointed or the list is terminated.

X. HOW TO PASS THE INTERVIEW TEST

The examination for which you applied requires an oral interview test. You have already taken the written test and you are now being called for the interview test – the final part of the formal examination.

You may think that it is not possible to prepare for an interview test and that there are no procedures to follow during an interview. Our purpose is to point out some things you can do in advance that will help you and some good rules to follow and pitfalls to avoid while you are being interviewed.

What is an interview supposed to test?

The written examination is designed to test the technical knowledge and competence of the candidate; the oral is designed to evaluate intangible qualities, not readily measured otherwise, and to establish a list showing the relative fitness of each candidate – as measured against his competitors – for the position sought. Scoring is not on the basis of "right" and "wrong," but on a sliding scale of values ranging from "not passable" to "outstanding." As a matter of fact, it is possible to achieve a relatively low score without a single "incorrect" answer because of evident weakness in the qualities being measured.

Occasionally, an examination may consist entirely of an oral test – either an individual or a group oral. In such cases, information is sought concerning the technical knowledges and abilities of the candidate, since there has been no written examination for this purpose. More commonly, however, an oral test is used to supplement a written examination.

Who conducts interviews?

The composition of oral boards varies among different jurisdictions. In nearly all, a representative of the personnel department serves as chairman. One of the members of the board may be a representative of the department in which the candidate would work. In some cases, "outside experts" are used, and, frequently, a businessman or some other representative of the general public is asked to serve. Labor and management or other special groups may be represented. The aim is to secure the services of experts in the appropriate field.

However the board is composed, it is a good idea (and not at all improper or unethical) to ascertain in advance of the interview who the members are and what groups they represent. When you are introduced to them, you will have some idea of their backgrounds and interests, and at least you will not stutter and stammer over their names.

What should be done before the interview?

While knowledge about the board members is useful and takes some of the surprise element out of the interview, there is other preparation which is more substantive. It *is* possible to prepare for an oral interview – in several ways:

1) Keep a copy of your application and review it carefully before the interview

This may be the only document before the oral board, and the starting point of the interview. Know what education and experience you have listed there, and the sequence and dates of all of it. Sometimes the board will ask you to review the highlights of your experience for them; you should not have to hem and haw doing it.

2) Study the class specification and the examination announcement

Usually, the oral board has one or both of these to guide them. The qualities, characteristics or knowledges required by the position sought are stated in these documents. They offer valuable clues as to the nature of the oral interview. For example, if the job involves supervisory responsibilities, the announcement will usually indicate that knowledge of modern supervisory methods and the qualifications of the candidate as a supervisor will be tested. If so, you can expect such questions, frequently in the form of a hypothetical situation which you are expected to solve. NEVER go into an oral without knowledge of the duties and responsibilities of the job you seek.

3) Think through each qualification required

Try to visualize the kind of questions you would ask if you were a board member. How well could you answer them? Try especially to appraise your own knowledge and background in each area, *measured against the job sought*, and identify any areas in which you are weak. Be critical and realistic – do not flatter yourself.

4) Do some general reading in areas in which you feel you may be weak

For example, if the job involves supervision and your past experience has NOT, some general reading in supervisory methods and practices, particularly in the field of human relations, might be useful. Do NOT study agency procedures or detailed manuals. The oral board will be testing your understanding and capacity, not your memory.

5) Get a good night's sleep and watch your general health and mental attitude

You will want a clear head at the interview. Take care of a cold or any other minor ailment, and of course, no hangovers.

What should be done on the day of the interview?

Now comes the day of the interview itself. Give yourself plenty of time to get there. Plan to arrive somewhat ahead of the scheduled time, particularly if your appointment is in the fore part of the day. If a previous candidate fails to appear, the board might be ready for you a bit early. By early afternoon an oral board is almost invariably behind schedule if there are many candidates, and you may have to wait. Take along a book or magazine to read, or your application to review, but leave any extraneous material in the waiting room when you go in for your interview. In any event, relax and compose yourself.

The matter of dress is important. The board is forming impressions about you – from your experience, your manners, your attitude, and your appearance. Give your personal appearance careful attention. Dress your best, but not your flashiest. Choose conservative, appropriate clothing, and be sure it is immaculate. This is a business interview, and your appearance should indicate that you regard it as such. Besides, being well groomed and properly dressed will help boost your confidence.

Sooner or later, someone will call your name and escort you into the interview room. *This is it.* From here on you are on your own. It is too late for any more preparation. But remember, you asked for this opportunity to prove your fitness, and you are here because your request was granted.

What happens when you go in?

The usual sequence of events will be as follows: The clerk (who is often the board stenographer) will introduce you to the chairman of the oral board, who will introduce you to the other members of the board. Acknowledge the introductions before you sit down. Do not be surprised if you find a microphone facing you or a stenotypist sitting by. Oral interviews are usually recorded in the event of an appeal or other review.

Usually the chairman of the board will open the interview by reviewing the highlights of your education and work experience from your application – primarily for the benefit of the other members of the board, as well as to get the material into the record. Do not interrupt or comment unless there is an error or significant misinterpretation; if that is the case, do not hesitate. But do not quibble about insignificant matters. Also, he will usually ask you some question about your education, experience or your present job – partly to get you to start talking and to establish the interviewing "rapport." He may start the actual questioning, or turn it over to one of the other members. Frequently, each member undertakes the questioning on a particular area, one in which he is perhaps most competent, so you can expect each member to participate in the examination. Because time is limited, you may also expect some rather abrupt switches in the direction the questioning takes, so do not be upset by it. Normally, a board member will not pursue a single line of questioning unless he discovers a particular strength or weakness.

After each member has participated, the chairman will usually ask whether any member has any further questions, then will ask you if you have anything you wish to add. Unless you are expecting this question, it may floor you. Worse, it may start you off on an extended, extemporaneous speech. The board is not usually seeking more information. The question is principally to offer you a last opportunity to present further qualifications or to indicate that you have nothing to add. So, if you feel that a significant qualification or characteristic has been overlooked, it is proper to point it out in a sentence or so. Do not compliment the board on the thoroughness of their examination – they have been sketchy, and you know it. If you wish, merely say, "No thank you, I have nothing further to add." This is a point where you can "talk yourself out" of a good impression or fail to present an important bit of information. Remember, *you close the interview yourself.*

The chairman will then say, "That is all, Mr. _____, thank you." Do not be startled; the interview is over, and quicker than you think. Thank him, gather your belongings and take your leave. Save your sigh of relief for the other side of the door.

How to put your best foot forward

Throughout this entire process, you may feel that the board individually and collectively is trying to pierce your defenses, seek out your hidden weaknesses and embarrass and confuse you. Actually, this is not true. They are obliged to make an appraisal of your qualifications for the job you are seeking, and they want to see you in your best light. Remember, they must interview all candidates and a non-cooperative candidate may become a failure in spite of their best efforts to bring out his qualifications. Here are 15 suggestions that will help you:

1) Be natural – Keep your attitude confident, not cocky

If you are not confident that you can do the job, do not expect the board to be. Do not apologize for your weaknesses, try to bring out your strong points. The board is interested in a positive, not negative, presentation. Cockiness will antagonize any board member and make him wonder if you are covering up a weakness by a false show of strength.

2) Get comfortable, but don't lounge or sprawl

Sit erectly but not stiffly. A careless posture may lead the board to conclude that you are careless in other things, or at least that you are not impressed by the importance of the occasion. Either conclusion is natural, even if incorrect. Do not fuss with your clothing, a pencil or an ashtray. Your hands may occasionally be useful to emphasize a point; do not let them become a point of distraction.

3) Do not wisecrack or make small talk

This is a serious situation, and your attitude should show that you consider it as such. Further, the time of the board is limited – they do not want to waste it, and neither should you.

4) Do not exaggerate your experience or abilities

In the first place, from information in the application or other interviews and sources, the board may know more about you than you think. Secondly, you probably will not get away with it. An experienced board is rather adept at spotting such a situation, so do not take the chance.

5) If you know a board member, do not make a point of it, yet do not hide it

Certainly you are not fooling him, and probably not the other members of the board. Do not try to take advantage of your acquaintanceship – it will probably do you little good.

6) Do not dominate the interview

Let the board do that. They will give you the clues – do not assume that you have to do all the talking. Realize that the board has a number of questions to ask you, and do not try to take up all the interview time by showing off your extensive knowledge of the answer to the first one.

7) Be attentive

You only have 20 minutes or so, and you should keep your attention at its sharpest throughout. When a member is addressing a problem or question to you, give him your undivided attention. Address your reply principally to him, but do not exclude the other board members.

8) Do not interrupt

A board member may be stating a problem for you to analyze. He will ask you a question when the time comes. Let him state the problem, and wait for the question.

9) Make sure you understand the question

Do not try to answer until you are sure what the question is. If it is not clear, restate it in your own words or ask the board member to clarify it for you. However, do not haggle about minor elements.

10) Reply promptly but not hastily

A common entry on oral board rating sheets is "candidate responded readily," or "candidate hesitated in replies." Respond as promptly and quickly as you can, but do not jump to a hasty, ill-considered answer.

11) Do not be peremptory in your answers

A brief answer is proper – but do not fire your answer back. That is a losing game from your point of view. The board member can probably ask questions much faster than you can answer them.

12) Do not try to create the answer you think the board member wants

He is interested in what kind of mind you have and how it works – not in playing games. Furthermore, he can usually spot this practice and will actually grade you down on it.

13) Do not switch sides in your reply merely to agree with a board member

Frequently, a member will take a contrary position merely to draw you out and to see if you are willing and able to defend your point of view. Do not start a debate, yet do not surrender a good position. If a position is worth taking, it is worth defending.

14) Do not be afraid to admit an error in judgment if you are shown to be wrong

The board knows that you are forced to reply without any opportunity for careful consideration. Your answer may be demonstrably wrong. If so, admit it and get on with the interview.

15) Do not dwell at length on your present job

The opening question may relate to your present assignment. Answer the question but do not go into an extended discussion. You are being examined for a *new* job, not your present one. As a matter of fact, try to phrase ALL your answers in terms of the job for which you are being examined.

Basis of Rating

Probably you will forget most of these "do's" and "don'ts" when you walk into the oral interview room. Even remembering them all will not ensure you a passing grade. Perhaps you did not have the qualifications in the first place. But remembering them will help you to put your best foot forward, without treading on the toes of the board members.

Rumor and popular opinion to the contrary notwithstanding, an oral board wants you to make the best appearance possible. They know you are under pressure – but they also want to see how you respond to it as a guide to what your reaction would be under the pressures of the job you seek. They will be influenced by the degree of poise you display, the personal traits you show and the manner in which you respond.

ABOUT THIS BOOK

This book contains tests divided into Examination Sections. Go through each test, answering every question in the margin. We have also attached a sample answer sheet at the back of the book that can be removed and used. At the end of each test look at the answer key and check your answers. On the ones you got wrong, look at the right answer choice and learn. Do not fill in the answers first. Do not memorize the questions and answers, but understand the answer and principles involved. On your test, the questions will likely be different from the samples. Questions are changed and new ones added. If you understand these past questions you should have success with any changes that arise. Tests may consist of several types of questions. We have additional books on each subject should more study be advisable or necessary for you. Finally, the more you study, the better prepared you will be. This book is intended to be the last thing you study before you walk into the examination room. Prior study of relevant texts is also recommended. NLC publishes some of these in our Fundamental Series. Knowledge and good sense are important factors in passing your exam. Good luck also helps. So now study this Passbook, absorb the material contained within and take that knowledge into the examination. Then do your best to pass that exam.

EXAMINATION SECTION

EXAMINATION SECTION
TEST 1

DIRECTIONS: Each question or incomplete statement is followed by several suggested answers or completions. Select the one that BEST answers the question or completes the statement. *PRINT THE LETTER OF THE CORRECT ANSWER IN THE SPACE AT THE RIGHT.*

1. Assume that a certain file has a safe edge. This is an edge that has   1.____
   - A. no teeth
   - B. the teeth pointing backward
   - C. the teeth pointing forward
   - D. fine criss-cross teeth

2. The one of the following which is the proper tool for threading a round rod is a   2.____
   - A. tap   B. countersink   C. counterbore   D. die

3. A rasp is a   3.____
   - A. type of chisel
   - B. type of file cleaner
   - C. type of coarse file
   - D. kind of plane

4. The one of the following which is the proper tool to use to tighten a round nut which has a series of notches cut in its outer surface is a(n) _____ wrench.   4.____
   - A. box   B. spanner   C. Stillson   D. monkey

5. Small leaks resulting from poor threads on steel or wrought-iron water pipes will often stop because the leaky threads are in time filled with   5.____
   - A. sediment   B. stalactite   C. rust   D. soapstone

6. A metal that can be rolled or beaten into very fine sheets is said to be   6.____
   - A. anodized   B. malleable   C. tempered   D. ferrous

7. To *rod* a sewer pipe means MOST likely to   7.____
   - A. clean it out by means of rods
   - B. keep the pipe clear of debris by placing a grating of rods at the intake
   - C. support the sewer pipe with horizontal reinforcing metal rods
   - D. shore up the pipe

8. Of the following abrasives, the one which is the LEAST coarse is   8.____
   - A. No. 2 emery cloth
   - B. crocus cloth
   - C. No. 1 sandpaper
   - D. No. 1/0 sandpaper

9. In order to permit free passage of water in one direction only and prevent a reversal of flow in the pipe, it is necessary to use a _____ valve.   9.____
   - A. gate   B. check   C. globe   D. needle

10. Assume that a cubic foot of water contains 7 1/2 gallons. The number of gallons of water which could be contained in a rectangular tank 3 feet long, 2 feet wide, and 2 feet deep is MOST NEARLY   10.____
    - A. 12   B. 45   C. 90   D. 120

11. The weight, in pounds, of a cubic foot of fresh water is MOST NEARLY

    A. 8.5   B. 32.4   C. 62.4   D. 98.6

12. The total weight, in pounds, of ten bags of Portland cement is MOST NEARLY _____ pounds.

    A. 108   B. 187   C. 940   D. 1,200

13. If a concrete mix is said to be 1:2:4, this would mean that the mix is made up of 1 part by 1

    A. volume of cement to 2 parts by volume of sand to 4 parts by volume of coarse aggregate
    B. volume of cement to 2 parts by volume of coarse aggregate to 4 parts by volume of sand
    C. volume of coarse aggregate to 2 parts by volume of sand to 4 parts by volume of cement
    D. weight of cement to 2 parts by weight of coarse aggregate to 4 parts by weight of sand

14. The ratio of the weight of a substance to the weight of an equal volume of water is called the _____ of the substance.

    A. specific volume   B. specific gravity
    C. viscosity   D. fractional weight

15. Of the following, the pipe fitting which has four openings which permits connecting a line at right angles to another line is called a(n)

    A. side outlet street L B. double elbow
    C. tee   D. cross

16. To tighten a nut where only a short swing of the wrench handle is possible, it is BEST to use a _____ wrench.

    A. ratchet   B. hook spanner
    C. Stillson   D. Bristo

17. Of the following, the proper tool to use to remove the burr from the inside of a pipe is a

    A. half round file   B. reamer
    C. mandrel   D. chisel

18. Fittings commonly used with copper pipe should be made of

    A. brass   B. cast iron
    C. malleable iron   D. pure tin

19. With respect to pipe, the abbreviation I.P.S. means

    A. Internal Pipe Size   B. Iron Pipe Size
    C. Iron Pipe Shape   D. International Pipe Size

20. A Stillson wrench is the proper wrench to use when tightening a
    A. square nut B. hexagonal nut
    C. valve gland nut D. pipe fitting

21. The one of the following which is the proper tool to use for cutting wood along the grain is a _____ saw.
    A. rip B. panel C. cross-cut D. back

22. The one of the following which is the proper tool to use to cut internal screw threads is a
    A. broach B. die C. tap D. stock

23. A center punch is the proper tool used to
    A. cut out the center of a gasket
    B. dent metal prior to drilling
    C. drive nails beneath the surface of the wood
    D. punch a small hole in sheet metal

24. The one of the following knots which can be safely used for tying together the ends of two dry ropes of the same size is a
    A. granny knot B. clove hitch
    C. half hitch D. square knot

25. The PRIMARY purpose of a trap under a plumbing fixture is to
    A. act as a seal against sewer gas
    B. permit cleaning out the drain line
    C. permit the recovery of valuables accidentally dropped into the fixture
    D. permit the making of tests on the drain line

26. The one of the following which contains exactly 10 board feet is a board 10 feet long, ____ inches wide, _____ inch(es) thick.
    A. 24; 1 B. 12; 2 C. 12; 1 D. 10; 1

27. Short pieces of pipe threaded on both ends are called
    A. nipples B. couplings C. bushing D. sleeves

28. The unit of electrical capacitance is the
    A. ampere B. farad C. henry D. cycle

29. As used in the electrical industry, BX means
    A. best grade of electrical wire
    B. type B extension wire
    C. metal greenfield
    D. insulated wires in flexible metal tubing

Questions 30-33.

DIRECTIONS: Questions 30 to 33, inclusive, are to be answered in accordance with the following paragraph.

One of the categories of nuisance is a chemical one and relates to the dissolved oxygen of the watercourse. The presence in sewage and industrial wastes of materials capable of undergoing biochemical oxidation and resulting in reduction of oxygen in the watercourse leads to a partial or complete depletion of this oxygen. This, in turn, leads to the subsequent production of malodorous products of decomposition, to the destruction of aquatic plant life and major fish life and to conditions offensive to sight and smell.

30. The word *malodorous* as used in the above paragraph means MOST NEARLY   30.____

    A. fragrant   B. fetid   C. wholesome   D. redolent

31. From the above paragraph, because of pollution, the amount of dissolved oxygen in the waterways is   31.____

    A. released   B. multiplied   C. lessened   D. saturated

32. The word *categories* as used in the above paragraph means MOST NEARLY   32.____

    A. divisions   B. clubs   C. symbols   D. products

33. The word *offensive* as used in the above paragraph means MOST NEARLY   33.____

    A. pliable   B. complaint
    C. deferential   D. disagreeable

34. The terminal voltage of 5 dry cells connected in a series is _____ of one(each) cell.   34.____

    A. 1/5 the voltage   B. the same as the voltage
    C. 5 times the voltage   D. determined by the current

35. If a 15 ampere fuse blows out and blows out again after inserting a new fuse, it is BEST to   35.____

    A. replace it with a 10 ampere fustat
    B. replace it with two 10 ampere fuses connected in series
    C. replace it with a 20 ampere fuse
    D. have the circuit checked to find the trouble

36. Ordinary soft solder is a mixture of lead and   36.____

    A. sulphur   B. brass   C. zinc   D. tin

37. The electrolyte used in the ordinary flashlight-type dry cell is   37.____

    A. calcium chloride   B. ammonium chloride
    C. manganese dioxide   D. sulfuric acid

38. An electrical transformer is an electrical device used primarily to 38.____

    A. raise or lower A.C. voltages
    B. change the frequency of alternating current
    C. rectify currents from A.C. to D.C.
    D. change currents from D.C. to A.C.

39. Of the following, the MAIN reason for the grounding of electrical equipment and circuits is to 39.____

    A. save power
    B. increase the voltage
    C. protect personnel from electric shock
    D. prevent serious short circuits

40. In order to properly ground portable electric hand tools, it is USUALLY necessary to use a 40.____

    A. solenoid
    C. fuse
    B. circuit breaker
    D. three prong plug

41. The current in a simple electrical circuit can be calculated by dividing the voltage by the resistance in ohms. Assume that the resistance of a certain circuit is 60 ohms and its voltage is 120 volts, 60 cycle A.C. The current in this circuit will be MOST NEARLY _____ ampere(s). 41.____

    A. 1/2   B. 2   C. 1   D. 30

42. The one of the following which is the MOST common type of motor that may be used with an A.C. or D.C. source of supply is the _____ motor. 42.____

    A. shunt
    C. compound
    B. squirrel cage
    D. series

43. The electrolyte in the ordinary storage battery is 43.____

    A. nitric acid
    C. manganese dioxide
    B. sulphuric acid
    D. ammonium chloride

44. The one of the following terms which is used in expressing the rating of a storage battery is 44.____

    A. ampere-hours
    C. volt-ampere
    B. amperes
    D. watt-hours

45. The size of the SMALLEST graduation on the ordinary 6-foot folding rule is *usually* 45.____

    A. 1/8"   B. 1/16"   C. 1/32"   D. 1/64"

46. A given saw has 8 points per inch. This saw is PROBABLY a _____ saw. 46.____

    A. cross-cut   B. hack   C. veneer   D. back

47. Assume that it takes 6 men 8 days to do a certain job. Working at the same same speed, the number of days that it will take 4 men to do this job is

   A. 9 B. 10 C. 12 D. 14

48. The sum of 3 5/8 + 4 1/4 + 6 1/2 + 7 1/8 is

   A. 20 7/8 B. 21 1/4 C. 21 1/2 D. 22 1/8

49. The fraction which is equal to .0625 is

   A. 1/64 B. 3/64 C. 1/16 D. 5/8

50. The volume, in cubic feet, of a rectangular coal bin 8 ft. long by 5 ft. wide by 7 ft. high is MOST NEARLY

   A. 40 B. 56 C. 186 D. 280

KEY (CORRECT ANSWERS)

1. A	11. C	21. A	31. C	41. B
2. D	12. C	22. C	32. A	42. D
3. C	13. A	23. B	33. D	43. B
4. B	14. B	24. D	34. C	44. A
5. C	15. D	25. A	35. D	45. B
6. B	16. A	26. C	36. D	46. A
7. A	17. B	27. A	37. B	47. C
8. B	18. A	28. B	38. A	48. C
9. B	19. B	29. D	39. C	49. C
10. C	20. D	30. B	40. D	50. D

TEST 2

DIRECTIONS: Each question or incomplete statement is followed by several suggested answers or completions. Select the one that BEST answers the question or completes the statement. *PRINT THE LETTER OF THE CORRECT ANSWER IN THE SPACE AT THE RIGHT.*

Questions 1-7

DIRECTIONS: Questions 1 to 7, inclusive, are to be answered in accordance with the following information.

At sea level, the atmosphere can exert a pressure of 14.7 pounds per square inch. This pressure is capable of sustaining a column of water having a height equal to 14.7 pounds, multiplied by 2.304 (the height of water in feet which will exert one pound per square inch pressure). No pump built can produce a perfect vacuum. The atmospheric pressure exerting its force on the surface of the water from which suction is being taken forces the water up through the suction to the pump. From this, it is evident that the maximum height which a water pump of this type can lift water is determined ultimately by the atmospheric pressure. The tightness of the pump and its ability to create a vacuum also have a bearing.

1. The meaning of the word *vacuum* as used in the above article is a
    A. space entirely devoid of matter
    B. sealed tube filled with gas
    C. bottle-shaped vessel with a double wall
    D. cleaning device

2. With reference to the above article, if a pump could produce a perfect vacuum, the MAXIMUM height, in feet, that it could lift water at sea level is MOST NEARLY
    A. 33.9   B. 29.4   C. 23.3   D. 14.7

3. With reference to the above article, a column of water having a height of 4.6 feet at sea level will exert a pressure of MOST NEARLY _____ pound(s) per square inch.
    A. 3   B. 2   C. 1   D. 1/2

4. The word *atmosphere* as used in the above article means
    A. the pull of gravity
    B. perfect vacuum
    C. the whole mass of air surrounding the earth
    D. the weight of water at sea level

5. The word *bearing* as used in the above article means MOST NEARLY
    A. direction   B. connection
    C. divergence   D. convergence

6. The word *evident* as used in the above article means MOST NEARLY   6.____

   A. disconcerting   B. obscure   C. equivocal   D. manifest

7. The word *maximum* as used in the above article means MOST NEARLY   7.____

   A. best   B. median   C. adjacent   D. greatest

8. Assume that a car travels at a constant speed of 36 miles per hour. The speed of this car, in feet per second, is MOST NEARLY (one mile equals 5,280 ft.)   8.____

   A. 3   B. 24.6   C. 52.8   D. 879.8

9. If one-third of a 19-foot length of lumber is cut off, the length of the remaining piece will measure APPROXIMATELY   9.____

   A. 8'8"   B. 9'8"   C. 12'8"   D. 13'8"

10. The circumference of a circle having a diameter of 10" is MOST NEARLY _____ inches.   10.____

    A. 3.14   B. 18.72   C. 24.96   D. 31.4

11. Assume that in the purchase of paint, the seller quotes a discount of 10%. If the price per gallon is $6.35, the actual payment in dollars per gallon is MOST NEARLY   11.____

    A. $5.72   B. $5.95   C. $6.25   D. $6.50

12. On a 1" bolt that has 10 threads per inch, if the nut is turned 6 complete turns, the distance, in inches, that the nut will move along the bolt is MOST NEARLY   12.____

    A. .3   B. .6   C. .9   D. 1

13. Assume that at one end of a 6-inch horizontal line, an 8-inch vertical line is drawn at right angles to the horizontal line. The length, in inches, between the ends of the two lines is MOST NEARLY   13.____

    A. 6   B. 8   C. 10   D. 12

Questions 14-21.

DIRECTIONS: Questions 14 to 21, inclusive, are to be answered in accordance with the following information.

In his 2012 annual report to the Mayor, the Public Works Commissioner stated that the city's basic water pollution control program begun in 1996 and costing $425 million so far would be completed in five or six years at a cost of $275 million more. However, he said, the city must spend an additional $175 million more on its marginal pollution control program to protect present and proposed beaches. Under the basic program, the city will have eliminated the last major discharges of raw sewage into the harbor. Over 800 million gallons, two thirds of the city's spent water each day, is now treated at 12 plants, to which six new plants will be added, enabling the city to treat the estimated 1.8 billion gallons that will be discharged daily in 2030. The department had about $200 million worth of municipal construction under way in 2012, and completed $85.5 millions' worth.

14. According to the above, the city will add _____ new plants.   14._____
    A. 18   B. 12   C. 6   D. 4

15. The amount of municipal construction under way in 2012 was _____ million.   15._____
    A. $85.5   B. $175   C. $200   D. $425

16. It is estimated that in 2030, the city will treat daily _____ gallons.   16._____
    A. 700 million   B. 800 million
    C. 900 million   D. 1.8 billion

17. According to the above article, the total cost of the water pollution program   17._____
    begun in 1996 will be _____ million.
    A. $275   B. $425   C. $700   D. $815

18. According to the above article, to protect present and proposed beaches, the   18._____
    city must spend an additional _____ million.
    A. $175   B. $275   C. $425   D. $450

19. The above article concerns the statements of the Commissioner of Public Works   19._____
    in his _____ annual report to the Mayor.
    A. 1996   B. 2002   C. 2012   D. 2013

20. The word *discharged* as used in the above article means MOST NEARLY   20._____
    A. emitted   B. erased   C. refuted   D. repelled

21. The word *pollution* as used in the above article means MOST NEARLY   21._____
    A. condensation   B. purification
    C. contamination   D. distillation

22. A tool commonly used to cut off the head of a rivet is a   22._____
    A. cold chisel B. cape chisel C. band saw   D. file

23. A metal washer is MOST often used with a _____ screw.   23._____
    A. wood   B. lag   C. hand   D. machine

24. A good safety rule to follow is that water should NOT be used to extinguish   24._____
    fires in or around electrical apparatus. Of the following, the PRIMARY reason
    for this is that water
    A. will damage the insulation
    B. will corrode the electrical conductors
    C. may cause the circuit fuse to blow
    D. may conduct electric current and cause a shock hazard

25. One should be extremely careful to keep open flames and sparks away from storage batteries when they are being charged because the

    A. sulphate given off during this operation is highly flammable
    B. hydrogen given off during this operation is highly flammable
    C. oxygen given off during this operation is extremely flammable
    D. static electricity of the battery may cause combustion

26. A good safety rule to follow is that an electric hand tool, such as a portable electric drill, should never be lifted or carried by its service cord.
Of the following, the PRIMARY reason for this rule is that the

    A. tool might swing and be damaged by striking some hard object
    B. cord might be pulled off its terminals and become short circuited
    C. tool may slip out of the hand as it is hard to get a good grip on a slick rubber cord
    D. rubber covering of the cord might overstretch

27. When a man is working on a 15-foot ladder with its top placed against a wall, the MAXIMUM safe distance that he may reach out to one side of the ladder is

    A. as far out as he can reach lifting one foot off the rung for balance
    B. as far out as he can reach without bending his body more than 45 from the vertical
    C. one-third the length of the ladder
    D. as far out as his arm's length

28. When NOT in use, oily waste rags should be stored in

    A. water-tight oak barrels   B. open metal containers
    C. sealed cardboard boxes   D. self-closing, metal containers

29. Assume that one of your co-workers has suffered an electric shock. Artificial respiration should be started on him immediately if he is

    A. unconscious and breathing   B. conscious and in a daze
    C. unconscious and not breathing D. conscious and badly burned

30. Assume that the top of a 12-foot portable straight ladder is placed against a wall but is not held by a man or fastened in any way. In order to be safe, the ladder should be placed so that the distance from the wall to the foot of the ladder is

    A. not over 3 feet   B. not over 4 feet
    C. at least 4 feet   D. at least 5 feet

31. Of the following, the one which is an acceptable method of caring for wooden ladders is to

    A. coat the ladder with clear shellac
    B. paint the ladder with red lead followed by a second coat of the desired color
    C. paint the ladder with a coat of paint of the desired color
    D. apply a sealer coat before painting with a second coat of the desired color

32. The MOST important safety precaution to follow when using an electric drill press is to

   A. wear safety shoes
   B. drill at a slow speed
   C. use plenty of cutting oil
   D. clamp the work firmly

33. The proper method of lifting heavy objects is to stand

   A. far enough away from the load so that, with knees bent, the back is at an angle of 45, then lift by straightening the back
   B. close to the load, with feet solidly placed and slightly apart and knees bent; then lift by straightening the legs, keeping the back as nearly vertical as possible
   C. close to the load, with feet solidly placed and far apart, knees bent; then lift by straightening the legs, keeping the body at an angle of 30°
   D. far away from the load, with knees bent and the back at an angle of 45°, then lift by straightening the knees and slowly straightening the back

34. An oilstone is often made of

   A. silicon   B. carborundum   C. tungsten   D. emery

35. To draw a circle, you should use a(n)

   A. compass   B. caliper   C. awl   D. gage

36. A *mushroomed* head is a common defect of a

   A. rivet
   B. hammer
   C. chisel
   D. screwdriver

37. The tool USUALLY used to drive a lag screw is a(n)

   A. open end wrench
   B. Stillson wrench
   C. screwdriver
   D. Allen wrench

38. It is BEST to lubricate machinery

   A. whenever you feel the oil is running low
   B. only if the machinery needs it
   C. when the machine begins to vibrate
   D. on a regular schedule

39. When repairing machinery that is to be reassembled, punch marks are often placed on parts that are next to each other.
    The reason for this is to

   A. make sure you assemble the pieces in proper order
   B. make it easier to line up the parts in proper position
   C. keep count of the number of pieces that belong to this machine
   D. provide a stop so that parts cannot be assembled too tightly

Questions 40-46.

DIRECTIONS: Questions 40 to 46, inclusive, are to be answered in accordance with the following paragraph.

At 2:30 P.M. on Monday, October 25, Mr. Paul Jones, a newly appointed Sewage Treatment Worker, started on a routine inspectional tour of the settling tanks and other sewage treatment works installations of the plant to which he was assigned. At 2:33 P.M., Mr. Jones discovered a co-worker, Mr. James P. Brown, lying unconscious on the ground. Mr. Jones quickly reported the facts to his immediate superior, Mr. Jack Rota, who immediately telephoned for an ambulance. Mr. Rota then rushed to the site and placed a heavy woolen blanket over the victim. Mr. Brown was taken to the Ave. H hospital by an ambulance driven by Mr. Dave Smith, which arrived at the sewage disposal plant at 3:02 P.M. Patrolman Robert Daly, badge number 12520, had arrived before the ambulance and recorded all the details of the incident, including the statements of Mr. Jones, Mr. Rota, and Mr. Nick Nespola, a Stationary Engineer (Electric), who stated that he saw the victim when he fell to the ground.

40. The time which elapsed between the start of the sewage treatment worker's routine inspection and the arrival of the ambulance was MOST NEARLY _____ minutes.

    A. 3   B. 28   C. 29   D. 32

41. The name of the sewage treatment worker's immediate superior was

    A. James P. Brown
    B. Jack Rota
    C. Paul Jones
    D. Robert Daly

42. The name of the patrolman was

    A. James P. Brown
    B. Jack Rota
    C. Paul Jones
    D. Robert Daly

43. Referring to the above, the incident occurred on

    A. Monday, Oct. 25
    B. Monday, October 26
    C. Tuesday, Oct. 25
    D. Tuesday, October 26

44. The victim was found at exactly

    A. 2:30 A.M.   B. 2:33 P.M.   C. 2:33 A.M.   D. 2:30 P.M.

45. The sewage treatment worker's name was

    A. James P. Brown
    B. Jack Rota
    C. Paul Jones
    D. Dave Smith

46. The man named Nick Nespola was the

    A. Stationary Engineer (Electric)
    B. patrolman
    C. victim
    D. ambulance driver

47. When sharpening a tool on a grindstone, the tool is often dipped in water. The MAIN reason for this is to

    A. prevent overheating of the tool
    B. lubricate the grindstone
    C. produce a sharper edge on the tool
    D. anneal the tool

47._____

48. It is BEST to use a screwdriver having a square shank

    A. when clearance is limited
    B. on sheet metal screws
    C. on small screws
    D. where a wrench is to be used to help turn the screwdriver

48._____

49. Brass liners are often placed over the jaws of a bench vise to

    A. grip the work better
    B. prevent damage to the work
    C. protect the vise
    D. make it easier to adjust the work

49._____

50. Other than the bulb, the part of a fluorescent light that must be changed MOST often as it wears is the

    A. switch   B. ballast   C. control   D. starter

50._____

KEY (CORRECT ANSWERS)

1. A	11. A	21. C	31. A	41. B
2. A	12. B	22. A	32. D	42. D
3. B	13. C	23. D	33. B	43. A
4. C	14. C	24. D	34. B	44. B
5. B	15. C	25. B	35. A	45. C
6. D	16. D	26. B	36. C	46. A
7. D	17. C	27. D	37. A	47. A
8. C	18. A	28. D	38. D	48. D
9. C	19. C	29. C	39. B	49. B
10. D	20. A	30. A	40. D	50. D

EXAMINATION SECTION
TEST 1

DIRECTIONS: Each question or incomplete statement is followed by several suggested answers or completions. Select the one that BEST answers the question or completes the statement. *PRINT THE LETTER OF THE CORRECT ANSWER IN THE SPACE AT THE RIGHT.*

1. The flow of sewage into the treatment plant is USUALLY controlled by a   1.____

   A. gate valve
   B. sluice gate
   C. tainter gate
   D. parshall gate

2. Regulator gates USUALLY close when the sewage in the interceptor sewer reaches a predetermined   2.____

   A. velocity
   B. pressure
   C. temperature
   D. elevation

3. A bar screen serves the same purpose as a   3.____

   A. filter
   B. grit collector
   C. trash rack
   D. sluice gate

4. Material that is removed from the sewage by the fine screen is MOST frequently   4.____

   A. blown by compressed air to the grit storage tank
   B. ground up and returned to the sewage
   C. burnt as fuel for the plant
   D. dried in the sludge drying beds and then disposed at sea

5. The one of the following pieces of equipment that is operated in conjunction with air pressure is a(n)   5.____

   A. centrifugal pump
   B. venturi
   C. ejector
   D. sump pump

6. One of the methods used to prime a centrifugal pump is to   6.____

   A. raise the air pressure in the pump
   B. bleed the suction line
   C. apply a vacuum to the pump
   D. open the suction valve

7. The one of the following types of pumps MOST frequently used to pump thickened sludge is the _____ type.   7.____

   A. ejector
   B. centrifugal
   C. gear
   D. piston

8. A plant is called an *Activated Sludge Plant* when the   8.____

   A. thickened sludge can be used as fertilizer
   B. gases from the sludge digestion tanks are burnt as fuel
   C. sludge must be dried before being disposed
   D. partly treated sewage is mixed with sludge

15

9. Where a digester tank has either a floating or a rising cover, it is made airtight by means of a(n)

   A. water seal
   B. sliding rubber gasket
   C. leather *bellows*
   D. oiled steel ring

10. Grease and fats are USUALLY removed from the sewage by

    A. skimming the liquid in the sedimentation tanks
    B. pumping the liquid from the sump in the grit chamber
    C. decanting the liquid in the digestion tank
    D. backwashing the fine screens

11. The type of plant in which *flocculation* MOST frequently occurs is the _____ plant.

    A. aerated sludge
    B. chemical precipitation
    C. plain screening
    D. filtration

12. Chlorine leaks are BEST detected by use of

    A. orthotoludin
    B. litmus paper
    C. ammonia
    D. copperas

13. Settling tanks operate effectively by _____ the sewage.

    A. slowing the speed of
    B. increasing the speed of
    C. changing the direction of flow of
    D. adding air to

14. A *venturi* is used in a sewage treatment plant in order to

    A. clean the diffusers
    B. control the amount of sewage in the wet well
    C. measure the flow of sewage
    D. reduce the pressure of the gases used as fuel

15. Sludge tanks are USUALLY heated by means of

    A. forced warm air
    B. hot water
    C. radiant heat
    D. electric coils

16. Chlorine is USUALLY added to sewage by

    A. adding the gas directly to the sewage
    B. mixing a small quantity of the sewage with the chlorine and then adding the mixture to the main body of sewage
    C. mixing the chlorine with water, and then adding the mixture to the sewage
    D. combining the gas with the air used in the aeration tank

17. The MAIN reason for defective operation of an aeration tank is that

    A. sewage flow is too slow
    B. of clogged diffuser plates
    C. tank temperature is too low
    D. too much air is supplied

18. The type of pump that seldom requires a relief valve is MOST likely a _____ pump. 18.____

    A. reciprocating B. gear
    C. piston D. centrifugal

19. The MAIN purpose of a foot valve in a centrifugal pump is to 19.____

    A. prevent the liquid from flowing back down the suction line
    B. equalize the pressure on both sides of the pump
    C. make it easier to prime the pump
    D. block passage of material that is too large to pump

20. The MAIN reason for lubricating machinery is to 20.____

    A. lower operating temperature
    B. keep down noise and vibration
    C. reduce friction
    D. lower cost of operation

21. The one of the following items that has the LOWEST viscosity is 21.____

    A. cup grease B. kerosene
    C. #10 oil D. #40 oil

22. The one of the following statements that is MOST NEARLY correct is: 22.____

    A. High speed machinery is most frequently lubricated by grease
    B. For most applications, either grease or oil can be used
    C. When in doubt, it is best to use the heavier of two grades of oil available
    D. Oil becomes *thinner* as the operating temperature increases

23. The function of a circuit breaker is MOST similar to that of a 23.____

    A. switch B. fuse C. rheostat D. transformer

24. Noisy operation of a motor is MOST frequently caused by 24.____

    A. a shorted armature B. over-voltage
    C. worn bearings D. a grounded casing

25. Consumption of electrical energy is registered on a(n) 25.____

    A. volt-ohm meter B. ammeter
    C. watt-hour meter D. ohm meter

26. A dirty commutator is BEST cleaned by using 26.____

    A. sandpaper B. soap and water
    C. emery cloth D. kerosene

27. The one of the following items that is MOST frequently used to prevent an electric motor from being overloaded is a 27.____

    A. warning signal B. governor
    C. thermal cut-out D. rheostat

28. The one of the following metals that is MOST commonly used for outboard bearings is 28.____

    A. zinc B. brass C. magnesium D. babbit

29. The use of pipe joint compound when making up a screwed joint results in a watertight joint and also

    A. cleans the threads
    B. makes the joint hard
    C. lubricates the threads
    D. prevents cross threading

30. A pipe is generally threaded by using a

    A. die   B. tap   C. yoke   D. swedge

31. The type of motor that MOST frequently does NOT use brushes is the

    A. universal type
    B. series wound D.C. motor
    C. synchronous motor
    D. induction motor

32. Compressed air can be used to clean generator and motor windings provided the air is

    A. heated
    B. blown at a high velocity
    C. used at a pressure of at least 90 lbs./sq.in.
    D. dry

33. The use of a cold chisel with a *mushroomed* head is

    A. *good*, because the mushrooming cushions the blow
    B. *bad*, because the head cannot be hit squarely
    C. *good*, because there is more area on the head to hit
    D. *bad*, because chips might fly from the head

34. After brass or black iron pipe has been cut, it should be

    A. counterbored
    B. reamed
    C. countersunk
    D. squared

35. The one of the following that is used to change the speed of certain types of electric motors is a (n)

    A. commutator
    B. brush
    C. rheostat
    D. armature

36. The type of pipe that is MOST frequently made with bell and spigot ends is

    A. brass
    B. steel
    C. cast iron
    D. transite

37. The one of the following that is used to connect two pipes together in a straight line is a

    A. manifold   B. divider   C. band   D. union

38. The difference between a stud and a bolt is that the stud has

    A. a finer thread
    B. no head
    C. a round head
    D. a coarser thread

39. A set screw is often used to

    A. bolt two pieces of flanged pipe together
    B. screw together matching parts in a motor casing
    C. clamp a piece to a work table
    D. secure a pulley to a shaft

40. Soft jaw inserts sometimes used to protect the surface of a piece of metal that is held in a vise are MOST frequently made of

    A. zinc   B. tin   C. brass   D. pewter

41. The BEST type of wrench to use on a large square nut is a _____ wrench.

    A. monkey   B. spanner   C. stillson   D. spintite

42. The BEST method of cleaning files is to use a

    A. file card   B. knife
    C. scriber   D. fibre brush

43. The BEST lubricant to use when cutting threads on steel pipe is _____ oil.

    A. pike   B. penetrating
    C. lard   D. coal

44. The BEST type of valve to use to control the flow of liquid to a delicate gauge is a _____ valve.

    A. gate   B. needle   C. globe   D. check

45. Water hammer is caused MAINLY by

    A. pumping sewage to too high a head
    B. interrupting the flow of sewage too rapidly
    C. debris floating in the sewage
    D. excessive corrosion in the pipes

46. Suppose a centrifugal pump is pumping less sewage than it is capable of handling. Of the following, the one that is NOT a possible reason for this is that the

    A. speed of pump is too slow
    B. pump is not properly primed
    C. stuffing box packing is defective
    D. suction line is partly clogged

47. The one of the following types of pumps that will give a smooth continuous flow of liquid rather than a pulsating flow is the _____ type.

    A. reciprocating   B. rotary
    C. gear   D. centrifugal

48. For pumping against a very high head, the BEST type of pump to use is a _____ type.

    A. reciprocating   B. propeller
    C. mixed flow   D. centrifugal

5 (#1)

49. To increase the volume of delivery of a reciprocating pump, USUALLY the

   A. angle of the impeller is increased
   B. inlet valve is opened wider
   C. piston stroke is lengthened
   D. discharge valve is opened wider

50. The capacity of a pump is MOST frequently expressed in

   A. cubic feet per day
   B. gallons per day
   C. cubic feet per minute
   D. gallons per minute

KEY (CORRECT ANSWERS)

1. B	11. B	21. B	31. D	41. A
2. D	12. C	22. D	32. D	42. A
3. C	13. A	23. B	33. D	43. C
4. B	14. C	24. C	34. B	44. B
5. C	15. B	25. C	35. C	45. B
6. C	16. C	26. A	36. C	46. B
7. D	17. B	27. C	37. D	47. D
8. D	18. D	28. D	38. B	48. A
9. A	19. A	29. C	39. D	49. C
10. A	20. C	30. A	40. C	50. D

TEST 2

DIRECTIONS: Each question or incomplete statement is followed by several suggested answers or completions. Select the one that BEST answers the question or completes the statement. *PRINT THE LETTER OF THE CORRECT ANSWER IN THE SPACE AT THE RIGHT.*

1. The sum of the following dimensions: 1 5/8, 2 1/4, 4 1/16, 3 3/16, is   1.____

   A. 10 15/16   B. 11   C. 11 1/8   D. 11 1/4

2. Assume that six men, working together at the same rate of speed, can complete a certain job in 3 hours.   2.____
   If, however, there were only four men available to do this job, and they all worked at the same rate of speed, to complete this job would take MOST NEARLY _____ hours.

   A. 4 1/4   B. 4 1/2   C. 4 3/4   D. 5

3. Due to unforeseen difficulties, a job which would normally take 17 hours to complete was actually completed in 21 hours.   3.____
   This represents a percent increase over the normal time of MOST NEARLY

   A. 19%   B. 2.4%   C. 24%   D. 124%

4. The veteran should approach the problem of safety with the idea that   4.____

   A. there will always be accidents
   B. most accidents can be prevented
   C. the best method of preventing accidents is to post safety rules for the men to follow
   D. punishing the man with the worst accident record will reduce the number of accidents occurring

5. The one of the following that is NOT a common cause of accidents occurring when working around machinery is   5.____

   A. wearing loose clothing
   B. wearing gloves
   C. having insufficient illumination
   D. having slippery floors

Questions 6-8.

DIRECTIONS: Questions 6 through 8, inclusive, are to be answered in accordance with the following information.
   A certain job requires 4 men working the number of hours and at the salary rate indicated in the accompanying table.

Name	No. of Hours	Salary/Hr.
Brown	30	$15.00
Jones	22	$19.50
Walter	40	$10.50
Thomas	25	$17.22

6. According to the above table, the salary received by Thomas on this job is MOST NEARLY

   A. $426.00   B. $427.50   C. $429.00   D. $430.50

7. According to the above table, the man who received the MOST wages chargeable to this job is

   A. Brown   B. Jones   C. Walter   D. Thomas

8. According to the above table, the total amount of wages chargeable to this job is MOST NEARLY

   A. $1,726.50   B. $1,717.50   C. $1,729.50   D. $1,737.50

9. Of the following statements, the one that represents the SAFEST practice in a shop is: Adjustments should be made on.

   A. running machinery only if another man can be assigned to guard the man making the actual adjustment
   B. running machinery only if proper protective equipment is worn
   C. running machinery only when the machine is grounded
   D. machinery only after the machine has been stopped

10. Regarding work performed on electrical circuits, the one of the following that is unsafe is to

    A. use #10 wire instead of #12
    B. ground the junction boxes
    C. replace a 15 ampere circuit breaker with a 20 ampere one
    D. open the main switch before working on the wiring

11. Of the following, the MOST important reason for making detailed reports of all accidents is to

    A. have a record of who to blame for the accident
    B. be able to properly assess the cost of the accident
    C. reduce the number of *compensation* claims
    D. determine the causes of accidents and eliminate future accidents

12. As a veteran sewage treatment worker, you can BEST promote safety in your operations by

    A. carefully investigating and reporting the circumstances of any accident
    B. suggesting safer methods of operation
    C. training subordinates in proper safety
    D. disciplining subordinates who engage in unsafe acts

13. Oil-soaked rags are BEST stored in a

    A. neat pile in a readily accessible corner
    B. metal container with a tight cover
    C. metal box that has holes for adequate ventilation
    D. closet on a shelf above the ground

14. The one of the following actions that is NOT the cause of injury when working with hand tools is

    A. working with defective tools
    B. using the wrong tool for the job
    C. working too carefully
    D. using a tool improperly

15. Artificial respiration is the FIRST action you should take when a man becomes unconscious either as a result of drowning or as a result of

    A. chlorine poisoning   B. electric shock
    C. falling   D. clothing catching fire

Questions 16-17.

DIRECTIONS: Questions 16 and 17 should be answered in accordance with the following paragraph.

Sewage treatment plants are designed so that the sewage flow reaches the plant by gravity. In some instances, a small percentage of the sewerage system may be below the planned level of the plant. Economy in construction and other factors may indicate that the raising of that lower portion of the flow by means of pumps, to the desired plant elevation, is more desirable than lowering the plant structure. Some plants operate with this feature.

16. According to the above paragraph,

    A. a small percentage of the sewage reaches the plant by means of gravity
    B. all sewage reaches the plant by means of gravity
    C. where sewage cannot reach the plant by gravity it is pumped
    D. pumping is used so that all sewage can reach the plant

17. According to the above paragraph, the reason that some plants are built above the level of the sewerage system is that

    A. these plants operate more efficiently this way
    B. gravity will naturally bring the sewage in at a lower level
    C. pumping of the sewage is more expensive
    D. these plants are cheaper to build this way

Questions 18-20.

DIRECTIONS: Questions 18 through 20, inclusive, should be answered in accordance with the following paragraph.

Accident proneness is a subject which deserves much move objective and competent study than it has received to date. In discussing accident proneness, it is important to differentiate between the employee who is a "repeater" and one who is truly accident prone. It is obvious that any person put on work of which he knows little without thorough training in safe practice for the work in question will be liable to injury until he does learn the "how" of it. Few workmen left to their own devices will develop adequate safe practices. Therefore, they must be trained. Only those who fail to respond to proper training should be regarded as accident prone. The repeater whose accident record can be explained by a correctible physical defect, by correctible plant or machine hazards, by assignment to work for which he is not suited because of physical deficiencies or special abilities, cannot be fairly called "accident prone."

18. According to the above paragraph, a person is considered accident prone if

    A. he has accidents regardless of the fact that he has been properly trained
    B. he has many accidents
    C. it is possible for him to have accidents
    D. he works at a job where accidents are possible

19. According to the above paragraph,

    A. workers will learn the safe way of doing things if left to their own intelligence
    B. most workers must be trained to be safe
    C. a worker who has had more than one accident has not been properly trained
    D. intelligent workers are always safe

20. According to the above paragraph, a person would not be called accident prone if the cause of his accidents was

    A. a lack of interest in the job
    B. recklessness
    C. a low level of intelligence
    D. eyeglasses that don't fit properly

Questions 21-23.

DIRECTIONS: Questions 21 through 23, inclusive, should be answered in accordance with the following paragraph.

Sharpening a twist drill by hand is a skill that is mastered only after much practice and careful attention to the details. Therefore, whenever possible, use a tool grinder in which the drills can be properly positioned, clamped in place, and set with precision for the various angles. This machine grinding will enable you to sharpen the drills accurately. As a result, they will last longer and will produce more accurate holes.

21. According to the above paragraph, one reason for sharpening drills accurately is that the drills

    A. can then be used in a hand drill as well as a drill press
    B. will last longer
    C. can then be used by unskilled persons
    D. cost less

22. According to the above paragraph,

    A. it is easier to sharpen a drill by machine than by hand
    B. drills cannot be sharpened by hand
    C. only a skilled mechanic can learn to sharpen a drill by hand
    D. a good mechanic will learn to sharpen drills by hand

23. As used in the above paragraph, the word *precision* means MOST NEARLY

    A. accuracy   B. ease   C. rigidity   D. speed

Questions 24-27.

DIRECTIONS: Questions 24 through 27, inclusive, should be answered in accordance with the following paragraph.

Centrifugal pumps have relatively fewer moving parts than reciprocating pumps, and no valves. While reciprocating pumps when new are usually more efficient than centrifugal pumps, the latter retain their efficiency longer. Most rotary pumps are also without valves, but they have closely meshed parts between which high pressures may be set up after they begin to wear. In general, centrifugal pumps can be made much smaller than reciprocating pumps giving the same result. There is an exception, in that positive displacement pumps delivering small volumes at high heads are smaller than equivalent centrifugal pumps. Centrifugal pumps cost less when first purchased than other comparable pumps. The original outlay may be as little as one-third or one-half that of a reciprocating pump suitable for the same purpose.

24. The type of pump NOT mentioned in the above paragraph is the _____ type.   24.____

   A. rotary
   B. propeller
   C. reciprocating
   D. centrifugal

25. According to the above paragraph, the type of pump that sometimes has valves and sometimes does NOT is the   25.____

   A. rotary
   B. propeller
   C. reciprocating
   D. centrifugal

26. According to the above paragraph, centrifugal pumps are   26.____

   A. *always smaller* than reciprocating pumps
   B. *smaller* than reciprocating pumps only when designed to deliver small quantities at low pressures
   C. *larger* than reciprocating pumps only when designed to deliver small quantities at high pressures
   D. *larger* than reciprocating pumps only when designed to deliver large quantities at low pressures

27. The advantage of centrifugal pumps that is NOT mentioned in the above paragraph is that   27.____

   A. the centrifugal pump retains its efficiency longer
   B. it is impossible to create an excessive pressure when using a centrifugal pump
   C. there are fewer parts to wear out in a centifugal pump
   D. the centrifugal pump is cheaper

Questions 28-30.

DIRECTIONS: Questions 28 through 30, inclusive, should be answered in accordance with the following paragraph.

Gaskets made of relatively soft materials are placed between the meeting surfaces of hydraulic fittings in order to increase the tightness of the seal. They should be composed of materials that will not be affected by the liquid to be enclosed, nor by the conditions under which the system operates, including maximum pressure and temperature. They should be able to maintain the amount of clearance required between meeting surfaces. One of the materials most widely used in making gaskets is neoprene. Since neoprene is flexible, it is often used in sheet form at points where a gasket must expand enough to allow air to accumulate, as with cover plates on supply tanks. Over a period of time, oil tends to deteriorate the material used in making neoprene gaskets. The condition of the gasket must, therefore, be checked whenever the unit is disassembled. Since neoprene gasket material is soft and flexible, it easily becomes misshapen, scratched or torn. Great care is, therefore, necessary in handling neoprene. Shellac, gasket sealing compounds or "pipe dope" should never be used with sheet neoprene, unless absolutely necessary for satisfactory installation.

28. Of the following, the one that is NOT mentioned in the above paragraph as a requirement for a good gasket material is that the material must be

    A. cheap
    B. unaffected by heat developed in a system
    C. relatively soft
    D. capable of maintaining required clearances

29. According to the above paragraph, neoprene will be affected by

    A. air
    B. temperature
    C. pressure
    D. oil

30. According to the above paragraph, care is necessary in handling neoprene because

    A. its condition must be checked frequently
    B. it tears easily
    C. pipe dope should not be used
    D. it is difficult to use

Questions 31-35.

DIRECTIONS: Questions 31 through 35, inclusive, should be answered in accordance with the following statements and instructions.

Column A below lists defects that often happen to equipment that is used in a sewage disposal plant. Column B shows the equipment that is used in such a plant. In the space at the right next to the number of the defect listed in Column A, select the letter in Column B representing the piece of equipment with which this defect is MOST closely associated.

COLUMN A		COLUMN B
31. Broken shear pin	A.	Centrifugal pump
32. Worn collector ring	B.	Wound rotor motor
33. Pitted impeller	C.	Bar screen
34. Worn chain	D.	Methane-gas engine
35. Crankpin bearing		

36. It is often said that in selecting a man for a job, dependability is more important than seniority. This is because 36.____

    A. it is difficult to judge the amount of work an older man can do
    B. an older man will know how to *avoid* work better
    C. the dependable man is the man you can count on to do the job as called for
    D. the dependable man will require fewer instructions

37. *A man may be conscientious, and yet not be efficient.* This statement MOST likely means that 37.____

    A. a man will not be able to do a job properly unless he has special training
    B. a man may want to do a job well, but may not know how to go about doing it
    C. if a man is efficient, he may not be conscientious
    D. the more conscientious a man is the less efficient he will be

38. If you were a senior sewage treatment worker, a good way of building up the morale of men assigned to you would be to 38.____

    A. overlook minor infractions of the rules
    B. pass the blame for bad assignments to your superiors
    C. treat the men fairly
    D. cover up for men who have made mistakes in their jobs

39. Threatening your subordinates with penalties for neglect of duty is 39.____

    A. *good* practice just to frighten them, even though the penalties will not be inflicted
    B. *poor* practice since men should never be threatened
    C. *good* practice if the penalty is actually going to be inflicted
    D. *poor* practice because men ought to work properly without threats

40. Of the following, the BEST indication that men are dissatisfied with their jobs is that they 40.____

    A. offer suggestions on improving operations
    B. appoint a grievance committee
    C. all join a union
    D. frequently leave for other jobs

41. If a senior sewage treatment worker must reprimand one of the men under him, the reprimand should be given 41.____

    A. in a loud tone of voice so that the man is properly impressed
    B. firmly but quietly
    C. the next day when the senior can get the man alone
    D. in front of the entire crew so that the rest of the men know what is right

42. If a senior sewage treatment worker is not sure of how a job should be done, he should 42.____

    A. make believe he does so that his men will not discover his lack of knowledge
    B. get someone else to do the job
    C. ask his superior how the job should be done
    D. put the job off until he can learn from another crew how it should be done

43. A senior sewage treatment worker makes a mistake, and admits it to his men. This practice is _____, because the men _____.

    A. *good;* will respect him more
    B. *poor;* will not trust his judgment anymore
    C. *good;* will then learn to check everything he does before wasting time doing jobs improperly
    D. *poor;* should not know why a job is being done in the way it is

44. A supervisor can BEST earn the respect of his men by

    A. never criticizing his men
    B. taking the blame for all actions of his men
    C. defending his men from all criticism, regardless of whether the criticism is deserved or not
    D. defending his men from unsupported criticism

45. As a senior sewage treatment worker, you have been ordered by the engineer to do a job in a certain manner which you think is not a good way of doing the job. You should

    A. tell the engineer you should be permitted to do the job in whatever way you feel best
    B. avoid doing the job
    C. do the job, but tell your men that you are not responsible for the method being used
    D. explain your objections to the engineer, but then do the job in whatever manner the engineer decides

46. The MOST important requirement for a good supervisor is to have

    A. physical strength
    B. the ability to handle men
    C. manual dexterity
    D. good appearance

47. A good senior sewage treatment worker should

    A. give all the disagreeable assignments to the laziest worker
    B. give all the good assignments to the best worker
    C. give disagreeable assignments to those men who have special training for them
    D. rotate disagreeable assignments among the men

48. A new sewage treatment worker has been assigned to work under you as a senior. The MOST important information you should get from the new man is

    A. his age
    B. the type of work he likes to do
    C. his previous experience
    D. how well he gets along with other men

49. A member of your crew, who frequently comes to you with unjustified complaints, comes to you again with another complaint.
    You should

    A. cut the man short and tell him to stop complaining unnecessarily
    B. listen to the complaint, but do nothing about it
    C. listen to the complaint, and then tell the man the complaint is not justified
    D. check the complaint to see if it is justified

50. To insure that the men working under him are doing their work properly, a senior sewage treatment worker should 50._____

    A. check their work frequently
    B. have the men prepare a written report about the work
    C. assign one individual to be responsible for each job
    D. keep a record of the supplies they use

KEY (CORRECT ANSWERS)

1. C	11. D	21. B	31. C	41. B
2. B	12. C	22. A	32. B	42. C
3. C	13. B	23. A	33. A	43. A
4. B	14. C	24. B	34. C	44. D
5. B	15. B	25. A	35. D	45. D
6. D	16. B	26. C	36. C	46. B
7. A	17. D	27. B	37. B	47. D
8. C	18. A	28. A	38. C	48. C
9. D	19. B	29. D	39. C	49. D
10. C	20. D	30. B	40. D	50. A

EXAMINATION SECTION
TEST 1

DIRECTIONS: Each question or incomplete statement is followed by several suggested answers or completions. Select the one that BEST answers the question or completes the statement. *PRINT THE LETTER OF THE CORRECT ANSWER IN THE SPACE AT THE RIGHT.*

1. Reprimanding a crew member before other workers is a

    A. *good* practice; the reprimand serves as a warning to the other workers
    B. *bad* practice; people usually resent criticism made in public
    C. *good* practice; the other workers will realize that the supervisor is fair
    D. *bad* practice; the other workers will take sides in the dispute

2. Of the following actions, the one which is LEAST likely to promote good work is for the group leader to

    A. praise workers for doing a good job
    B. call attention to the opportunities for promotion for better workers
    C. threaten to recommend discharge of workers who are below standard
    D. put into practice any good suggestion made by crew members

3. A supervisor notices that a member of his crew has skipped a routine oiling of a machine.
   Of the following, the BEST action for the supervisor to take is to

    A. promptly question the worker about the incident
    B. immediately assign another man to oil the machine
    C. bring up the incident the next time the worker asks for a favor
    D. say nothing about the incident but watch the worker carefully in the future

4. Assume you have been told to show a new worker how to operate a piece of equipment. Your FIRST step should be to

    A. ask the worker if he has any questions about the equipment
    B. permit the worker to operate the equipment himself while you carefully watch to prevent damage
    C. demonstrate the operation of the equipment for the worker
    D. have the worker read an instruction booklet on the maintenance of the equipment

5. Whenever a new man was assigned to his crew, the supervisor would introduce him to all other crew members, take him on a tour of the plant, tell him about bus schedules and places to eat.
   This practice is

    A. *good;* the new man is made to feel welcome
    B. *bad;* supervisors should not interfere in personal matters
    C. *good;* the new man knows that he can bring his personal problems to the supervisor
    D. *bad;* work time should not be spent on personal matters

6. The MOST important factor in successful leadership is the ability to

    A. obtain instant obedience to all orders
    B. establish friendly personal relations with crew members
    C. avoid disciplining crew members
    D. make crew members want to do what should be done

7. Explaining the reasons for departmental procedure to workers tends to

    A. waste time which should be used for productive purposes
    B. increase their interest in their work
    C. make them more critical of departmental procedures
    D. confuse them

8. If you want a job done well, do it yourself.
   For a supervisor to following this advice would be

    A. *good;* a supervisor is responsible for the work of his crew
    B. *bad;* a supervisor should train his men, not do their work
    C. *good;* a supervisor should be skilled in all jobs assigned to his cre
    D. *bad;* a supervisor loses respect when he works with his hands

9. When a supervisor discovers a mistake in one of the jobs for which his crew is responsible, it is MOST important for him to find out

    A. whether anybody else knows about the mistake
    B. who was to blame for the mistake
    C. how to prevent similar mistakes in the future
    D. whether similar mistakes occurred in the past

10. A supervisor who has to explain a new procedure to his crew should realize that questions from the crew usually show that they

    A. are opposed to the new procedure
    B. are completely confused by the explanation
    C. need more training in the new procedure
    D. are interested in the explanation

11. A supervisor assigns one of his crew to sweep the area around the trash racks. A short time later, the supervisor notices that the trash rack area has not been swept. Of the following, the BEST way for the supervisor to handle this is to

    A. ask the crew member why he has not swept the area
    B. reprimand the crew member for not obeying orders
    C. assign another crew member to sweep the area
    D. sweep the area himself

12. Suppose that a member of your crew complains that you are *playing favorites* in assigning work.
    Of the following, the BEST method of handling the complaint is to

    A. deny it and refuse to discuss the matter with the worker
    B. take the opportunity to tell the worker what is wrong with his work

C. ask the worker for examples to prove his point and try to clear up any misunderstanding
D. promise to be more careful in making assignments in the future

13. A member of your crew comes to you with a complaint. After discussing the matter with him, it is clear that you have convinced him that his complaint was not justified.
    At this point, you should

    A. permit him to drop the matter
    B. make him admit his error
    C. pretend to see some justification in his complaint
    D. warn him against making unjustified complaints

13.____

14. Suppose that a supervisor has in his crew an older man who works rather slowly. In other respects, this man is a good worker; he is seldom absent, works carefully, never loafs, and is cooperative.
    The BEST way for the supervisor to handle this worker is to

    A. try to get him to work faster and less carefully
    B. give him the most disagreeable jobs
    C. request that he be given special training
    D. permit him to work at his own speed

14.____

15. Suppose that a member of your crew comes to you with a suggestion he thinks will save time in doing a job. You realize immediately that it won't work.
    Under these circumstances, your BEST action would be to

    A. thank the worker for the suggestion and forget about it
    B. explain to the worker why you think it won't work
    C. tell the worker to put the suggestion in writing
    D. ask the other members of your crew to criticize the suggestion

15.____

Questions 16-18.

DIRECTIONS: Questions 16 through 18 are to be answered on the basis of the following paragraph.

Thermostats should be tested in hot water for proper opening. A bucket should be filled with sufficient water to cover the thermostat and fitted with a thermometer suspended in the water so that the sensitive bulb portion does not rest directly on the bucket. The water is then heated on a stove. As the temperature of the water passes the 160-165° range, the thermostat should start to open and should be completely opened when the temperature has risen to 185-190°. Lifting the thermostat into the air should cause a pronounced closing action, and the unit should be closed entirely within a short time.

16. The thermostat described above is a device which opens and closes with changes in the

    A. position   B. pressure
    C. temperature   D. surroundings

16.____

17. According to the above paragraph, the closing action of the thermostat should be tested by

    A. working the thermostat back and forth
    B. permitting the water to cool gradually
    C. adding cold water to the bucket
    D. removing the thermostat from the bucket

18. The bulb of the thermometer should NOT rest directly on the bucket because

    A. the bucket gets hotter than the water
    B. the thermometer might be damaged in that position
    C. it is difficult to read the thermometer in that position
    D. the thermometer might interfere with operation of the thermostat

Questions 19-21.

DIRECTIONS: Questions 19 through 21 are to be answered on the basis of the following paragraph.

All idle pumps should be turned daily by hand, and should be run under power at least once a week. Whenever repairs are made on a pump, a record should be kept so that it will be possible to judge the success with which the pump is performing its functions. If a pump fails to deliver liquid, there may be an obstruction in the suction line, the pump's parts may be badly worn, or the packing defective.

19. According to the above paragraph, pumps

    A. in use should be turned by hand every day
    B. which are not in use should be run under power every day
    C. which are in daily use should be run under power several times a week
    D. which are not in use should be turned by hand every day

20. According to the above paragraph, the reason for keeping records of repairs made on pumps is to

    A. make certain that proper maintenance is being performed
    B. discover who is responsible for improper repairs
    C. rate the performance of the pumps
    D. know when to replace worn parts

21. The one of the following causes of pump failure which is NOT mentioned in the above paragraph is

    A. excessive suction lift   B. clogged lines
    C. bad packing   D. worn parts

Questions 22-24.

DIRECTIONS: Questions 22 through 24 are to be answered on the basis of the following paragraph.

The bearings of all electrical equipment should be subjected to careful inspection at scheduled periodic intervals in order to secure maximum life. The newer type of sleeve bearings requires very little attention since the oil does not become contaminated and oil leakage is negligible. Maintenance of the correct oil level is frequently the only upkeep required for years of service with this type of bearing.

22. According to the above paragraph, the MAIN reason for making periodic inspections of electrical equipment is to 22.____

    A. reduce waste of lubricants
    B. prevent injury to operators
    C. make equipment last longer
    D. keep operators *on their toes*

23. According to the above paragraph, the bearings of electrical equipment should be inspected 23.____

    A. whenever the equipment isn't working properly
    B. whenever there is time for inspections
    C. at least once a year
    D. at regular times

24. According to the above paragraph, when using newer type of sleeve bearings, 24.____

    A. oil leakage is slight
    B. the oil level should be checked every few years
    C. oil leakage is due to carelessness
    D. oil soon becomes dirty

25. The MAIN reason for treating sewage before emptying it into the ocean is to 25.____

    A. prevent pollution of the water
    B. remove disagreeable odors
    C. protect fishing areas
    D. obtain valuable by-products

KEY (CORRECT ANSWERS)

1. B
2. C
3. A
4. C
5. A

6. D
7. B
8. B
9. C
10. D

11. A
12. C
13. A
14. D
15. B

16. C
17. D
18. A
19. D
20. C

21. A
22. C
23. D
24. A
25. A

TEST 2

DIRECTIONS: Each question or incomplete statement is followed by several suggested answers or completions. Select the one that BEST answers the question or completes the statement. *PRINT THE LETTER OF THE CORRECT ANSWER IN THE SPACE AT THE RIGHT.*

Questions 1-3.

DIRECTIONS: Questions 1 through 3, inclusive, are to be answered in accordance with the information given in the paragraph below.

The soda-acid fire extinguisher is the commonest type of water solution extinguisher in which pressure is used to expel the water. The chemicals used are sodium bicarbonate (baking soda) and sulfuric acid. The sodium bicarbonate is dissolved in water, and this solution is the extinguishing agent. The extinguishing, value of the stream is that of an equal quantity of water.

1. According to the above paragraph, the soda-acid extinguisher, compared to others of the same type, is the   1.____

    A. most widely used
    B. most effective in putting out fire
    C. cheapest to operate
    D. easiest to operate

2. In the soda-acid extinguisher, the fire is put out by a solution of sodium bicarbonate and   2.____

    A. sulfuric acid
    B. baking soda
    C. soda-acid
    D. water

3. According to the above paragraph, the sodium bicarbonate solution, compared to water, is   3.____

    A. *more* effective in putting out fires
    B. *less* effective in putting out fires
    C. *equally* effective in putting out fires
    D. *more or less* effective, depending upon the type of fire

Questions 4-6.

DIRECTIONS: Questions 4 through 6, inclusive, are to be answered in accordance with the information given in the paragraph below.

Some gases which may be inhaled have an irritant effect on the respiratory tract. Among them are ammonia fumes, hydrogen sulfide, nitrous fumes, and phosgene. Persons who have been exposed to irritant gases must lie down at once and keep absolutely quiet until the doctor arrives. The action of some of these gases may be delayed, and at first the victim may show few or no symptoms.

4. According to the above paragraph, the part of the body that is most affected by irritant gases is the

   A. heart B. lungs C. skin D. nerves

5. According to the above paragraph, a person who has inhaled an irritant gas should be

   A. given artificial respiration
   B. made to rest
   C. wrapped in blankets
   D. made to breathe smelling salts

6. A person is believed to have come in contact with an irritant gas but he does not become sick immediately. According to the above paragraph, we may conclude that the person

   A. did not really come in contact with the gas
   B. will become sick later
   C. came in contact with a small amount of gas
   D. may possibly become sick later

7. The BEST way for a supervisor to reduce the number of accidents among his workers is to

   A. draw up detailed safety procedures
   B. constantly inspect the operation for dangerous practices
   C. carefully investigate the cause of every accident
   D. develop safety consciousness in his workers

8. The MAIN reason for enclosing switches and other current-carrying parts of electrical systems is to

   A. exclude dirt and moisture
   B. protect workers from shock
   C. increase the capacity of the equipment
   D. prevent damage to the equipment

9. Sewage treatment workers who work near electrical equipment should avoid touching wires particularly when wearing

   A. rubber-soled shoes B. wet clothing
   C. loose-fitting clothing D. nylon clothing

10. A leak in a chlorine tank is dangerous because chlorine

    A. may cause an explosion B. may corrode equipment
    C. is an irritating gas D. is highly flammable

11. Suppose that a member of your crew falls down a flight of stairs and severely injures his leg.
    While waiting for the doctor, you should try to

    A. make the injured man comfortable and prevent further injury
    B. put a splint on his leg if it appears to be broken
    C. question the injured man about the cause of the accident
    D. exercise the injured leg to prevent muscle tightening

12. Suppose that you see some acid splash into the eyes of a fellow worker. The one of the following actions that you should take FIRST is to

    A. bandage his eyes with a clean dressing
    B. place boric acid ointment in his eyes
    C. make him lie down and close his eyes
    D. wash his eyes with large amounts of clean water

13. Suppose that you discover an unconscious man who has fallen across a *live* electric wire.
    Of the following, the action that you should take FIRST is to

    A. break the contact between the man and the live wire
    B. give the man artificial respiration
    C. loosen the man's clothing and treat him for shock
    D. apply sterile dressings to the man's burns

14. It is important to know the location of pressure points when treating persons suffering from

    A. shock   B. bleeding   C. poisoning   D. burns

15. The one of the following diseases which may be caused by the pollution of drinking water by sewage is

    A. malaria
    B. typhoid fever
    C. tuberculosis
    D. muscular dystrophy

16. The one of the following gases which is a valuable byproduct of the treatment of sewage is

    A. methane
    B. chlorine
    C. hydrogen sulfide
    D. ammonia

17. In the city sewage system, MOST digested sludge is

    A. used as soil fertilizer
    B. dumped into the ocean
    C. used as land fill
    D. processed into soap

18. The MAIN reason for painting metal equipment in a sewage plant is to

    A. cut down on repairs and replacement of equipment
    B. improve the appearance of the plant
    C. make it easier to inspect the equipment
    D. eliminate the need for cleaning the equipment

19. A pump is able to fill a tank holding 15,000 gallons in 2 hours and 30 minutes. Pumping at the same rate, an empty 60,000 gallon tank can be filled in _____ hours.

    A. 10   B. 10/1/2   C. 11   D. 11 1/2

20. Assume you want to add 10,000 gallons of water to a tank. If you pump water into the tank at the rate of 100 gallons per minute for one hour and 50 gallons per minute after the first hour, the total time required to add the 10,000 gallons is MOST NEARLY

    A. 1 hour and 20 minutes
    B. 2 hours
    C. 2 hours and 20 minutes
    D. 3 hours

21. A tank 25 feet long, 15 feet wide, and 10 feet deep is enlarged by extending the length another 25 feet.
    The enlarged tank will be able to hold _____ more than the original tank.

    A. 50%   B. 100%   C. 150%   D. 200%

Questions 22-24.

DIRECTIONS: Questions 22 through 24, inclusive, are to be answered in accordance with the information given below.

At midnight of each day, readings are made of gas consumption meters. Readings for 8 days are as follows:

Sunday	6873 cu.ft.	Thursday	3246 cu.ft.
Monday	8147 cu.ft.	Friday	4962 cu.ft.
Tuesday	0065 cu.ft.	Saturday	6823 cu.ft.
Wednesday	1480 cu.ft.	Sunday	7179 cu.ft.

22. According to the above table, the total gas consumed for the week was MOST NEARLY _____ cu.ft.

    A. 1000   B. 4000   C. 7000   D. 10,000

23. Gas consumption for Tuesday was MOST NEARLY _____ cu.ft.

    A. 500   B. 1000   C. 2000   D. 8000

24. The day on which gas consumption was LOWEST was

    A. Monday   B. Tuesday   C. Wednesday   D. Thursday

25. The yearly summer survey of harbor pollution is made by the department of

    A. health
    C. public works
    B. marine and aviation
    D. sanitation

KEY (CORRECT ANSWERS)

1.	A	11.	A
2.	D	12.	D
3.	C	13.	A
4.	B	14.	B
5.	B	15.	B
6.	D	16.	A
7.	D	17.	B
8.	B	18.	A
9.	B	19.	A
10.	C	20.	C

21. B
22. D
23. C
24. A
25. C

EXAMINATION SECTION
TEST 1

DIRECTIONS: Each question or incomplete statement is followed by several suggested answers or completions. Select the one that *BEST* answers the question or completes the statement. *PRINT THE LETTER OF THE CORRECT ANSWER IN THE SPACE AT THE RIGHT.*

1. In a modification of the conventional activated sludge process known as Modified Aeration, the percentage of returned sludge to the aeration tank is, MOST nearly, 1.____

    A. 10 B. 20 C. 30 D. 40

2. The amount of chlorine, in pounds per million gallons, to produce 0.5 ppm residual in most primary effluents will, *most nearly,* be between 2.____

    A. 10 to 40 B. 50 to 70 C. 100 to 200 D. 300 to 500

3. In a conventional activated sludge treatment plant, air is applied at a rate of, most *nearly,* 3.____

    A. 1 to 1 1/2 cubic feet per gallon of sewage
    B. 3 to 3 1/2 cubic feet per gallon of sewage
    C. 4 to 5 1/2 cubic feet per gallon of sewage
    D. 7 to 7 1/2 cubic feet per gallon of sewage

4. Of the following temperature ranges, the *one* which is the *MOST* efficient for sludge digester operation is 4.____

    A. 45° F and 50° F
    B. 55° F and 65° F
    C. 70° F and 75° F
    D. 85° F and 95° F

5. The sewage detention time in an aeration tank using modified aeration is, *most nearly,* 5.____

    A. 2 hours B. 4 hours C. 6 hours D. 8 hours

6. The BTU per cubic foot value of sludge gas from a well established and properly operated digestion tank is, most *nearly,* 6.____

    A. 150 B. 350 C. 450 D. 650

7. BOD is an abbreviation for 7.____

    A. Bacteria Operating Demand
    B. Biosorption Operating Demand
    C. Biochemical Oxygen Demand
    D. Biofilter Oxygen Demand

8. The one of the following that is normally used to control the flow of sewage to the treatment plant from the intercepting sewer is the 8.____

    A. float valve
    B. sluice gate
    C. gate valve
    D. regulator gate

9. A sludge gas encountered at sewage treatment plants that is corrosive and damaging to metals is

   A. carbon dioxide
   B. ethane
   C. nitrogen
   D. hydrogen sulphide

10. When sludge is withdrawn from a sludge gas collector tank with a fixed color, a compensating volume of fresh sludge or water or gas must be put into the tank to prevent the development of

    A. leakage
    B. positive pressures
    C. negative pressures
    D. condensation

11. Devices in sewage treatment plants whose function is to break or cut up solids found in sewage are known as

    A. barmimutors
    B. diffusers
    C. tricklers
    D. grinders

12. The sludge treatment process whereby the volume of sludge going to the digester is reduced is known as

    A. thickening
    B. elutriation
    C. chemical conditioning
    D. wet oxidation

13. *Most* of the suspended solids are separated or removed from the sewage by

    A. aeration   B. washing   C. elutriation   D. sedimentation

14. The *one* of the following that is usually operated by compressed air is a

    A. reducer
    B. baffle
    C. sump pump
    D. sewage ejector

15. The *PRIMARY* function of a grit chamber in a sewage treatment plant is to remove

    A. paper   B. worms   C. gravel   D. algae

16. A deep two-storied storage sewage tank with an upper sedimentaton chamber and a lower chamber is known as a _____ tank.

    A. detritus   B. imhoff   C. septic   D. elocculating

17. The *one* of the following which *BEST* characterizes activated sludge is that it is

    A. black in color and has small particles
    B. blue in color and has large particles
    C. brown in color and has some dissolved oxygen
    D. beige in color and has a great amount of dissolved oxygen

18. The *optimum* PH value of the sludge in a digester should be

    A. 10   B. 7   C. 3   D. 2

19. In the Activated Sludge Process, the *one* of the following steps that may be taken to prevent or control sludge bulkings is to

    A. decrease aeration in time and rate
    B. chlorinate returned activated sludge

C. increase the solids content carried in aeration tanks
D. raise the pH value to 7.8

20. In starting a digester unit, the QUICKEST results can be obtained by

    A. seeding   B. shredding   C. dosing   D. chlorinating

21. Sludge digestion carried out in the absence of free oxygen is known as

    A. wet oxidation   B. heat drying
    C. anaerobic decomposition   D. aerobic decomposition

22. "Frothing" is MOST frequently attributable to

    A. short circuiting of aeration tanks
    B. septic sewage in primary tank
    C. high concentration of fungus
    D. detergent compounds in the sewage

23. The process of removing floating grease or scum from the surface of sewage in a tank is called

    A. squeegeeing   B. siphoning
    C. skimming   D. sloughing

24. Of the following, the one which BEST represents a primary treatment device for sewage is the

    A. stabilization pond   B. intermittent sand filter
    C. septic tank   D. aeration tank

25. Freshly poured concrete surfaces normally exposed to air should be cured for a minimum period of

    A. 4 days   B. 5 days   C. 6 days   D. 7 days

26. One of your men on the job is injured at a work site and is unconscious. The BEST course of action for you to follow is to

    A. give him liquids to drink
    B. have him remain in a lying position until medical help arrives
    C. immediately move him to the first-aid station
    D. attempt to arouse him to consciousness by shaking him

27. The type of portable fire extinguisher that is MOST effective in controlling a fire around live electrical equipment is the

    A. foam type   B. soda-acid type
    C. carbon-dioxide type   D. water type

28. The hazards of electric shock resulting from operation of a portable electric tool in a damp location can be reduced by

    A. grounding the tool
    B. holding the tool with one hand
    C. running the tool at low speed
    D. using a baffle

29. The *one* of the following that is the *proper* first aid to administer to a conscious person suffering from chlorine inhalation is 29.____

   A. an alocholic drink
   B. black coffee
   C. a pulmotor
   D. a cold shower

30. Of the following actions, the *best one* to take *FIRST* after smoke is seen coming from an electric control device is to 30.____

   A. shut off the power to it
   B. call the main office for advice
   C. look for a wiring diagram
   D. throw water on it

KEY (CORRECT ANSWERS)

1.	A	16.	B
2.	C	17.	C
3.	A	18.	B
4.	D	19.	B
5.	A	20.	A
6.	D	21.	C
7.	C	22.	D
8.	B	23.	C
9.	D	24.	C
10.	C	25.	D
11.	A	26.	B
12.	A	27.	C
13.	D	28.	A
14.	D	29.	B
15.	C	30.	A

TEST 2

DIRECTIONS: Each question or incomplete statement is followed by several suggested answers or completions. Select the one that BEST answers the question or completes the statement. *PRINT THE LETTER OF THE CORRECT ANSWER IN THE SPACE AT THE RIGHT.*

1. Of the following, the BEST fastener to use when attaching a pipe support bracket to a concrete wall is a(n)   1.____

    A. toggle bolt
    B. expansion bolt
    C. carriage bolt
    D. lag bolt

2. The MAIN reason for mixing a "thinner" into paint is to   2.____

    A. *clear up* air bubbles
    B. *stop* the paint from bleeding
    C. *spread* the paint easily
    D. *make* the paint color lighter

3. Schedule 40 pipe is a designation for   3.____

    A. asbestos cement pipe
    B. steel pipe
    C. transite pipe
    D. clay pipe

4. The function of a check valve in a pipeline is to   4.____

    A. relieve excessive pressure
    B. remove air
    C. meter the flow
    D. prevent reverse flow

5. The device on an electric motor which will prevent overheating is called a   5.____

    A. rheostat
    B. bus bar
    C. solenoid
    D. thermal relay

6. The oil recommended for the gear box of a 20-ton sewage plant crane is, *most nearly*,   6.____

    A. SAE 80   B. SAE 120   C. SAE 160   D. SAE 200

7. Where pump ball bearings may be subjected to water washing, the lubricating grease should have a   7.____

    A. white lead base
    B. red lead base
    C. sodium soap base
    D. lithum soap base

8. A chlorine leak can normally be detected by   8.____

    A. a lighted candle
    B. its smell
    C. a dry rag
    D. an oil-soaked rag

9. The moving wooden planks in a tank used to scrape sludge from the bottom of a tank are known as   9.____

    A. cleats   B. flights   C. rails   D. levers

10. A device with an edge or notch used for measuring liquid flow is known as a   10.____

    A. Parshall Flume
    B. Plainer Bowlus
    C. Venturi
    D. Weir

11. The *one* of the following types of pumps that is WIDELY used for pumping sewage is

    A. reciprocating   B. rotary   C. simplex   D. centrifugal

12. Prior to starting a newly installed pump, you should

    A. open the motor disconnect switch
    B. expose the pump to outside weather conditions
    C. turn the shaft by hand to see that it rotates freely
    D. disconnect the vent and drain the plugs

13. A maintenance program for a new piece of operating equipment should BEST be set up in accordance with the

    A. location of the unit
    B. location of personnel
    C. manufacturer's recommendations
    D. monthly plant capacity

14. The *one* of the following fasteners that has threads at *both* ends is called a

    A. screw   B. stud   C. blivet   D. drift bolt

15. The *one* of the following that is installed between two pipe flanges to seal the connection is called a

    A. sheave   B. gasket   C. boss   D. fillet

16. A wet undigested sludge containing a large amount of grease will MOST probably

    A. clog the opening of the filter
    B. have no effect on the efficiency of the filters
    C. cause rapid deterioration of the filter
    D. cause the filter to shrink and snap

17. The floating cover for a sludge gas storage tank is kept under a gauge pressure of, *most nearly,*

    A. 0 to 2 ounces   B. 3 to 5 ounces
    C. 6 to 9 ounces   D. 10 to 12 ounces

18. The tool that is used to remove the burrs from the end of 1/2" diameter steel pipe after cutting it with a pipe cutter is known as a

    A. bit   B. reamer   C. tap   D. caliper

19. Of the following common obstructions found in sewer lines, the *one* that occurs MOST frequently is

    A. roots   B. debris   C. grease   D. grit

20. The *one* of the following that is the MAIN reason for putting orders in writing is to

    A. protect the person who receives it
    B. protect the person who prepared the order
    C. make it easier to check mistakes
    D. protect the agency should something unforeseen occur

21. For records to provide an essential basis for future changes or expansions of the sewage treatment plant, the records must be

    A. accurate
    B. lengthy
    C. detailed in ink
    D. hand-written in pencil

22. The volume, in cubic feet, of a slab of concrete that is 5'-0" wide, 6'-0" long, and 0'-6" in depth is, *most nearly*,

    A. 15.0 B. 13.5 C. 12.0 D. 10.5

23. The sum of the following pipe lengths, 22 1/8", 7 3/4", 19 7/16", and 4 3 5/8", is:

    A. 91 7/8" B. 92 1/16" C. 92 1/4" D. 92 15/16"

24. The area in square feet of a plant floor that is 42 feet wide and 75 feet long is

    A. 3150 B. 3100 C. 3075 D. 2760

25. Of the following types of gauges, the *one* that indicates pressure above and below atmospheric pressures is known as a

    A. pressure B. vacuum C. Bourdan D. compound

26. A U-tube manometer is used to measure

    A. deflection B. height C. radiation D. pressure

27. If an air-conditioning unit shorted out and caught fire, the *BEST* fire extinguisher to use would be a _____ extinguisher.

    A. water
    B. foam
    C. carbon dioxide
    D. soda acid

28. Of the following, the *best* action to take to help someone whose eyes have been splashed with lye is to *FIRST*

    A. wash out the eyes with clean water
    B. wash out the eyes with a salt water solution
    C. apply a sterile dressing over the eyes
    D. do nothing to the eyes, but telephone for medical help

Questions 29-30.

DIRECTIONS: Questions numbered 29 and 30 are to be answered in accordance with the information given in the following paragraph:

A sludge lagoon is an excavated area in which digested sludge is desired. Lagoon depths vary from six to eight feet. There are no established criteria for the required capacity of a lagoon. The sludge moisture content is reduced by evaporation and drainage. Volume reduction is slow, especially in cold and rainy weather. Weather and soil conditions affect concentration. The drying period ranges from a period of several months to several years. After the sludge drying period has ended, a bulldozer or tractor can be used to remove the sludge. The dried sludge can be used for fill of low ground. A filled dried lagoon can be developed into a lawn. Lagoons can be used for emergency storage when the sludge beds are full. Lagoons are popular because they are inexpensive to build and operate. They have a disadvantage of being unsightly. A hazard to lagoon operation is the possibility of draining partly digested sludge to the lagoon that creates a fly and odor nuisance.

29. In accordance with the given paragraph, sludge lagoons have the *disadvantage* of being 29.____

    A. unsightly
    B. too deep
    C. concentrated
    D. wet

30. In accordance with the given paragraph, moisture content is *reduced* by 30.____

    A. digestion
    B. evaporation
    C. oxidation
    D. removal

KEY (CORRECT ANSWERS)

1.	B	16.	A
2.	C	17.	B
3.	B	18.	B
4.	D	19.	A
5.	D	20.	B
6.	B	21.	A
7.	D	22.	A
8.	B	23.	D
9.	B	24.	A
10.	D	25.	D
11.	D	26.	D
12.	C	27.	C
13.	C	28.	A
14.	B	29.	A
15.	A	30.	B

EXAMINATION SECTION
TEST 1

DIRECTIONS: Each question or incomplete statement is followed by several suggested answers or completions. Select the one that BEST answers the question or completes the statement. *PRINT THE LETTER OF THE CORRECT ANSWER IN THE SPACE AT THE RIGHT.*

1. To measure the diameter of a replacement pump shaft, a(n) _____ should be used.   1._____

    A. surveyor's chain
    B. micrometer
    C. metallic tape
    D. engineer's scale

2. A _____ is used to bypass storm flow in a combined-sewerage system.   2._____

    A. drop inlet
    B. side weir
    C. hydraulic jump
    D. baffle

3. The PRIMARY element in a control system is the   3._____

    A. transmitter
    B. receiver
    C. sensor
    D. controller

4. The use of water to break down complex substances into simpler ones is called   4._____

    A. dissolving
    B. hydrolysis
    C. coagulation
    D. hydrostasis

5. In its progress through a pumping station, wastewater FIRST passes through a   5._____

    A. comminutor
    B. chlorine room
    C. wet well
    D. barminutor

6. Which of the following is NOT one of the main operational factors for a barminutor?   6._____

    A. Amount of debris in wastewater
    B. Number of units in service
    C. Head loss through unit
    D. Removal of floatables

7. Which of the following precautions must be taken before attempting to repair a surface aerator?   7._____

    A. Shut down aerator
    B. Drain aeration tank
    C. Secure header assembly
    D. Test atmosphere for toxic gases

8. Which of the following source types would MOST likely influence the pH of wastewater?   8._____

    A. Industrial
    B. Commercial
    C. Agricultural
    D. Domestic

9. Each of the following items should be carefully controlled in an activated sludge plant in order to prevent sludge bulking EXCEPT   9._____

    A. filamentous growth
    B. length of aeration time
    C. return sludge rate
    D. sludge age

10. Sludge blanket depths may be measured by the use of

    A. ultrasonic transmitters and receivers
    B. pressure gages
    C. floats connected to cables
    D. bubbler tubes

11. The vertical distance from the normal water surface to the top of the confining wall of a pond or tank is called the

    A. freeboard   B. force main
    C. header   D. stop log

12. Suspended solids in the effluent from a trickling filter plant may be caused by

    A. heavy sloughing from the filters
    B. precipitation of solids in the secondary filter
    C. condensation of effluent on secondary equipment
    D. flotation of solids in the primary clarifier

13. What is MOST often produced during the decomposition of domestic wastes?

    A. Phenols   B. Oxygen
    C. Hydrogen sulfide   D. Sulfur

14. Air compressor vibration sensing devices are used to measure each of the following EXCEPT

    A. flow   B. velocity
    C. acceleration   D. displacement

15. The height or energy of liquids above a certain point is measured in terms of

    A. discharge rate   B. volume
    C. flow   D. head

16. Factors in the design of sanitary sewers include each of the following EXCEPT

    A. maximum rate for an entire service area's domestic sewage within a specified time period
    B. maximum rates from commercial and industrial areas
    C. infiltration allowance for entire service area
    D. maximum rates from domestic and industrial/commercial sources combined

17. Which of the following could prevent a pump from starting?

    A. Tripped circuit breakers
    B. Air leaks in suction line
    C. High discharge head
    D. Lack of priming

18. Through which stage would wastewater undergoing chemical-physical treatment pass FIRST?

    A. Precipitation   B. Stripping
    C. Flocculation   D. Slaking

19. Which of the following could be considered a normal operating condition for micro-screens?

   A. High flow
   B. High pH level
   C. Low pH flow
   D. Toxic wastes

20. The tank in which sludges are placed in order to allow decomposition is known as the

   A. emulsion
   B. dessicator
   C. digester
   D. percolator

21. The conversion of large solid sludge particles into fine particles that can be dissolved or suspended in water is called

   A. hydrolysis
   B. liquefaction
   C. comminution
   D. recirculation

22. A mixture in which two or more liquid substances are held in suspension is called a(n)

   A. solution
   B. electrolyte
   C. emulsion
   D. reagent

23. What is the term for a mass of sludge containing a highly concentrated population of microorganisms?

   A. Septic
   B. Seed
   C. Shock load
   D. Slug

24. Which of the following forms of nitrogen is LEAST important to the wastewater treatment process?

   A. Nitrate   B. Ammonia   C. Elemental   D. Organic

25. What is the term for water leaving a centrifuge after the removal of most solids?

   A. Cation exchange
   B. Centration
   C. Flocculation
   D. Turbidity

KEY (CORRECT ANSWERS)

1. B
2. B
3. C
4. B
5. C

6. D
7. A
8. A
9. D
10. A

11. A
12. A
13. C
14. A
15. D

16. D
17. A
18. C
19. D
20. C

21. B
22. C
23. B
24. C
25. B

TEST 2

DIRECTIONS: Each question or incomplete statement is followed by several suggested answers or completions. Select the one that BEST answers the question or completes the statement. *PRINT THE LETTER OF THE CORRECT ANSWER IN THE SPACE AT THE RIGHT.*

1. The MOST effective treatment process for destroying or removing bacteria from waste-water is through

    A. activated sludge process
    B. trickling filter
    C. chlorination
    D. sedimentation

    1.____

2. Which of the following tasks is NOT associated with the starting of a comminutor?

    A. Check positioning of inlet and outlet gases
    B. Inspect for frayed cables
    C. Adjust cutter blades
    D. Inspect for lubrication and oil leaks

    2.____

3. One of the objectives of digester mixing is

    A. the use of waste gas to run mixers
    B. adequate cooling throughout digester contents
    C. the release of hydrogen sulfide gas
    D. microorganic inoculation of raw sludge

    3.____

4. Which type of bacteria would give the STRONGEST indication of the possible presence of pathogenic bacteria in waste-water?

    A. Coliform   B. Filamentous
    C. Heterotrophic   D. Facultative

    4.____

5. Cryogenic oxygen plants should be shut down for maintenance every

    A. six months   B. year
    C. two years   D. five years

    5.____

6. At the _____ stage in the biological treatment process, aerobic bacteria uses dissolved oxygen to convert carbon compounds to carbon dioxide.

    A. clarifying   B. carbonaceous
    C. nitrification   D. coagulation

    6.____

7. _____ is NOT an influential factor in the settleability of solids in a clarifier.

    A. Detention time
    B. Flow velocity
    C. The movement of sludge scrapers
    D. Temperature

    7.____

55

8. Which concentration of total organic carbon, in milligrams per liter, would be considered *moderate* in wastewater?

   A. 50   B. 100   C. 200   D. 300

9. Which of the following is a volume reduction alternative in sludge processing?

   A. Centrifugation
   B. Chemical conditioning
   C. Flotation
   D. Drying

10. The hydraulic loading for a phosphate stripper depends on the

    A. dissolved oxygen of the activated sludge
    B. pH of wastewater
    C. BOD loading of the unit
    D. ability of the aerobic phosphate stripper to remain aerobic

11. The range of typical carrying capacities, in gallons per minute, of package-plant pumping stations is

    A. less than 600
    B. 200-700
    C. 100-1,600
    D. 700-10,000

12. When a sludge becomes too light and refuses to settle properly in a clarifier, this is known as

    A. centration
    B. precipitation
    C. comminution
    D. bulking

13. In a wet well, level control systems include each of the following EXCEPT

    A. bubblers   B. hearts   C. floats   D. electrodes

14. Which of the following is NOT one of the primary sources of odors in a wastewater treatment plant?

    A. Unwashed grit
    B. The carbon adsorption process
    C. Sludge incinerators
    D. Waste-gas burning

15. A chemical property used in the classification of irrigation waters is

    A. pH
    B. total dissolved solids
    C. BOD
    D. aeration

16. Which of the following is NOT a potential use for the dissolved air flotation process?

    A. Solids recovery
    B. Coagulation
    C. Wastewater treatment
    D. Water recovery

17. Each of the following is a principal factor determining the use of pumping stations in sewage collection EXCEPT the

    A. elevation of the area or district to be serviced
    B. location of natural drainage areas in relation to the service area
    C. cost of a pumping station
    D. cost of trunk sewer construction

18. Through which stage would wastewater undergoing chemical-physical treatment pass LAST? 18.____

    A. Carbon adsorption
    B. Lime recovery
    C. Flocculation
    D. Slaking

19. Which of the following practices is NOT included in the maintenance of equipment in package operation plants? 19.____

    A. Changing oil in the speed reducer
    B. Adjusting aeration equipment
    C. Washing tank walls and channels
    D. Inspecting the air-lift pump

20. What chemical solution is capable of neutralizing acids or bases without greatly altering pH? 20.____
    A(n)

    A. blank   B. alkaline   C. buffer   D. digester

21. Which of the following types of pumps is a displacement pump? 21.____

    A. Centrifugal
    B. Electromagnetic
    C. Peripheral
    D. Diaphragm

22. A sludge whose solid portion can be separated from the liquid is referred to as 22.____

    A. anhydrous
    B. soluble
    C. hydrolytic
    D. dewaterable

23. Which of the following could indicate that a high organic waste load has reached the activated sludge process? 23.____
    A(n)

    A. *increase* in DO residual in the aeration tank
    B. *increase* in turbidity in the effluent from the secondary chamber
    C. *decrease* in nutrients in the effluent from the secondary chamber
    D. *decrease* in aeration

24. The term for the clogging of the filtering medium or a microscreen or a vacuum filter is 24.____

    A. corrosion
    B. head loss
    C. coagulation
    D. blinding

25. Through which stage in an activated sludge treatment plant would wastewater pass LAST? 25.____

    A. Grit chamber
    B. Chlorine contact chamber
    C. Settling tanks
    D. Trickling filters

KEY (CORRECT ANSWERS)

1. C
2. B
3. D
4. A
5. B
6. B
7. C
8. C
9. D
10. A

11. B
12. D
13. B
14. B
15. B
16. B
17. C
18. A
19. A
20. C

21. D
22. D
23. B
24. D
25. B

EXAMINATION SECTION
TEST 1

DIRECTIONS: Each question or incomplete statement is followed by several suggested answers or completions. Select the one that BEST answers the question or completes the statement. *PRINT THE LETTER OF THE CORRECT ANSWER IN THE SPACE AT THE RIGHT.*

1. To check for the entrance of toxic wastes into a treatment plant, each of the following may be reliably observed as indicators EXCEPT

   A. changes in color of incoming wastewater
   B. waste recording equipment
   C. odors
   D. bulking of sludge in the clarifier

2. An increase in _____ could cause a demand for more oxygen in an aeration tank.

   A. inert or inorganic wastes
   B. pH
   C. toxic substances
   D. microorganisms

3. Chlorine may be added for hydrogen sulfide control in the

   A. collection lines
   B. aeration tank
   C. plant effluent
   D. trickling filter

4. The range of typical carrying capacities, in gallons per minute, of intermediate pumping stations is

   A. less than 600
   B. 200-700
   C. 100-1,600
   D. 700-10,000

5. A low sulfanator injector vacuum reading could be caused by

   A. missing gasket
   B. high back pressure
   C. high-volume injector flow
   D. wrong orifice

6. Before starting a rotating biological contactor process, each of the following should be checked EXCEPT

   A. lubrication
   B. biomass
   C. clearance
   D. tightness

7. The capacity for water or wastewater to neutralize acids is expressed in terms of

   A. pH
   B. oxygen demand
   C. alkalinity
   D. acidity

8. Which of the following is NOT one of the available methods for determining stormwater flow for the purpose of storm sewer design?

A. Rainfall and runoff correlation studies
B. Inlet method
C. Hydrograph method
D. Outlet method

9. What is the term for the accumulation of residue that appears on trickling filters and must be removed periodically?

    A. Sludges   B. Slurries   C. Slugs   D. Sloughings

10. A sludge containing a high number of living organisms is referred to as

    A. raw   B. activated   C. primary   D. toxic

11. Which of the following is NOT a plant location where liquid mixing is commonly practiced?

    A. Ponds
    B. Hydraulic jumps in open channels
    C. Pipelines
    D. Venturi flumes

12. Which of the following industries releases primarily inorganic wastes in its effluent?

    A. Paper
    C. Gravel washing
    B. Petroleum
    D. Dairy

13. Which of the following collection system variables could upset a plant's activated sludge process?

    A. Discharge by industrial cleaning operations
    B. Chlorination of return sludge flows
    C. Decreases in influent flows
    D. Recycling of digester supernatant

14. The second-stage BOD is also referred to as the _____ stage.

    A. carbonaceous
    C. flocculation
    B. pretreatment
    D. nitrification

15. When organic matter decomposes to form foul-smelling products associated with the lack of free oxygen, this condition is known as

    A. shock loading
    C. sloughing
    B. septicity
    D. sidestreaming

16. Which type of bacteria has the HIGHEST optimum temperature for treatment?

    A. Mesophilic
    C. Thermophilic
    B. Cryophilic
    D. Psychrophilic

17. The COD test

    A. estimates the total oxygen consumed
    B. measures the carbon oxygen demand
    C. provides results more quickly than the BOD test
    D. measures only the nitrification oxygen demand

18. Which of the following is NOT considered a major factor that may cause variations in lab test results?   18._____

    A. The nature of the material being examined
    B. Testing equipment
    C. Sampling procedures
    D. The quantity of material being examined

19. The treatment process that MOST effectively removes suspended solids from wastewater is   19._____

    A. sedimentation   B. flocculation
    C. skimming   D. comminution

20. Which of the following is a thickening alternative in sludge processing?   20._____

    A. Flotation   B. Incineration
    C. Elutriation   D. Wet oxidation

21. The device that continuously adds the flow of wastewater into a plant is the   21._____

    A. aggregate   B. turbidity meter
    C. titrator   D. totalizer

22. Two types of measurement required in connection with the operation of a treatment plant are   22._____

    A. effluent and downstream
    B. temperature and dissolved oxygen
    C. in-plant and receiving water
    D. temperature and receiving water

23. You may NOT dispose of excess activated sludge waste from package plants   23._____

    A. at a nearby treatment plant
    B. by anaerobic digestion
    C. by removal by septic tank pumper
    D. by aeration in a holding tank, then deposit in a sanitary landfill

24. What is the term for the combination of activated sludge with raw wastewater in a treatment plant?   24._____

    A. Median   B. Liquefaction
    C. Effluent   D. Mixed liquor

25. Landfills produce poisonous _____ gas as a byproduct of decomposition.   25._____

    A. methane   B. nitrogen
    C. chlorofluorocarbons   D. argon

KEY (CORRECT ANSWERS)

1. B
2. D
3. A
4. D
5. B

6. B
7. C
8. D
9. D
10. B

11. A
12. C
13. A
14. D
15. B

16. C
17. C
18. D
19. B
20. A

21. D
22. C
23. B
24. D
25. A

TEST 2

DIRECTIONS: Each question or incomplete statement is followed by several suggested answers or completions. Select the one that BEST answers the question or completes the statement. *PRINT THE LETTER OF THE CORRECT ANSWER IN THE SPACE AT THE RIGHT.*

1. Which of the following types of pumps is a kinetic pump? 1.____

   A. Rotary
   B. Piston plunger
   C. Hydraulic ram
   D. Blow case

2. What device is used to keep floated solids out of the effluent in dissolved air flotation thickeners? 2.____

   A. Cloth screens
   B. Microscreens
   C. Effluent baffles
   D. Water sprays

3. The _____ is NOT one of the primary factors affecting the flow of wastewater and sewage in sewers. 3.____

   A. viscosity of the liquid
   B. cross-sectional area of the system conduit
   C. time of day
   D. pipe surface

4. What is the term for washing a digested sludge in the plant effluent? 4.____

   A. Masking
   B. Elutriation
   C. Hydrolysis
   D. Slaking

5. _____ is NOT an objective in periodically pumping sludge from the primary clarifier to the digester. 5.____

   A. Prevention of pump clogging
   B. Prevention of digester overload
   C. Allowance for thicker sludge pumping
   D. Maintenance of good clarifier conditions

6. The toxic chemical LEAST likely to be encountered by treatment plant operators is(are) 6.____

   A. mercury
   B. acids
   C. fluorocarbons
   D. bases

7. Which concentration of total dissolved solids, in milligrams per liter, would be the MINIMUM required in order to be considered *strong* in wastewater? 7.____

   A. 250   B. 500   C. 850   D. 1,200

8. What is the term for the treatment process in which a tank or reactor is filled, the water is treated, and the tank is emptied? 8.____

   A. Flocculation
   B. Centration
   C. Batch process
   D. Pond process

9. The mixing of a compound with water to produce a true chemical reaction is to 9.____

   A. dissolve   B. slake   C. strip   D. hydrate

2 (#2)

10. If the difference in elevation between inflow and outflow sewers is greater than 1.5 feet, which device is needed?

   A. Side weir
   B. Drop inlet
   C. Baffles
   D. Inlet casting

11. Intermittent releases or discharges of industrial wastes are known as

   A. slurries
   B. slugs
   C. splashes
   D. stop logs

12. Results from the settleability test of activated sludge solids may be used to

   A. calculate BOD
   B. determine probable flow rates at which sludges may clog equipment
   C. calculate sludge age
   D. determine ability of solids to separate from liquid in final clarifier

13. The device used to measure the temperature of an effluent is a

   A. thermometer
   B. Bourdon tube
   C. thermocouple
   D. pug mill

14. Which source is typically the HEAVIEST contributor of total solids in a service area's wastewater supply?

   A. Industrial wastes
   B. Domestic wash waters
   C. Storm runoff
   D. Human biological wastes

15. The term for liquid removed from a settled sludge is

   A. hydrolyte
   B. supernatant
   C. aliquot
   D. slurry

16. A unit of wastewater moving through the treatment system without dispersing or mixing with the rest of the wastewater in the system is called

   A. centration
   B. plug flow
   C. putrefaction
   D. slugging

17. What is the term for the groups or clumps of bacteria or particles that have clustered together during the treatment process?

   A. Coagulants
   B. Slurries
   C. Floes
   D. Slugs

18. The purpose of PRIMARY sedimentation is to remove

   A. settleable and floatable material
   B. roots, rags, and large debris
   C. suspended and dissolved solids
   D. sand and gravel

19. _____ would NOT cause an increase in effluent coliform levels at a treatment plant.

   A. Mixing problems
   B. An increase in effluent BOD
   C. Solids accumulation in the contact chamber
   D. High chlorine residual

20. What is the term used to describe bacteria that can live under either aerobic or anaerobic conditions?

    A. Cultured
    B. Agglomerated
    C. Filamentous
    D. Facultative

21. Which devices are NOT used during pretreatment?

    A. Racks
    B. Comminutors
    C. Screens
    D. Coagulators

22. Through which stage in an activated sludge treatment plant would wastewater pass FIRST?

    A. Grit chambers
    B. Bar racks
    C. Settling tanks
    D. Primary sedimentation

23. The inorganic gas LEAST likely to be found around a treatment plant is

    A. ammonia
    B. methane
    C. hydrogen sulfide
    D. mercaptans

24. The soils in an effluent disposal on land program may be tested using each of the following procedures EXCEPT

    A. BOD
    B. conductivity
    C. pH
    D. cation exchange capacity

25. Which of the following is a conditioning alternative in sludge processing?

    A. Centrifugation
    B. Drying
    C. Composing
    D. Elutriation

KEY (CORRECT ANSWERS)

1.	C	11.	B
2.	C	12.	D
3.	C	13.	C
4.	B	14.	A
5.	A	15.	B
6.	C	16.	B
7.	C	17.	C
8.	C	18.	A
9.	B	19.	D
10.	B	20.	D

21.	D
22.	B
23.	D
24.	A
25.	D

EXAMINATION SECTION
TEST 1

DIRECTIONS: Each question or incomplete statement is followed by several suggested answers or completions. Select the one that BEST answers the question or completes the statement. *PRINT THE LETTER OF THE CORRECT ANSWER IN THE SPACE AT THE RIGHT.*

1. One of your men is doing a new job incorrectly.
   The BEST action for you to take is to

   A. criticize him in the presence of the other men
   B. criticize him in private
   C. bring him up on charges
   D. show him how to do it correctly

   1.____

2. Of the following, the BEST reason why it is unacceptable policy for you to become too friendly with the men you supervise is that the men may

   A. try to take advantage of your friendship
   B. resent your familiarity
   C. wish to borrow money from you
   D. be transferred to another unit

   2.____

3. Of the following, the attitude for you to have toward your men in order to accomplish your job BEST is to be

   A. harsh and uncompromising
   B. firm and fair
   C. easygoing and forgiving
   D. aloof and unsocial

   3.____

4. A man in your gang complains that the work is dirty.
   Of the following, the BEST action for you to take is to

   A. give the man only the clean jobs
   B. tell the man that the dirt is part of the working conditions
   C. tell the man to quit if he does not like the working conditions
   D. bring the man up on charges

   4.____

5. Although you estimate that you will need 4 men to do a certain job, you bring 6 men to do the job.
   This practice is considered by authorities to be

   A. *good,* since you will be sure to get the job done on time
   B. *good,* since some men may get sick on the job and may be unable to work
   C. *poor,* since men may stand around doing nothing
   D. *poor,* since the work will not be divided evenly

   5.____

6. One of your men tends to *goof off* whenever he has the chance.
   Of the following, the BEST procedure to follow first with respect to this man is to

   A. have him transferred to another unit
   B. deduct the estimated wasted time from his time off
   C. give him the hardest jobs
   D. watch him closely

   6.____

67

7. If four men work seven hours during the day, the number of man-hours of work done is

   A. 4 B. 7 C. 11 D. 28

8. You should check that you have all the equipment and material you need for the day before work is started. Of the following, the BEST reason for personally making this check is that

   A. the men under your supervision cannot be trusted
   B. the men are usually too busy to check the material and equipment
   C. it is your responsibility to see that everything is in order
   D. it is very difficult to get help for checking once you are in the field

9. One of your men is injured on the job.
   The FIRST thing you should do is to

   A. assist the injured man
   B. find out the circumstances of the accident
   C. call the office to notify your supervisor of the accident
   D. fill out the paperwork relating to the accident

10. When investigating a complaint by a home owner of sewage backing up in a house, you find that the house trap in the basement is blocked.
    Of the following, the PROPER action for you to take is to

    A. call in a plumber for the home owner
    B. clean out the house trap
    C. tell the home owner to call in a plumber
    D. disconnect the house trap from the piping, clean it out, and reinstall the trap

11. If it takes four men fourteen days to do a certain job, seven men, working at the same rate, should be able to do the same job in _____ days.

    A. 8 B. 7 C. 6 D. 5

12. The men you supervise suggest that work be started an hour earlier so that they can leave an hour earlier at the end of the day.
    Of the following, the BEST action for you to take is to

    A. ignore the request
    B. start work an hour earlier
    C. tell them you will forward their suggestion to your superior
    D. report the men for insubordination

13. One of the men under your supervision tells you he is ill and would like to leave the job. Of the following, the BEST action for you to take is to

    A. grant the request
    B. report the man for trying to goof off
    C. take the man personally to the department doctor
    D. tell the man he has to work the rest of the day or he will lose a day's pay

3 (#1)

14. One of your men scheduled to arrive at 8 A.M. calls you at noon to inform you that he will not be in because of personal business.
    Of the following, the BEST action for you to take FIRST is to

    A. tell him to take it off sick leave
    B. call the office and ask for a replacement
    C. tell the man he should have called in on or about 8 A.M.
    D. tell him to charge the absence to lateness

14._____

15. Assume that you are in the field and have completed your work 2 hours before quitting time. The men spend the remaining 2 hours sitting in a restaurant.
    This practice is considered by authorities to be

    A. *good*, as the men put in a full day
    B. *good*, as make–work is a poor policy
    C. *poor*, because it creates a bad public image
    D. *poor*, as it disrupts the restaurant's business

15._____

16. As a foreman, you insist that all mechanical equipment you use be PROPERLY serviced and maintained by your men. This policy is

    A. *poor*, since you may be pressuring the men
    B. *poor*, since the men may not cooperate
    C. *good*, since it helps prevent breakdown in equipment which can cause work to stop
    D. *good*, since the equipment is serviced on the men's time so that you get more work out of the men

16._____

17. Assume that the men you supervise are cleaning out a catchbasin and uncover a gun.
    Of the following, the BEST action to take is to

    A. notify the police department of the discovery
    B. throw the gun away because it probably does not work
    C. keep the gun since you may be able to repair it
    D. dismantle the gun before disposing of it because it may be loaded

17._____

18. While your crew is working, a passer–by stops and asks you what they are doing.
    Of the following, the BEST action to take is to

    A. tell him to mind his own business
    B. briefly explain your operation
    C. tell him to write a letter to the sewer department
    D. ignore the man and call the police if he persists

18._____

19. Your men should be careful not to break manhole covers. Of the following, the BEST reason for taking this precaution is that

    A. the cost of the manhole cover will be taken out of your paycheck
    B. the manhole cover can't be replaced
    C. manhole covers cost money to replace
    D. broken manhole covers are difficult to get rid of

19._____

20. While on the job, you teach your duties to one of the laborers. 20._____
    This practice is considered by authorities to be
    A. *poor,* because it shows favoritism
    B. *poor,* because this laborer may undermine your authority
    C. *good,* because the laborer will then be able to pass a promotion examination
    D. *good,* because the laborer can replace you in an emergency

KEY (CORRECT ANSWERS)

1.	D	11.	A
2.	A	12.	C
3.	B	13.	A
4.	B	14.	C
5.	C	15.	C
6.	D	16.	C
7.	D	17.	A
8.	C	18.	B
9.	A	19.	C
10.	C	20.	D

TEST 2

DIRECTIONS: Each question or incomplete statement is followed by several suggested answers or completions. Select the one that BEST answers the question or completes the statement. *PRINT THE LETTER OF THE CORRECT ANSWER IN THE SPACE AT THE RIGHT.*

1. The BEST reason for you to advise your men to be alert at all times while working in the street is that

    A. working in the street could be dangerous
    B. they may see some criminal activity
    C. somebody from the main office may be observing your men
    D. they may create a bad public image if they are not always alert

    1._____

2. It is GOOD practice to complete a report on an accident as soon as possible after the accident occurs MAINLY because

    A. paperwork should be submitted to the office on the same day an accident occurs
    B. if you do not you may forget some of the necessary details
    C. this gives you more time to change the report if this should be necessary
    D. the department can then immediately prepare its defense

    2._____

3. Official directives state that you are to report immediately by telephone if a manhole cover or basin grate is missing.
   Of the following, the BEST reason for having this requirement is to

    A. permit the cover or grate to be ordered if it is not on hand
    B. be able to assess the responsibility for this condition
    C. prevent an accident
    D. enable the sanitation department to clean the street

    3._____

4. A complainant is a

    A. city agency that responds to a complaint
    B. person filing a complaint
    C. crew member that responds to a complaint
    D. lawyer who defends a client against a complaint

    4._____

5. In filling out an accident form, there is a section entitled *Accident Type*.
   Of the following, the one that is an accident type is

    A. struck by falling object
    B. operated without authority
    C. worked too slowly
    D. engaged in horseplay

    5._____

6. On an accident report, there is an item labeled *Nature of Injury*.
   Of the following, the one that belongs in this category is

    A. fracture   B. carelessness
    C. defective equipment D. loose clothing

    6._____

7. Of the following, the LEAST serious of the defects filed in a sewer report is

    A. broken casting   B. missing casting
    C. noisy manhole cover D. backed up sewer

    7._____

71

8. When signing a time sheet, the employee must sign his name and his number. The BEST of the following reasons for requiring his number in addition to his name is

   A. to be sure the employee has not entered the wrong time on the time sheet
   B. to make it easier to contact the employee
   C. his signature may be difficult to read
   D. the employee is paid based on his number which is fed into the IBM machine

8._____

9. One of the men in your unit states that he will take off the next day to attend his father-in-law's funeral and wants to know if he can change the absence to sick leave. Of the following, the BEST answer you can give him is that

   A. he can charge half the time to sick leave and half to annual leave
   B. the rules do not permit this to be done
   C. this can only be done if his father-in-law had lived with him
   D. sick leave can be used this way only if he had 10 years or more in service

9._____

10. In addition to the Department of Water Resources, the Environmental Protection Administration consists of the

    A. Board of Water Supply, the Department of Sanitation, and the Department of Air Resources
    B. Department of Sanitation, the Department of Municipal Services, and the Department of Air Resources
    C. Department of Sanitation and the Department of Municipal Services
    D. Department of Sanitation and the Department of Air Resources

10._____

11. The government calendar year starts on _____ 1.

    A. June   B. July   C. May   D. January

11._____

12. A truck leaves the garage at 9:26 A.M. and returns the same day at 3:43 P.M. The period of time that the truck was away from the garage is MOST NEARLY _____ hours _____ minutes.

    A. 5; 17   B. 5; 43   C. 6; 17   D. 6; 26

12._____

13. Of the following, the BEST method for a foreman to use to teach a man how to lift a manhole cover safely is to

    A. tell him how to do it
    B. make a sketch showing the correct method to use
    C. actually lift a cover with the man watching
    D. let the man try to lift the cover and correct any mistakes

13._____

14. Assume that one of the laborers you supervise is unable to read well and that you have advised him to go evenings to school to learn to read and write English. According to good supervisory practice, the advice is considered to be

    A. *poor*, because it is none of your business
    B. *poor*, because a laborer does not have to know how to read
    C. *good*, because he can then go on to get a high school diploma
    D. *good*, because he will be able to read signs and avoid danger on the job

14._____

15. Assume that a new piece of mechanical equipment is brought to the job.
    Of the following, the BEST way for the men to learn the proper use of the equipment is to

    A. have a representative of the company that manufactures the equipment come to the job and demonstrate its use
    B. let the men try out the equipment and learn the operation of the equipment by using it
    C. let the men read the instruction manual carefully before trying out the equipment
    D. deliver a lecture to the men that have to use the equipment on the proper use of the equipment

16. Assume that you are training a group of men on the adjustment of a high-pressure relief valve.
    Of the following, the FIRST topic you should discuss with the men is

    A. the conditions under which it is necessary to adjust the relief valve
    B. how to order parts for the relief valve
    C. how the springs in the relief valve work
    D. how to take apart the relief valve

17. Assume that a new man is assigned to your unit and you explain to him exactly what is expected of him.
    This procedure is

    A. *poor,* because the new man will feel that you are threatening him
    B. *poor,* because this leaves the new man with no freedom to do the job as he feels best
    C. *good,* because then the new man can quit if he does not like the foreman
    D. *good,* because the new man will know what is required of him

18. A foreman explains to a man a way of doing a particular job and the man says he does not understand.
    Of the following, the BEST action for the foreman to take is to

    A. repeat the explanation
    B. let the man remain ignorant
    C. transfer the man to another unit
    D. tell the man he may understand the procedure at a later time

19. A new piece of equipment is ordered and the men who will use it are trained in its use before the equipment arrives on the job.
    This practice is

    A. *poor,* because the order may be cancelled and time wasted
    B. *poor,* because it takes longer to train men when the equipment is not present
    C. *good,* because it keeps the men busy when they do not have anything to do
    D. *good,* because the equipment can immediately be put to use

20. You observe a man using a piece of equipment incorrectly. Of the following, the BEST action for you to take is to

    A. have somebody else work with the equipment
    B. transfer the man to another unit
    C. bring the man up on charges
    D. show him how to use the equipment correctly

20.____

KEY (CORRECT ANSWERS)

1.	A	11.	D
2.	B	12.	C
3.	C	13.	C
4.	B	14.	D
5.	A	15.	A
6.	A	16.	A
7.	C	17.	D
8.	C	18.	A
9.	B	19.	D
10.	D	20.	D

EXAMINATION SECTION

TEST 1

DIRECTIONS: Each question or incomplete statement is followed by several suggested answers or completions. Select the one that BEST answers the question or completes the statement. *PRINT THE LETTER OF THE CORRECT ANSWER IN THE SPACE AT THE RIGHT.*

1. Of the following, the one MOST important quality required of a good supervisor is
   A. ambition   B. leadership   C. friendliness   D. popularity

2. It is often said that a supervisor can delegate authority but never responsibility. This means MOST NEARLY that
   A. a supervisor must do his own work if he expects it to be done properly
   B. a supervisor can assign someone else to do his work, but in the last analysis, the supervisor himself must take the blame for any actions followed
   C. authority and responsibility are two separate things that cannot be borne by the same person
   D. it is better for a supervisor never to delegate his authority

3. One of your men who is a habitual complainer asks you to grant him a minor privilege.
   Before granting or denying such a request, you should consider
   A. the merits of the case
   B. that it is good for group morale to grant a request of this nature
   C. the man's seniority
   D. that to deny such a request will lower your standing with the men

4. A supervisory practice on the part of a foreman which is MOST likely to lead to confusion and inefficiency is for him to
   A. give orders verbally directly to the man assigned to the job
   B. issue orders only in writing
   C. follow up his orders after issuing them
   D. relay his orders to the men through co-workers

5. It would be POOR supervision on a foreman's part if he
   A. asked an experienced maintainer for his opinion on the method of doing a special job
   B. make it a policy to avoid criticizing a man in front of his co-workers
   C. consulted his assistant supervisor on unusual problems
   D. allowed a cooling-off period of several days before giving one of his men a deserved reprimand

6. Of the following behavior characteristics of a supervisor, the one that is MOST likely to lower the morale of the men he supervises is
   A. diligence
   B. favoritism
   C. punctuality
   D. thoroughness

7. Of the following, the BEST method of getting an employee who is not working up to his capacity to produce more work is to
   A. have another employee criticize his production
   B. privately criticize his production but encourage him to produce more
   C. criticize his production before his associates
   D. criticize his production and threaten to fire him

8. Of the following, the BEST thing for a supervisor to do when a subordinate has done a very good job is to
   A. tell him to take it easy
   B. praise his work
   C. reduce his workload
   D. say nothing because he may become conceited

9. Your orders to your crew are MOST likely to be followed if you
   A. explain the reasons for these orders
   B. warn that all violators will be punished
   C. promise easy assignments to those who follow these orders best
   D. say that they are for the good of the department

10. In order to be a good supervisor, you should
    A. impress upon your men that you demand perfection in their work at all times
    B. avoid being blamed for your crew's mistakes
    C. impress your superior with your ability
    D. see to it that your men get what they are entitled to

11. In giving instructions to a crew, you should
    A. speak in as loud a tone as possible
    B. speak in a coaxing, persuasive manner
    C. speak quietly, clearly, and courteously
    D. always use the word *please* when giving instructions

12. Of the following factors, the one which is LEAST important in evaluating an employee and his work is his
    A. dependability
    B. quantity of work done
    C. quality of work done
    D. education and training

13. When a District Superintendent first assumes his command, it is LEAST important for him at the beginning to observe
    A. how his equipment is designed and its adaptability
    B. how to reorganize the district for greater efficiency
    C. the capabilities of the men in the district
    D. the methods of operation being employed

14. When making an inspection of one of the buildings under your supervision, the BEST procedure to follow in making a record of the inspection is to
    A. return immediately to the office and write a report from memory
    B. write down all the important facts during or as soon as you complete the inspection
    C. fix in your mind all important facts so that you can repeat them from memory if necessary
    D. fix in your mind all important facts so that you can make out your report at the end of the day

15. Assume that your superior has directed you to make certain changes in your established procedure. After using this modified procedure on several occasions, you find that the original procedure was distinctly superior and you wish to return to it.
    You should
    A. let your superior find this out for himself
    B. simply change back to the original procedure
    C. compile definite data and information to prove your case to your superior
    D. persuade one of the more experienced workers to take this matter up with your superior

16. An inspector visited a large building under construction. He inspected the soil lines at 9 A.M., water lines at 10 A.M., fixtures at 11 A.M., and did his office work in the afternoon. He followed the same pattern daily for weeks.
    This procedure was
    A. *good*, because it was methodical and he did not miss anything
    B. *good*, because it gave equal time to all phases of the plumbing
    C. *bad*, because not enough time was devoted to fixtures
    D. *bad*, because the tradesmen knew when the inspection would occur

17. Assume that one of the foremen in a training course, which you are conducting, proposes a poor solution for a maintenance problem.
    Of the following, the BEST course of action for you to take is to
    A. accept the solution tentatively and correct it during the next class meeting
    B. point out all the defects of this proposed solution and wait until somebody thinks of a better solution
    C. try to get the class to reject this proposed solution and develop a better solution
    D. let the matter pass since somebody will present a better solution as the class work proceeds

18. As a supervisor, you should be seeking ways to improve the efficiency of shop operations by means such as changing established work procedures.
    The following are offered as possible actions that you should consider in changing established work procedures:
    I. Make changes only when your foremen agree to them
    II. Discuss changes with your supervisor before putting them into practice

III. Standardize any operation which is performed on a continuing basis
IV. Make changes quickly and quietly in order to avoid dissent
V. Secure expert guidance before instituting unfamiliar procedures
Of the following suggested answers, the one that describes the actions to be taken to change established work procedures is
   A. I, IV, V   B. II, III, V   C. III, IV, V   D. All of the above

19. A supervisor determined that a foreman, without informing his superior, delegated responsibility for checking time cards to a member of his gang. The supervisor then called the foreman into his office where he reprimanded the foreman.
This action of the supervisor in reprimanding the foreman was
    A. *proper*, because the checking of time cards is the foreman's responsibility and should not be delegated
    B. *proper*, because the foreman did not ask the supervisor for permission to delegate responsibility
    C. *improper*, because the foreman may no longer take the initiative in solving future problems
    D. *improper*, because the supervisor is interfering in a function which is not his responsibility

20. A capable supervisor should check all operations under his control.
Of the following, the LEAST important reason for doing this is to make sure that
    A. operations are being performed as scheduled
    B. he personally observes all operations at all times
    C. all the operations are still needed
    D. his manpower is being utilized efficiently

21. A supervisor makes it a practice to apply fair and firm discipline in all cases of rule infractions, including those of a minor nature.
This practice should PRIMARILY be considered
    A. *bad*, since applying discipline for minor violations is a waste of time
    B. *good*, because not applying discipline for minor infractions can lead to a more serious erosion of discipline
    C. *bad*, because employees do not like to be disciplined for minor violations of the rules
    D. *good*, because violating any rule can cause a dangerous situation to occur

22. A maintainer would PROPERLY consider it poor supervisory practice for a foreman to consult with him on
    A. which of several repair jobs should be scheduled first
    B. how to cope with personal problems at home
    C. whether the neatness of his headquarters can be improved
    D. how to express a suggestion which the maintainer plans to submit formally

23. Assume that you have determined that the work of one of your foremen and the men he supervises is consistently behind schedule. When you discuss this situation with the foreman, he tells you that his men are poor workers and then complains that he must spend all of his time checking on their work.
The following actions are offered for your consideration as possible ways of solving the problem of poor performance of the foreman and his men:
   I. Review the work standards with the foreman and determine whether they are realistic.
   II. Tell the foreman that you will recommend him for the foreman's training course for retraining.
   III. Ask the foreman for the names of the maintainers and then replace them as soon as possible.
   IV. Tell the foreman that you expect him to meet a satisfactory level of performance.
   V. Tell the foreman to insist that his men work overtime to catch up to the schedule.
   VI. Tell the foreman to review the type and amount of training he has given the maintainers.
   VII. Tell the foreman that he will be out of a job if he does not produce on schedule.
   VIII. Avoid all criticism of the foreman and his methods.
   Which of the following suggested answers CORRECTLY lists the proper actions to be taken to solve the problem of poor performance of the foreman and his men?
   A. I, II, IV, VI B. I, III, V, VII C. II, III, VI, VIII D. IV, V, VI, VIII

24. When a conference or a group discussion is tending to turn into a *bull session* without constructive purpose, the BEST action to take is to
   A. reprimand the leader of the bull session
   B. redirect the discussion to the business at hand
   C. dismiss the meeting and reschedule it for another day
   D. allow the bull session to continue

25. Assume that you have been assigned responsibility for a program in which a high production rate is mandatory. From past experience, you know that your foremen do not perform equally well in the various types of jobs given to them. Which of the following methods should you use in selecting foremen for the specific types of work involved in the program?
   A. Leave the method of selecting foremen to your supervisor
   B. Assign each foreman to the work he does best
   C. Allow each foreman to choose his own job
   D. Assign each foreman to a job which will permit him to improve his own abilities

KEY (CORRECT ANSWERS)

1. B
2. B
3. A
4. D
5. D

6. B
7. B
8. B
9. A
10. D

11. C
12. D
13. B
14. B
15. C

16. D
17. C
18. B
19. A
20. B

21. B
22. A
23. A
24. B
25. B

TEST 2

DIRECTIONS: Each question or incomplete statement is followed by several suggested answers or completions. Select the one that BEST answers the question or completes the statement. *PRINT THE LETTER OF THE CORRECT ANSWER IN THE SPACE AT THE RIGHT.*

1. A foreman who is familiar with modern management principles should know that the one of the following requirements of an administrator which is LEAST important is his ability to
    A. coordinate work
    B. plan, organize, and direct the work under his control
    C. cooperate with others
    D. perform the duties of the employees under his jurisdiction

    1.____

2. When subordinates request his advice in solving problems encountered in their work, a certain chief occasionally answers the request by first asking the subordinate what he thinks should be done.
    This action by the chief is, on the whole,
    A. *desirable*, because it stimulates subordinates to give more thought to the solution of problems encountered
    B. *undesirable*, because it discourages subordinates from asking questions
    C. *desirable*, because it discourages subordinates from asking questions
    D. *undesirable*, because it undermines the confidence of subordinates in the ability of their supervisor

    2.____

3. Of the following factors that may be considered by a unit head in dealing with the tardy subordinate, the one which should be given LEAST consideration is the
    A. frequency with which the employee is tardy
    B. effect of the employee's tardiness upon the work of other employees
    C. willingness of the employee to work overtime when necessary
    D. cause of the employee's tardiness

    3.____

4. The MOST important requirement of a good inspectional report is that it should be
    A. properly addressed   B. lengthy
    C. clear and brief   D. spelled correctly

    4.____

5. Building superintendents frequently inquire about departmental inspectional procedures.
    Of the following, it is BEST to
    A. advise them to write to the department for an official reply
    B. refuse as the inspectional procedure is a restricted matter
    C. briefly explain the procedure to them
    D. avoid the inquiry by changing the subject

    5.____

6. Reprimanding a crew member before other workers is a
   A. *good* practice; the reprimand serves as a warning to the other workers
   B. *bad* practice; people usually resent criticism made in public
   C. *good* practice; the other workers will realize that the supervisor is fair
   D. *bad* practice; the other workers will take sides in the dispute

7. Of the following actions, the one which is LEAST likely to promote good work is for the group leader to
   A. praise workers for doing a good job
   B. call attention to the opportunities for promotion for better workers
   C. threaten to recommend discharge of workers who are below standard
   D. put into practice any good suggestion made by crew members

8. A supervisor notices that a member of his crew has skipped a routine step in his job.
   Of the following, the BEST action for the supervisor to take is to
   A. promptly question the worker about the incident
   B. immediately assign another man to complete the job
   C. bring up the incident the next time the worker asks for a favor
   D. say nothing about the incident but watch the worker carefully in the future

9. Assume you have been told to show a new worker how to operate a piece of equipment.
   Your FIRST step should be to
   A. ask the worker if he has any questions about the equipment
   B. permit the worker to operate the equipment himself while you carefully watch to prevent damage
   C. demonstrate the operation of the equipment for the worker
   D. have the worker read an instruction booklet on the maintenance of the equipment

10. Whenever a new man was assigned to his crew, the supervisor would introduce him to all other crew members, take him on a tour of the plant, tell him about bus schedules and places to eat.
    This practice is
    A. *good*; the new man is made to feel welcome
    B. *bad*; supervisors should not interfere in personal matters
    C. *good*; the new man knows that he can bring his personal problems to the supervisor
    D. *bad*; work time should not be spent on personal matters

11. The MOST important factor in successful leadership is the ability to
    A. obtain instant obedience to all orders
    B. establish friendly personal relations with crew members
    C. avoid disciplining crew members
    D. make crew members want to do what should be done

12. Explaining the reasons for departmental procedure to workers tends to
    A. waste time which should be used for productive purposes
    B. increase their interest in their work
    C. make them more critical of departmental procedures
    D. confuse them

13. If you want a job done well do it yourself.
    For a supervisor to follow this advice would be
    A. *good*; a supervisor is responsible for the work of his crew
    B. *bad*; a supervisor should train his men, not do their work
    C. *good*; a supervisor should be skilled in all jobs assigned to his crew
    D. *bad*; a supervisor loses respect when he works with his hands

14. When a supervisor discovers a mistake in one of the jobs for which his crew is responsible, it is MOST important for him to find out
    A. whether anybody else knows about the mistake
    B. who was to blame for the mistake
    C. how to prevent similar mistakes in the future
    D. whether similar mistakes occurred in the past

15. A supervisor who has to explain a new procedure to his crew should realize that questions from the crew USUALLY show that they
    A. are opposed to the new practice
    B. are completely confused by the explanation
    C. need more training in the new procedure
    D. are interested in the explanation

16. A good way for a supervisor to retain the confidence of his or her employees is to
    A. say as little as possible
    B. check work frequently
    C. make no promises unless they will be fulfilled
    D. never hesitate in giving an answer to any question

17. Good supervision is ESSENTIALLY a matter of
    A. patience in supervising workers   B. care in selecting workers
    C. skill in human relations   D. fairness in disciplining workers

18. It is MOST important for an employee who has been assigned a monotonous task to
    A. perform this task before doing other work
    B. ask another employee to help
    C. perform this task only after all other work has been completed
    D. take measures to prevent mistakes in performing the task

19. One of your employees has violated a minor agency regulation. The FIRST thing you should do is
    A. warn the employee that you will have to take disciplinary action if it should happen again
    B. ask the employee to explain his or her actions
    C. inform your supervisor and wait for advice
    D. write a memo describing the incident and place it in the employee's personnel file

20. One of your employees tells you that he feels you give him much more work than the other employees, and he is having trouble meeting your deadlines. You should
    A. ask if he has been under a lot of non-work related stress lately
    B. review his recent assignments to determine if he is correct
    C. explain that this is a busy time, but you are dividing the work equally
    D. tell him that he is the most competent employee and that is why he receives more work

21. A supervisor assigns one of his crew to complete a portion of a job. A short time later, the supervisor notices that the portion has not been completed. Of the following, the BEST way for the supervisor to handle this is to
    A. ask the crew member why he has not completed the assignment
    B. reprimand the crew member for not obeying orders
    C. assign another crew member to complete the assignment
    D. complete the assignment himself

22. Supposes that a member of your crew complains that you are *playing favorites* in assigning work.
    Of the following, the BEST method of handling the complaint is to
    A. deny it and refuse to discuss the matter with the worker
    B. take the opportunity to tell the worker what is wrong with his work
    C. ask the worker for examples to prove his point and try to clear up any misunderstanding
    D. promise to be more careful in making assignments in the future

23. A member of your crew comes to you with a complaint. After discussing the matter with him, it is clear that you have convinced him that his complaint was not justified.
    At this point, you should
    A. permit him to drop the matter
    B. make him admit his error
    C. pretend to see some justification in his complaint
    D. warn him against making unjustified complaints

24. Suppose that a supervisor has in his crew an older man who works rather slowly. In other respects, this man is a good worker; he is seldom absent, works carefully, never loafs, and is cooperative.

The BEST way for the supervisor to handle this worker is to
- A. try to get him to work faster and less carefully
- B. give him the most disagreeable job
- C. request that he be given special training
- D. permit him to work at his own speed

25. Suppose that a member of your crew comes to you with a suggestion he thinks will save time in doing a job. You realize immediately that it won't work.
Under these circumstances, your BEST action would be to
- A. thank the worker for the suggestion and forget about it
- B. explain to the worker why you think it won't work
- C. tell the worker to put the suggestion in writing
- D. ask the other members of your crew to criticize the suggestion

25.____

KEY (CORRECT ANSWERS)

1.	D		11.	D
2.	A		12.	B
3.	C		13.	B
4.	C		14.	C
5.	C		15.	D
6.	B		16.	C
7.	C		17.	C
8.	A		18.	D
9.	C		19.	B
10.	A		20.	B

21. A
22. C
23. A
24. D
25. B

86

READING COMPREHENSION
UNDERSTANDING AND INTERPRETING WRITTEN MATERIAL
EXAMINATION SECTION
TEST 1

DIRECTIONS: Each question or incomplete statement is followed by several suggested answers or completions. Select the one that BEST answers the question or completes the statement. *PRINT THE LETTER OF THE CORRECT ANSWER IN THE SPACE AT THE RIGHT.*

Questions 1-5.

DIRECTIONS: Questions 1 through 5 are to be answered SOLELY on the basis of the following paragraph.

The strength of the seal of a trap is closely proportional to the depth of the seal, regardless of the size of the trap. Unfortunately, an increase in the depth of the seal also increases the probability of solids being retained in the trap, and a limit of about a 4" depth of seal for traps that must pass solids has been imposed by some plumbing codes. The depth of seal most commonly found in simple traps is between $1\frac{1}{2}$" and 2". The Hoover Report recommends a minimum depth of 2" as a safeguard against seal rupture and a maximum depth of 4" to avoid clogging, fungus growths, and similar difficulties. Traps in rain-water leaders and other pipes carrying clear-water wastes only, and which are infrequently used, should have seal depths equal to or greater than 4". The increase in the volume of water retained in the trap helps very little in increasing the strength of the seal, but it does materially reduce the velocity of flow through the trap so as to increase the probability of the sedimentation of solids therein.

1. In accordance with the above, it may be said that traps carrying rain-water should have a seal of   1._____

   A. 5"   B. $3\frac{1}{2}$"   C. 2"   D. $1\frac{1}{2}$"

2. In accordance with the preceding paragraph, which one of the following statements is MOST NEARLY correct?   2._____

   A. Simple traps have a depth of seal between $1\frac{1}{2}$" to 4".
   B. A minimum depth of 4" is recommended to avoid seal rupture.
   C. The strength of the seal is proportional to the size of the trap.
   D. The higher the depth of seal, the more chance of collecting solids.

3. In accordance with the above, it may be said that increasing the volume of water retained in a trap may

   A. *greatly* increase the velocity of flow
   B. *slightly* increase the velocity of flow
   C. *greatly* increase the trap seal
   D. *slightly* increase the trap seal

3.___

4. Of the following, the title which BEST explains the main idea of this paragraph is

   A. TRAP SEAL DEPTHS
   B. THE EFFECTS OF SEDIMENTATION ON TRAP SEALS
   C. COMMON TRAP SIZES
   D. TRAP SIZES AND VELOCITY OF FLOW

4.___

5. Assume that the strength of a trap seal is indicated by 8 units when the trap depth is 2". In accordance with the above paragraph, increasing the depth of seal to 4" will cause the strength of the trap seal to be MOST NEARLY _____ units.

   A. 2   B. 4   C. 8   D. 16

5.___

Questions 6-10.

DIRECTIONS: Questions 6 through 10 are to be answered SOLELY on the basis of the following paragraph.

The thickness of insulation necessary for the most economical results varies with the steam temperature. The standard covering consists of 85 percent magnesia with 10 percent of long-fibre asbestos as a binder. Both magnesia and laminated asbestos—felt and other forms of mineral wool including glass wool—are also used for heat insulation. The magnesia and laminated asbestos coverings may be safely used at temperatures up to 600° F. Pipe insulation is applied in molded sections 3 feet long. The sections are attached to the pipe by means of galvanized iron wire or netting. Flanges and fittings can be insulated by direct application of magnesia cement to the metal without reinforcement. Insulation should always be maintained in good condition because it saves fuel. Routine maintenance of warm-pipe insulation should include prompt repair of damaged surfaces. Steam and hot water leaks concealed by insulation will be difficult to detect. Underground steam or hotwater pipes are best insulated using a concrete trench with removable cover.

6. The word *reinforcement,* as used above, means MOST NEARLY

   A. resistance   B. strengthening
   C. regulation   D. removal

6.___

7. According to the above paragraph, magnesia and laminated-asbestos coverings may be safely used at temperatures up to

   A. 800° F   B. 720° F   C. 675° F   D. 600° F

7.___

8. According to the above paragraph, insulation should ALWAYS be maintained in good condition because it

   A. is laminated   B. saves fuel
   C. is attached to the pipe   D. prevents leaks

8.___

9. According to the above paragraph, pipe insulation sections are attached to the pipe by means of

   A. binders
   B. mineral wool
   C. netting
   D. staples

10. According to the above paragraph, a leak in a hot-water pipe may be difficult to detect because when insulation is used, the leak is

    A. underground
    B. hidden
    C. routine
    D. cemented

Questions 11-15.

DIRECTIONS: Questions 11 through 15 are to be answered SOLELY on the basis of the following paragraph.

Reductions in pipe size of a building heating system are made with eccentric fittings and are pitched downward. The ends of mains with gravity return shall be at least 18" above the water line of the boiler. As condensate flows opposite to the stream, runouts are one size larger than the vertical pipe and are pitched upward. In a one-pipe system, an automatic air vent must be provided at each main to relieve air pressure and to let steam enter the radiator. As steam enters the radiator, a thermal device causes the vent to close, thereby holding the steam. Steam mains should not be less than two inches in diameter. The end of the steam main should have a minimum size of one-half of its greatest diameter. Small steam systems should be sized for a 2 oz. pressure drop. Large steam systems should be sized for a 4 oz. pressure drop.

11. The word *thermal,* as used in the above paragraph, means MOST NEARLY

    A. convector   B. heat   C. instrument   D. current

12. According to the above paragraph, the one of the following that is one size larger than the vertical pipe is the

    A. steam main
    B. valve
    C. water line
    D. runout

13. According to the above paragraph, small steam systems should be sized for a pressure drop of _____ ounces.

    A. 2   B. 3   C. 4   D. 5

14. According to the above paragraph, ends of mains with gravity return shall be AT LEAST

    A. 18" above the water line of the boiler
    B. one-quarter of the greatest diameter of the main
    C. twice the size of the vertical pipe in the main
    D. 18" above the steam line of the boiler

15. According to the above paragraph, the one of the following that is provided at each main to relieve air pressure is a(n)

    A. gravity return
    B. convector
    C. eccentric
    D. vent

Questions 16-17.

DIRECTIONS: Questions 16 and 17 are to be answered SOLELY on the basis of the following paragraph.

In determining the size of a storm drain, a number of factors must be taken into consideration. One factor which makes sizing the storm drain difficult is the matter of predicting rainfall over a given period. Using a maximum estimate of about 1 inch of rain in a 10-minute interval, the approximate volume of water that will fall on a roof or surface in one minute's time can be determined readily. Another factor is the pitch and material of a roof or surface upon which the rain falls. A surface that has a pitch and smooth surface would increase the flow of water into a drain pipe.

16. According to the above paragraph, the statement which includes all factors needed to determine the size of a drain pipe is the

    A. maximum rainfall on a surface
    B. pitch and surface of the area
    C. amount of water to be piped in a definite time interval
    D. area of the surface

17. A roof that has a 45° pitch would PROBABLY have a drain pipe size

    A. smaller than a roof with no pitch
    B. larger than a roof with no pitch
    C. equal to that of a flat roof
    D. equal to the amount of water falling in ten minutes

Questions 18-19.

DIRECTIONS: Questions 18 and 19 are to be answered SOLELY on the basis of the following paragraph.

Because of the large capacity of unit heaters, care should be taken to see that the steam piping leading to them is of sufficient size. Unit heaters should not be used on one-pipe systems. If the heating system contains direct radiators operated with steam under vacuum, it is best to have the unit heaters served by a separate main so that steam above atmospheric pressure can be supplied to the units, if desired, without interfering with the operation of the direct radiators.

18. According to the above paragraph, unit heaters are supplied with

    A. steam under vacuum
    B. steam from direct radiators
    C. separate steam lines
    D. steam preferably from a one-pipe system

19. According to the above paragraph, it may be said that unit heaters work BEST with

    A. steam above atmospheric pressure   B. direct radiators
    C. one-pipe system   D. vacuum systems

Questions 20-21.

DIRECTIONS: Questions 20 and 21 are to be answered SOLELY on the basis of the following paragraph.

Most heating units emit heat by radiation and convection. An exposed radiator emits approximately half of its heat by radiation, the amount depending upon the size and number of sections. In general, a thin radiator, such as a wall radiator, emits a larger proportion of its heat by radiation than does a thick radiator. When a radiator is enclosed or shielded, the proportion of heat emitted by radiation is reduced. The balance of the emission occurs by conduction to the air in contact with the heating surface, and this heated air rises by circulation due to convection and transmits this warm air to the space which is to be heated.

20. According to the above paragraph, when a radiator is enclosed, a GREATER portion of the heat is emitted to the room by 20.____

    A. convection	B. radiation
    C. conduction	D. transmission

21. According to the above paragraph, the amount of heat that a radiator emits is 21.____

    A. approximately half of its heat by radiation
    B. determined by the thickness of the radiator
    C. dependent upon whether it is exposed or enclosed
    D. dependent upon the size and number of sections of the radiator

Questions 22-25.

DIRECTIONS: Questions 22 through 25 are to be answered SOLELY on the basis of the following paragraph.

Safety valves are required to operate without chattering and to be set to close after blowing down not more than 4% of the set pressure, but not less than 2 lbs. in any case. For pressure between 100 and 300 lbs., inclusive, the blow down is required to be not less than 2% of the set pressure. The blow down adjustment is made and sealed by the manufacturer. The popping-point tolerance plus or minus is required not to exceed 2 lbs. for pressure up to and including 70 lbs., 3 lbs. for pressure 71 to 300 lbs., and 10 lbs. for pressure over 300 lbs.

22. A boiler is being installed to operate at a maximum allowable pressure of 10 lb., and the safety valve has been set to blow at this pressure. 22.____
    This valve should close after the boiler blows down to NOT MORE THAN _____ lb.

    A. 9.6	B. 4.0	C. 9.8	D. 8.0

23. A boiler is being installed to operate at a maximum allowable working pressure of 300 lb., and the safety valve is set to blow at this pressure. This valve should close after the boiler blows down to NOT MORE THAN _____ lb. 23.____

    A. 204	B. 298	C. 12	D. 6

24. A sealed safety valve is to be installed on a superheater header in a power steam generating plant. The marking on this valve shows that it is set to pop at 425 lb.
    This valve would operate satisfactorily if it popped at EITHER _____ or _____ lb.

    A. 425; 445
    B. 415; 435
    C. 372.5; 467.5
    D. 412.25; 437.75

25. A sealed safety valve is to be installed on a boiler in a high pressure steam generating station. The marking on the valve shows that it is set to pop at 300 lb.
    This valve would operate satisfactorily if it popped at EITHER _____ or _____ lb.

    A. 290; 310
    B. 297; 303
    C. 291; 309
    D. 288; 312

KEY (CORRECT ANSWERS)

1.	A	11.	B
2.	D	12.	D
3.	D	13.	A
4.	A	14.	A
5.	D	15.	D
6.	B	16.	C
7.	D	17.	B
8.	B	18.	C
9.	C	19.	A
10.	B	20.	A

21. D
22. D
23. A
24. B
25. B

TEST 2

DIRECTIONS: Each question or incomplete statement is followed by several suggested answers or completions. Select the one that BEST answers the question or completes the statement. *PRINT THE LETTER OF THE CORRECT ANSWER IN THE SPACE AT THE RIGHT.*

Questions 1-6.

DIRECTIONS: Questions 1 through 6 are to be answered SOLELY on the basis of the following paragraph.

FIRST AID INSTRUCTIONS

The main purpose of first aid is to put the injured person in the best possible position until medical help arrives. This includes the performance of emergency treatment for the purpose of saving a life if a doctor is not present. When a person is hurt, a crowd usually gathers around the victim. If nobody uses his head, the injured person fails to get the care he needs. You must stay calm and, most important, it is your duty to take charge at an accident. The first thing for you to do is to see, as best you can, what is wrong with the injured person. Leave the victim where he is until the nature and extent of his injury are determined. If he is unconscious, he should not be moved, except to lay him flat on his back if he is in some other position. Loosen the clothing of any seriously hurt person, and make him as comfortable as possible. Medical help should be called as soon as possible. You should remain with the injured person and send someone else to call the doctor. You should try to make sure that the one who calls for a doctor is able to give correct information as to the location of the injured person. In order to help the physician to know what equipment may be needed in each particular case, the person making the call should give the doctor as much information about the injury as possible.

1. If nobody uses his head at the scene of an accident, there is danger that

    A. no one will get the names of all the witnesses
    B. a large crowd will gather
    C. the victim will not get the care he needs
    D. the victim will blame the city for negligence

2. When an accident occurs, the FIRST thing you should do is

    A. call a doctor
    B. loosen the clothing of the injured person
    C. notify the victim's family
    D. try to find out what is wrong with the injured person

3. If you do NOT know the extent and nature of the victim's injuries, you should

    A. let the injured person lie where he is
    B. immediately take the victim to a hospital yourself
    C. help the injured person to his feet to see if he can walk
    D. have the injured person sit up on the ground while you examine him

4. If the injured person is breathing and unconscious, you should

   A. get some hot liquid such as coffee or tea into him
   B. give him artificial respiration
   C. lift up his head to try to stimulate blood circulation
   D. see that he lies flat on his back

5. If it is necessary to call a doctor, you should

   A. go and make the call yourself since you have all the information
   B. find out who the victim's family doctor is before making the call
   C. have someone else make the call who know the location of the victim
   D. find out which doctor the victim can afford

6. It is important for the caller to give the doctor as much information as is available regarding the injury so that the doctor

   A. can bring the necessary equipment
   B. can make out an accident report
   C. will be responsible for any malpractice resulting from the first aid treatment
   D. can inform his nurse on how long he will be in the field

Questions 7-8.

DIRECTIONS: Questions 7 and 8 are to be answered SOLELY on the basis of the following paragraph.

PRECIPITATION AND RUNOFF

In the United States, the average annual precipitation is about 30 inches, of which about 21 inches is lost to the atmosphere by evaporation and transpiration. The remaining 9 inches becomes runoff into rivers and lakes. Both the precipitation and runoff vary greatly with geography and season. Annual precipitation varies from more than 100 inches in parts of the northwest to only 2 or 3 inches in parts of the southwest. In the northeastern part of the country, including New York State, the annual average precipitation is about 45 inches, of which about 22 inches becomes runoff. Even in New York State, there is some variation from place to place and considerable variation from time to time. During extremely dry years, the precipitation may be as low as 30 inches and the runoff below 10 inches. In general, there are greater variations in runoff rates from smaller watersheds. A critical water supply situation occurs when there are three or four abnormally dry years in succession.

Precipitation over the state is measured and recorded by a network of stations operated by the U.S. Weather Bureau. All of the precipitation records and other data such as temperature, humidity, and evaporation rates are published monthly by the Weather Bureau in *Climatological Data*. Runoff rates at more than 200 stream-gauging stations in the state are measured and recorded by the U.S. Geological Survey in cooperation with various state agencies. Records of the daily average flows are published annually by the U.S. Geological Survey in *Surface Water Records of New York*. Copies may be obtained by writing to the Water Resources Division, United States Geological Survey, Albany, New York 23301.

7. From the above paragraphs, it is APPROPRIATE to conclude that

   A. critical supply situations do not occur
   B. the greater the rainfall, the greater the runoff
   C. there are greater variations in runoff from larger watersheds
   D. the rainfall in the southwest is greater than the average in the country

8. From the above paragraphs, it is APPROPRIATE to conclude that

   A. an annual rainfall of about 50 inches does not occur in New York State
   B. the U.S. Weather Bureau is only interested in rainfall
   C. runoff is equal to rainfall less losses to the atmosphere
   D. information about rainfall and runoff in New York State is unavailable to the public

Questions 9-10.

DIRECTIONS: Questions 9 through 10 are to be answered SOLELY on the basis of the following paragraph.

NATURAL LAKES

Large lakes may yield water of exceptionally fine quality except near the shore line and in the vicinity of sewer outlets or near outlets of large streams. Therefore, minimum treatment is required. The availability of practically unlimited quantities of water is also a decided advantage. Unfortunately, however, the sewage from a city is often discharged into the same lake from which the water supply is taken. Great care must be taken in locating both the water intake and the sewer outlet so that the pollution handled by the water treatment plant is a minimum.

Sometimes the distance from the shore where dependable, satisfactory water can be found is so great that the cost of water intake facilities is prohibitive for a small municipality. In such cases, another supply must be found, or water must be obtained from a neigh-boring large city. Lake water is usually uniform in quality from day to day and does not vary in temperature as much as water from a river or small impounding reservoir.

9. A DISADVANTAGE of drawing a water supply from a large lake is that

   A. expensive treatment is required
   B. a limited quantity of water is available
   C. nearby cities may dump sewage into the lake
   D. the water is too cold

10. An ADVANTAGE of drawing a water supply from a large lake is that the

    A. water is uniform in quality
    B. water varies in temperature
    C. intake is distant from the shore
    D. intake may be near a sewer outlet

Questions 11-13.

DIRECTIONS: Questions 11 through 13 are to be answered SOLELY on the basis of the following paragraph.

Excavation of trench—The trench shall be excavated as directed; one side of the street or avenue shall be left open for traffic at all times. In paved streets, the length of trench that may be opened between the point where the backfilling has been completed and the point where the pavement is being removed shall not exceed fifteen hundred feet for pipes 24 inches or less in diameter. For pipes larger than 24-inch, the length of open trenches shall not exceed one thousand feet. The completion of the backfilling shall be interpreted to mean the backfilling of the trench and the consolidation of the backfill so that vehicular traffic can be resumed over the backfill, and also the placing of any temporary pavement that may be required.

11. According to the above paragraph, the street

    A. can be closed to traffic in emergencies
    B. can be closed to traffic only when laying more than 1500 feet of pipe
    C. is closed to traffic as directed
    D. shall be left open for traffic at all times

12. According to the above paragraph, the MAXIMUM length of open trench permitted in paved streets depends on the

    A. traffic on the street
    B. type of ground that is being excavated
    C. water conditions met with in excavation
    D. diameter of the pipe being laid

13. According to the above paragraph, the one of the following items that is included in the *completion of the backfilling* is

    A. sheeting and bracing   B. cradle
    C. temporary pavement   D. bridging

Questions 14-16.

DIRECTIONS: Questions 14 through 16 are to be answered SOLELY on the basis of the following paragraph.

The Contractor shall notify the Engineer by noon of the day immediately preceding the date when he wishes to shut down any main; and if the time set be approved, the Contractor shall provide the men necessary to shut down the main at the time stipulated, and to previously notify all consumers whose supply may be affected. These men shall be under the direction of the Department employees, who will superintend all operations of valves and hydrants. Shutdowns for making connections will not be made unless and until the Contractor has everything on the ground in readiness for the work.

14. According to the above paragraph, before a contractor can make a shut-down, he MUST notify the

    A. police department   B. District Foreman
    C. Engineer   D. Highway Department

15. According to the above paragraph, the operation of the valves will be supervised by the   15.____

    A. Department employees
    B. Contractor's men
    C. Contractor's superintendent
    D. Engineer

16. According to the above paragraph, shut-downs for connections are made   16.____

    A. the day before the connection is to be made
    B. first and then consumers are notified
    C. at any time convenient to the Contractor
    D. when the Contractor has everything on the ground in readiness for the work

Questions 17-22.

DIRECTIONS: Questions 17 through 22 are to be answered SOLELY on the basis of the following paragraphs.

HOT WATER GENERATION

The hot water that comes from a faucet is called Domestic Hot Water. It is heated by a steam coil that runs through a storage tank full of water in the basement of each building.

As the tenants take the hot water, fresh cold water enters the tank and is heated. The temperature of this water is automatically kept at approximately 140° F.

The device which controls the temperature is called a temperature regulator valve. It is operated by a bellows, capillary tube, and thermo bulb which connects between the valve and the hot water being stored in the tank. This bulb, tube, and bellows contains a liquid which expands and contracts with changes in temperatures.

As the water in the tank reaches 140° F, the liquid in the thermo bulb expands and causes pressure to travel along the capillary tube and into the bellows. The expanded liquid forces the bellows to push the Temperature Regulator Valve Stem down, closing the valve. No more steam can enter the coil in the tank, and the water will get no hotter.

As the hot water is used by the tenants, cold water enters the tank and pulls the temperature down. This causes the liquid in the thermo bulb to cool and contract (shrink). The pressure is no longer in the bellows, and a spring pushes it up, allowing the valve to open and allowing steam to again enter the heating coil in the storage tank, raising the temperature of the Domestic Hot Water to 140° F.

17. Domestic hot water is heated by   17.____

    A. coal   B. electricity
    C. hot water   D. steam

18. The temperature of domestic hot water is MOST NEARLY   18.____

    A. 75° F   B. 100° F   C. 140° F   D. 212° F

19. The temperature of the hot water is controlled by a

   A. thermometer
   B. temperature regulator valve
   C. pressuretrol
   D. pressure gauge

20. The temperature regulator valve is operated by a combination of a

   A. thermometer and a thermo bulb
   B. thermometer and a pyrometer
   C. bellows, capillary tube, and a thermometer
   D. bellows, capillary tube, and a thermo bulb

21. Closing of the temperature regulator valve prevents _____ from entering the heating coil in the tank.

   A. water   B. steam
   C. electricity   D. air

22. As hot water is used by the tenants, the temperature of the water in the tank

   A. increases   B. decreases
   C. remains the same   D. approaches 212° F

Question 23.

DIRECTIONS: Question 23 is to be answered SOLELY on the basis of the following paragraph.

Lack of service meters has a definite effect on water consumption. Metering of all services of a city should reduce consumption to about 50 percent of the consumption without meters. Although metering reduces water consumption, there is a tendency for consumption to increase gradually after all services are metered.

23. According to the above paragraph, the one of the following statements that is CORRECT is:

   A. Consumption of water is cut approximately in half by metering, but once all services are metered, the consumption then increases gradually
   B. After all services are metered, water consumption continues to decrease steadily
   C. Metering of all services reduces the consumption of water by much more than half
   D. Water consumption is not affected by metering of all services

Question 24.

DIRECTIONS: Questions 24 is to be answered SOLELY on the basis of the following paragraph.

A venturi meter operates without moving parts and hence is the simplest type of meter in use so far as its construction is concerned. It is a velocity meter, and it is suitable for measuring only high rates of flow. Rates of flow below its capacity limit are not accurately measured. It is, therefore, not suitable for use in measuring the low intermittent demand of most consumers.

24. According to the above paragraph, the flow in a pipe which would MOST accurately be measured by a venturi meter is

   A. an intermittent flow below the meter's capacity
   B. a steady flow below the meter's capacity
   C. a steady flow at the meter's capacity
   D. intermittent flows above or below capacity of the meter

24.____

Question 25.

DIRECTIONS: Question 25 is to be answered SOLELY on the basis of the following paragraph.

A house service water supply connection may be taken from the sprinkler water supply connection to the public main if the diameter of the house service water supply connection is not greater than onehalf the diameter of the sprinkler water supply connection. No shutoff valve shall be placed on the sprinkler supply line other than the main shut-off valve for the building on the street side of the house service water supply connection. If such a connection is made and if a tap also exists for the house service water supply, the tap shall be plugged.

25. According to the above paragraph, the one of the following statements that is CORRECT is:

   A. A sprinkler water supply connection should be at least twice the diameter of any house service water supply connection taken from it
   B. A shut-off valve, in addition to the main shut-off valve, is required on sprinkler supply lines on the street side of the house service water supply connection
   C. Where a house service water supply is connected to the sprinkler water supply and there is a tap for the house service water supply, the tap may remain in service
   D. A house service water supply connection may be taken off each side of the main shut-off valve of the sprinkler water supply

25.____

KEY (CORRECT ANSWERS)

1.	C	11.	D
2.	D	12.	D
3.	A	13.	C
4.	D	14.	C
5.	C	15.	A
6.	A	16.	D
7.	B	17.	D
8.	C	18.	C
9.	C	19.	B
10.	A	20.	D

21. B
22. B
23. A
24. C
25. A

TEST 3

DIRECTIONS: Each question or incomplete statement is followed by several suggested answers or completions. Select the one that BEST answers the question or completes the statement. *PRINT THE LETTER OF THE CORRECT ANSWER IN THE SPACE AT THE RIGHT.*

Questions 1-4.

DIRECTIONS: Questions 1 through 4 are to be answered SOLELY on the basis of the following paragraph.

    Welds in sheet metal up to 1/16 inch in thickness can be made satisfactorily by flanging the edges of the joint. The edges are prepared by turning up a very thin lip or flange along the line of the joint. The height of this flange should be equal to the thickness of the sheet being welded. The edges should be aligned so that the flanges stand up, and the joint should be tack-welded every 5 or 6 inches. Heavy angles or bars should be clamped on each side of the joint to prevent distortion or buckling. No filler metal is required for making this joint. The raised edges are quickly melted by the heat of the welding flame so as to produce an even weld bead which is nearly flush with the original sheet metal surface. By controlling the speed of welding and the motion of the flame, good fusion to the under side of the sheets can be obtained without burning through.

1. According to the above paragraph, satisfactory welds may be made in sheet metal by flanging the edges.
   The MAXIMUM thickness of metal recommended is

   A. 20 gauge
   B. 18 gauge
   C. 1/16"
   D. 5/64"

2. According to the above paragraph, good fusion may be obtained without burning through of the metal by controlling the motion of the flame and the

   A. size of tip
   B. speed of welding
   C. oxygen flow
   D. acetylene flow

3. According to the above paragraph, if the thickness of the metal is 1/32", then the flange height should be

   A. 1/64" B. 1/32" C. 1/16" D. 1/8"

4. According to the above paragraph, distortion in the welding of sheet metal may be prevented by

   A. controlling the speed of welding
   B. use of a flange of correct height
   C. use of proper filler metal
   D. clamping angles on each side of the joint

Questions 5-12.

DIRECTIONS: Questions 5 through 12 are to be answered SOLELY on the basis of the Edison storage battery maintenance procedure below.

EDISON STORAGE BATTERY MAINTENANCE PROCEDURE

Take a voltage reading of each cell in the battery with a voltmeter. Any battery with two or more dead or reverse cells is to be removed and sent to the shop. All cell caps are to be opened, and the water level brought up to 2 3/4" above the plates. Any battery requiring a considerable amount of water must be called to the foreman's attention. All cell caps must be brushed clean and Edison battery oil applied to them. No batteries are to remain in service with cell caps broken or missing. The normal specific gravity reading of the solution must not be above 1.230 nor below 1.160. This reading is to be taken only on batteries which are found to be weak. Batteries with specific gravity lower than 1.160 must be sent to the shop. Be careful when disconnecting leads from the battery since a slight, turn of the connecting post will result in a dead cell due to the cell plates becoming short-circuited. When disconnecting leads, use a standard Edison terminal puller. When recording defective cells, give the battery number, the car number, and the position of the cell in the battery. No. 1 cell is the cell to which the positive battery lead is connected and so on up to the last cell, No. 26, to which the negative lead is connected.

5. A normal specific gravity reading would be

   A. 1.450   B. 1.294   C. 1.200   D. 1.180

6. Batteries with below normal specific gravity reading MUST

   A. always have water added
   B. be called to the foreman's attention
   C. not be given a voltmeter test
   D. be sent to the shop

7. The battery leads are disconnected by using

   A. gas pliers
   B. Edison battery oil to free them
   C. a screwdriver to pry them off
   D. a standard Edison terminal puller

8. To completely record a defective cell, _____ required.

   A. only one identifying number is
   B. two identifying numbers are
   C. three identifying numbers are
   D. four identifying numbers are

9. A battery MUST be taken out of service if it has

   A. one dead cell   B. broken cell caps
   C. one reversed cell   D. a low water level

10. The battery water level should be brought up above the plates by _____ inches.

    A. 2.75   B. 1.370   C. 1.264   D. 0.600

11. Specific gravity readings are to be taken only on batteries which

    A. are removed from service
    B. have missing cell caps
    C. are weak
    D. have a high water level

12. Dead cells are sometimes caused by

    A. a slight turn of the connecting post
    B. taking unnecessary gravity readings
    C. adding too little battery oil
    D. adding too much water

Questions 13-14.

DIRECTIONS: Questions 13 and 14 are to be answered SOLELY on the basis of the following paragraph.

It cannot be stressed too strongly that the greatest care should be taken in handling tools. If they are handled carelessly, serious accidents may result. Many accidents can be avoided if the back of the trowel is kept clean and if the trowel is not allowed to contain too much mortar. Where there is an *excess* of mortar, some might drop or splash into the plasterer's eyes. Any mortar which is dropped onto the hands, wrists, ankles, or underclothing should be removed immediately.

13. The MAIN point of the above paragraph is that

    A. all accidents will be avoided if tools are kept clean
    B. most accidents can be avoided by the use of protective gloves
    C. many accidents are caused by careless handling of tools
    D. trowels should be kept free of mortar at all times

14. In the above paragraph, the word *excess* means MOST NEARLY

    A. surplus   B. minor   C. scant   D. short

Questions 15-18.

DIRECTIONS: Questions 15 through 18 are to be answered SOLELY on the basis of the following paragraph.

There are two unfounded ideas that must be discarded before tackling the lube-simplification job. *Oil is oil* was a common expression from the middle of the nineteenth century up to the early 1900s. Then, as the century got well underway, *the pendulum swung in a wide arc.* At present, we find many oils being used, each with supposedly special properties. The large number of lube oils used at present results from the rapid growth at the same time of machine development and oil refining. The refiner acts to market new oils for each machine developed, and the machine manufacturer feels that each new mechanical unit is different from the others and needs a special lube oil. These feelings may be well-founded, but in many cases they are based on misinformation or blind faith in certain lube oil qualities. At the present time, operators and even lube engineers are finding it tough to keep track of all the claimed properties of all the lube oils.

15. It follows from the sense of this paragraph that the idea that *oil is oil* is unfounded because

    A. it was conceived in the middle of the nineteenth century
    B. the basic and varying properties of lube oils have now been shown to exist
    C. lube oil properties, though fully known, were kept secret for economic reasons
    D. there was no need for but one basic lube oil in the latter part of the nineteenth century

16. In the above paragraph, the phrase *the pendulum swung in a wide arc* means MOST NEARLY

    A. oil refining was unable to keep up with machinery development
    B. before 1900, lube oil engineers found it difficult to keep track of lube oil characteristics
    C. the simplification of lube oils and their application was developed about 1900
    D. many different lube oils with varying characteristics were marketed

17. As indicated in this paragraph, the simplification of the characteristics and the uses of lube oils is needed because the

    A. manufacturers develop new machines to overcome competition
    B. change in process at the refineries for a new lube oil is costly
    C. present market is flooded with many so-called *special purpose* lube oils
    D. *blind faith* of the operators in lube oil qualities should be rewarded

18. A reason given for the claimed need for special lube oil, as indicated in this paragraph, is that

    A. development of new lube oils created the need for new machine units
    B. lube oil engineers developed new tests and standards
    C. basic crudes, from which lube oil is obtained, allow different refining methods
    D. newly developed machines are so very different from each other

Questions 19-22.

DIRECTIONS: Questions 19 through 22 are to be answered SOLELY on the basis of the following paragraph.

ACCIDENT PREVENTION

Many accidents and injuries can be prevented if employees learn to be more careful. The wearing of shoes with thin or badly worn soles or open toes can easily lead to foot injuries from tacks, nails, and chair and desk legs. Loose or torn clothing should not be worn near moving machinery. This is especially true of neckties, which can very easily become caught in the machine. You should not place objects so that they block or partly block hallways, corridors, or other passageways. Even when they are stored in the proper place, tools, supplies, and equipment should be carefully placed or piled so as not to fall, nor have anything stick out from a pile. Before cabinets, lockers, or ladders are moved, the tops should be cleared of anything which might injure someone or fall off. If necessary, use a dolly to move these or other bulky objects.

Despite all efforts to avoid accidents and injuries, however, some will happen. If an employee is injured, no matter how small the injury, he should report it to his supervisor and have the injury treated. A small cut that is not attended to can easily become infected and can cause more trouble than some injuries which at first seem more serious. It never pays to take chances.

19. According to the above passage, the one statement that is NOT true is that

    A. by being more careful, employees can reduce the number of accidents that happen
    B. women should wear shoes with open toes for comfort when working
    C. supplies should be piled so that nothing is sticking out from the pile
    D. if an employee sprains his wrist at work, he should tell his supervisor about it

20. According to the above passage, you should NOT wear loose clothing when you are

    A. in a corridor   B. storing tools
    C. opening cabinets   D. near moving machinery

21. According to the above passage, before moving a ladder, you should

    A. test all rungs
    B. get a dolly to carry the ladder at all times
    C. remove everything from the top of the ladder which might fall off
    D. remove your necktie

22. According to the above passage, an employee who gets a slight cut should

    A. have it treated to help prevent infection
    B. know that a slight cut becomes more easily infected than a big cut
    C. pay no attention to it as it can't become serious
    D. realize that it is more serious than any other type of injury

Questions 23-25.

DIRECTIONS: Questions 23 through 25 are to be answered SOLELY on the basis of the following paragraph.

Keeping the city operating day and night requires the services of more than 400,000 civil service workers – roughly the number of people who live in Syracuse. This huge army of specialists works at more than 2,000 different jobs. The city's civil service workers are able to do everything that needs doing to keep our city running. Their only purpose is the well-being, comfort, and safety of the citizens of the city.

23. Of the following titles, the one that MOST nearly gives the meaning of the above paragraph is

    A. CIVIL SERVICE IN SYRACUSE
    B. EVERYONE WORKS
    C. JOB VARIETY
    D. SERVING THE CITY

24. According to the above paragraph, in order to keep the city operating 24 hours a day, 24.____
    A. half of the civil service workers work days and half work nights
    B. more than 400,000 civil service workers are needed on the day shift
    C. the city needs about as many civil service workers as there are people in Syracuse
    D. the services of some people who live in Syracuse is required

25. According to the above paragraph, it is MOST reasonable to assume that in the city's civil 25.____
    service,
    A. a worker can do any job that needs doing
    B. each worker works at a different job
    C. some workers work at more than one job
    D. some workers work at the same jobs

KEY (CORRECT ANSWERS)

1. C		11. C
2. B		12. A
3. B		13. C
4. D		14. A
5. C		15. B
6. D		16. D
7. D		17. C
8. C		18. D
9. B		19. B
10. A		20. D

21. C
22. A
23. D
24. C
25. D

ARITHMETICAL REASONING

EXAMINATION SECTION
TEST 1

DIRECTIONS: Each question or incomplete statement is followed by several suggested answers or completions. Select the one that BEST answers the question or completes the statement. *PRINT THE LETTER OF THE CORRECT ANSWER IN THE SPACE AT THE RIGHT.*

1. If it takes 2 men 9 days to do a job, how many men are needed to do the same job in 3 days?

   A. 4　　　B. 5　　　C. 6　　　D. 7

2. Suppose that a department operates 1,644 buildings. If one employee is needed for every 2 buildings, and one foreman is needed for every 18 employees, the number of foremen needed is CLOSEST to

   A. 45　　　B. 50　　　C. 55　　　D. 60

3. If 60 bars of soap cost the same as 2 gallons of wax, how many bars of soap can be bought for the price of 5 gallons of wax?

   A. 120　　　B. 150　　　C. 180　　　D. 300

4. An employee waxes 275 sq.ft. of floor on Monday, 352 sq.ft. on Tuesday, 179 sq.ft. on Wednesday, and 302 sq.ft. on Thursday.
   In order to average 280 sq.ft. of floor waxed a day, how many square feet of floor must he wax on Friday?

   A. 264　　　B. 278　　　C. 292　　　D. 358

5. A project covers 35 acres altogether. Lawns, playgrounds, and walks take up 28 acres and the rest is given over to buildings.
   What percentage of the total area is given over to buildings?

   A. 7%　　　B. 20%　　　C. 25%　　　D. 28%

6. When preparing for a mopping operation, fill the standard 16 quart bucket to the 3/4 full mark with warm water. Then add detergent at the rate of 2 oz. per gallon of water and disinfectant at the rate of 1 oz. to 3 gallons of water. According to these directions, the amount of detergent and disinfectant to add to 3/4 of a bucket of warm water is _____ oz. detergent and _____ oz. disinfectant.

   A. 4; 1/2　　　B. 5; 3/4　　　C. 6; 1　　　D. 8; 1 1/4

7. If corn brooms weigh 32 lbs. a dozen, the average weight of one corn broom is CLOSEST to _____ lbs. _____ oz.

   A. 2; 14　　　B. 2; 11　　　C. 2; 9　　　D. 2; 6

8. At the beginning of the year, a foreman has 7 dozen electric bulbs in stock. During the year, he receives a shipment of 14 dozen bulbs, and also replaces 5 burned out bulbs a month in each of 3 buildings in his area. How many electric bulbs does he have on hand at the end of the year? _____dozen.

   A. 3   B. 6   C. 8   D. 12

9. A project has 4 buildings, each 14 floors high. Each floor has 10 apartments. If 35% of the apartments in the project have 3 rooms or less, how many apartments have 4 or more rooms?

   A. 196   B. 210   C. 364   D. 406

10. An employee takes 1 hour and 30 minutes a day to sweep 30 flights of stairs. How many flights of stairs does he sweep in a month if he spends a total of 30 hours doing this job and works at the same rate?

    A. 200   B. 300   C. 600   D. 900

11. During a month, Employee A washed 30 windows, Employee B washed 4 times as many windows as Employee A, and Employee C washed half as many windows as Employee B. The TOTAL number of windows washed by all three men together during this month is

    A. 180   B. 210   C. 240   D. 330

12. How much would it cost to completely fence in the playground area shown at the right with fencing costing $7.50 a foot?
    A. $615.00
    B. $820.00
    C. $885.00
    D. $960.00

13. A drill bit measures .625 inches. The fractional equivalent, in inches, is

    A. 9/16   B. 5/8   C. 11/16   D. 3/4

14. The number of cubic yards of sand required to fill a bin measuring 12 feet by 6 feet by 4 feet is MOST NEARLY

    A. 8   B. 11   C. 48   D. 96

15. Assume that you are assigned to put down floor tiles in a room measuring 8 feet by 10 feet. Individual tiles measure 9 inches by 9 inches. The total number of floor tiles required to cover the entire floor is MOST NEARLY

    A. 107   B. 121   C. 142   D. 160

16. Lumber is usually sold by the board foot, and a board foot is defined as a board one foot square and one inch thick.
    If the price of one board foot of lumber is 90 cents and you need 20 feet of lumber 6 inches wide and 1 inch thick, the cost of the 20 feet of lumber is

    A. $9.00   B. $12.00   C. $18.00   D. $24.00

17. For a certain plumbing repair job, you need three lengths of pipe, 12 1/4 inches, 6 1/2 inches, and 8 5/8 inches.
    If you cut these three lengths from the same piece of pipe, which is 36 inches long, and each cut consumes 1/8 inch of pipe, the length of pipe REMAINING after you have cut out your three pieces should be _____ inches.

    A. 7 1/4   B. 7 7/8   C. 8 1/4   D. 8 7/8

18. A maintenance bond for a roadway pavement is in an amount of 10% of the estimated cost.
    If the estimated cost is $8,000,000, the maintenance bond is

    A. $8,000   B. $80,000   C. $800,000   D. $8,000,000

19. Specifications require that a core be taken every 700 square yards of paved roadway or fraction thereof. A 100 foot by 200 foot rectangular area would require _____ core(s).

    A. 1   B. 2   C. 3   D. 4

20. An applicant must file a map at a scale of 1" = 40'. Six inches on the map represents _____ feet on the ground.

    A. 600   B. 240   C. 120   D. 60

21. A 100' x 110' lot has an area of MOST NEARLY _____ acre.

    A. 1/8   B. 1/4   C. 3/8   D. 1/2

22. 1 inch is MOST NEARLY equal to _____ feet.

    A. .02   B. .04   C. .06   D. .08

23. The area of the triangle EFG shown at the right is MOST NEARLY _____ sq. ft.

    A. 36   B. 42   C. 48   D. 54

24. Specifications state: As further security for the faithful performance of this contract, the Comptroller shall deduct, and retain until the final payment, 10% of the value of the work certified for payment in each partial payment voucher, until the amount so deducted and retained shall equal 5% of the contract price or in the case of a unit price contract, 5% of the estimated amount to be paid to the Contractor under the contract.
    For a $300,000 contract, the amount to be retained at the end of the contract is

    A. $5,000   B. $10,000   C. $15,000   D. $20,000

25. Asphalt was laid for a length of 210 feet on the entire width of a street whose curb-to-curb distance is 30 feet. The number of square yards covered with asphalt is MOST NEARLY

    A. 210   B. 700   C. 2,100   D. 6,300

KEY (CORRECT ANSWERS)

1. C
2. A
3. B
4. C
5. B

6. C
7. B
8. B
9. C
10. C

11. B
12. C
13. B
14. B
15. C

16. A
17. C
18. C
19. D
20. B

21. B
22. D
23. A
24. C
25. B

SOLUTIONS TO PROBLEMS

1. (2)(9) = 18 man-days. Then, 18 ÷ 3 = 6 men

2. The number of employees = 1644 ÷ 2 = 822. The number of foremen needed = 822 ÷ 18 ≈ 45

3. 1 gallon of wax costs the same as 60 ÷ 2 = 30 bars of soap. Thus, 5 gallons of wax costs the same as (5)(30) = 150 bars of soap.

4. To average 280 sq.ft. for five days means a total of (5)(280) = 1400 sq.ft. for all five days. The number of square feet to be waxed on Friday = 1400 - (275+352+179+302) = 292

5. The acreage for buildings is 35 - 28 = 7. Then, 7/35 = 20%

6. (16)(3/4) = 12 quarts = 3 gallons. The amount of detergent, in ounces, is (2)(3) = 6. The amount of disinfectant is 1 oz.

7. One corn broom weighs 32 ÷ 12 = 2 2/3 lbs. ≈ 2 lbs. 11 oz.

8. Number of bulbs at the beginning of the year = (7)(12) + (14)(12) = 252. Number of bulbs replaced over an entire year = (5)(3)(12) = 180. The number of unused bulbs = 252 - 180 = 72 = 6 dozen.

9. Total number of apartments = (4)(14)(10) = 560. The number of apartments with at least 4 rooms = (.65)(560) = 364.

10. 30 ÷ 1 1/2 = 20. Then, (20)(30) = 600 flights of stairs

11. The number of windows washed by A, B, C were 30, 120, and 60. Their total is 210.

12. The two missing dimensions are 26 - 14 = 12 ft. and 33 - 9 = 24 ft. Perimeter = 9 + 12 + 33 + 26 + 24 + 14 = 118 ft. Thus, total cost of fencing = (118)($7.50) = $885.00

13. $.625 = \dfrac{625}{1000} = \dfrac{5}{8}$

14. (12)(6)(4) = 288 cu.ft. Now, 1 cu.yd. = 27 cu.ft.; 288 cu.ft. is equivalent to 10 2/3 or about 11 cu.yds.

15. 144 sq.in. = 1 sq.ft. The room measures (8 ft.)x(10 ft.) = 80 sq.ft. = 11,520 sq.in. Each tile measures (9)(9) = 81 sq.in. The number of tiles needed = 11,520 ÷ 81 = 142.2 or about 142.

16. 20 ft. by 6 in. = (20 ft.)(1/2 ft.) = 10 sq.ft. Then, (10X.90) = $9.00

17. There will be 3 cuts in making 3 lengths of pipe, and these 3 cuts will use (3)(1/8) = 3/8 in. of pipe. The amount of pipe remaining after the 3 pieces are removed = 36 - 12 1/4 - 6 1/2 - 8 5/8 - 3/8 = 8 1/4 in.

18. The maintenance bond = (.10)($8,000,000) = $800,000

19. $(100)(200) = 20,000$ sq.ft. $= 20,000 \div 9 \approx 2222$ sq.yds. Then, $2222 \div 700 \approx 3.17$. Since a core must be taken for each 700 sq.yds. plus any left over fraction, 4 cores will be needed.

20. Six inches means $(6)(40) = 240$ ft. of actual length.

21. $(100 \text{ ft.})(110 \text{ ft.}) = 11,000$ sq.ft. ≈ 1222 sq.yds. Then, since 1 acre $= 4840$ sq.yds., 1222 sq.yds. is equivalent to about 1/4 acre.

22. 1 in. $= 1/12$ ft. $\approx .08$ ft.

23. Area of $\triangle$ EFG $= (1/2)(8)(6) + (1/2)(4)(6) = 36$ sq.ft.

24. The amount to be retained $= (.05)(\$300,000) = \$15,000$

25. $(210)(30) = 6300$ sq.ft. Since 1 sq.yd. $= 9$ sq.ft., 6300 sq.ft. equals 700 sq.yds.

TEST 2

DIRECTIONS: Each question or incomplete statement is followed by several suggested answers or completions. Select the one that BEST answers the question or completes the statement. *PRINT THE LETTER OF THE CORRECT ANSWER IN THE SPACE AT THE RIGHT.*

1. The TOTAL length of four pieces of 2" pipe, whose lengths are 7'3 1/2", 4'2 3/16", 5'7 5/16", and 8'5 7/8", respectively, is

   A. 24'6 3/4" B. 24'7 15/16"
   C. 25'5 13/16" D. 25'6 7/8"

   1._____

2. Under the same conditions, the group of pipes that gives the SAME flow as one 6" pipe is (neglecting friction) _____ pipes.

   A. 3 3" B. 4 3" C. 2 4" D. 3 4"

   2._____

3. A water storage tank measures 5' long, 4' wide, and 6' deep and is filled to the 5 1/2' mark with water.
   If one cubic foot of water weighs 62 pounds, the number of pounds of water required to COMPLETELY fill the tank is

   A. 7,440 B. 6,200 C. 1,240 D. 620

   3._____

4. A hot water line made of copper has a straight horizontal run of 150 feet and, when installed, is at a temperature of 45°F. In use, its temperature rises to 190°F.
   If the coefficient of expansion for copper is 0.0000095" per foot per degree F, the total expansion, in inches, in the run of pipe is given by the product of 150 multiplied by 0.0000095 by

   A. 145 B. 145 x 12
   C. 145 divided by 12 D. 145 x 12 x 12

   4._____

5. To dig a trench 3'0" wide, 50'0" long, and 5'6" deep, the total number of cubic yards of earth to be removed is MOST NEARLY

   A. 30 B. 90 C. 140 D. 825

   5._____

6. If it costs $65 for 20 feet of subway rail, the cost of 150 feet of this rail will be

   A. $487.50 B. $512.00 C. $589.50 D. $650.00

   6._____

7. The number of cubic feet of concrete it takes to fill a form 10 feet long, 3 feet wide, and 6 inches deep is

   A. 12 B. 15 C. 20 D. 180

   7._____

8. The sum of 4 1/16, 5 1/4, 3 5/8, and 4 7/16 is

   A. 17 3/16 B. 17 1/4 C. 17 5/16 D. 17 3/8

   8._____

9. If you earn $10.20 per hour and time and one-half for working over 40 hours, your gross salary for a week in which you worked 42 hours would be

   A. $408.00 B. $428.40 C. $438.60 D. $770.80

   9._____

10. A drill bit, used to drill holes in track ties, has a diameter of 0.75 inches. When expressed as a fraction, the diameter of this drill bit is

    A. 1/4" B. 3/8" C. 1/2" D. 3/4"

11. Three dozen shovels were purchased for use.
    If the shovels were used at the rate of nine a week, the number of weeks that the three dozen lasted was

    A. 3 B. 4 C. 9 D. 12

12. Assume that you earn $20,000 per year.
    If twenty percent of your pay is deducted for taxes, social security, and pension, your weekly take-home pay will be MOST NEARLY

    A. $280 B. $308 C. $328 D. $344

13. If a measurement scaled from a drawing is one inch, and the scale of the drawing is 1/8 inch to the foot, then the one inch measurement would represent an ACTUAL length of

    A. 8 feet B. 2 feet
    C. 1/8 of a foot D. 8 inches

14. Tiles 12" x 12" are used to lay a floor having the dimensions 10'0" x 12'0".
    The MINIMUM number of tiles needed to completely cover the floor is

    A. 60 B. 96 C. 120 D. 144

15. The volume of concrete in a strip of sidewalk 30 feet long by 4 feet wide by 3 inches thick is _____ cubic feet.

    A. 30 B. 120 C. 240 D. 360

16. To change a quantity of cubic feet into an equivalent quantity of cubic yards, _____ the quantity by _____.

    A. multiply; 9 B. divide; 9
    C. multiply; 27 D. divide; 27

17. If a pump can deliver 50 gallons of water per minute, then the time needed for this pump to empty an excavation containing 5,800 gallons of water is _____ hour(s) _____ minutes.

    A. 2; 12 B. 1; 56 C. 1; 44 D. 1; 32

18. The sum of 3 1/6", 4 1/4", 3 5/8", and 5 7/16" is

    A. 15 9/16" B. 16 1/8" C. 16 23/48" D. 16 3/4"

19. If a measurement scaled from a drawing is 2 inches, and the scale of the drawing is 1/8 inch to the foot, then the two inch measurement would represent an ACTUAL length of

    A. 8 feet B. 4 feet
    C. 1/4 of a foot D. 16 feet

20. A room is 7'6" wide by 9'0" long with a ceiling height of 8'0". One gallon of flat paint will cover approximately 400 square feet of wall.
The number of gallons of this paint required to paint the walls of this room, making no deductions for windows or doors, is MOST NEARLY

    A. 1/4   B. 1/2   C. 2/3   D. 1

21. The cost of a certain job is broken down as follows:

    Materials $3,750
    Rental of equipment 1,200
    Labor   3,150

    The percentage of the total cost of the job that can be charged to materials is MOST NEARLY

    A. 40%   B. 42%   C. 44%   D. 46%

22. By trial, it is found that by using two cubic feet of sand, a 5 cubic foot batch of concrete is produced. Using the same proportions, the amount of sand required to produce 2 cubic yards of concrete is MOST NEARLY _____ cubic feet.

    A. 20   B. 22   C. 24   D. 26

23. It takes 4 men 6 days to do a certain job.
Working at the same speed, the number of days it will take 3 men to do this job is

    A. 7   B. 8   C. 9   D. 10

24. The cost of rawl plugs is $27.50 per gross. The cost of 2,448 rawl plugs is

    A. $467.50   B. $472.50   C. $477.50   D. $482.50

25. In a certain district, the area of a building may be no longer than 55% of the area of the lot on which it stands. On a rectangular lot 75 ft. by 125 ft., the maximum permissible area of building is, in square feet, MOST NEARLY

    A. 5,148   B. 5,152   C. 5,156   D. 5,160

KEY (CORRECT ANSWERS)

1.	D	11.	B
2.	B	12.	B
3.	D	13.	A
4.	A	14.	C
5.	A	15.	A
6.	A	16.	D
7.	B	17.	B
8.	D	18.	C
9.	C	19.	D
10.	D	20.	C

21. D
22. B
23. B
24. A
25. C

SOLUTIONS TO PROBLEMS

1. $3\frac{1}{6}"+4\frac{1}{4}"+3\frac{5}{8}"+5\frac{7}{16}"+=3\frac{8}{48}"+4\frac{12}{48}"+3\frac{30}{48}"+5\frac{21}{48}"=15\frac{71}{48}"=16\frac{23}{48}"$

2. The flow of a 6" pipe is measured by the cross-sectional area. Since diameter = 6", radius = 3", and so area = 9π sq.in. A single 3" pipe would have a cross-sectional area of $(3/2)\pi$ sq.in. = 2.25π sq.in. Now, 9 ÷ / 2.25 = 4. Thus, four 3" pipes is equivalent, in flow, to one 6" pipe.

3. (5x4x6) - (5x4x5 1/2) = 10. Then, (10)(62) = 620 pounds.

4. The total expansion = (150')(.0000095"/1 ft.)(190°-45°). So, the last factor is 145.

5. (3')(50')(5 1/2') = 825 cu.ft. Since 1 cu.yd. = 27 cu.ft., 825 cu.ft. cu.yds.

6. 150 ÷ 20 = 7.5. Then, (7.5)($65) = $487.50

7. (10')(3')(1/2') = 15 cu.ft.

8. $4\frac{1}{16}+5\frac{4}{16}+3\frac{10}{16}+4\frac{7}{16}=16\frac{22}{16}=17\frac{3}{8}$

9. Gross salary = ($10.20)(40) + ($15.30)(2) = $438.60

10. $75"=\frac{75}{100}"=\frac{3}{4}"$

11. 3 dozen = 36 shovels. Then, 36 ÷ 9 = 4 weeks

12. Since 20% is deducted, the take-home pay = ($20,000)(.80) = $16,000 for the year, which is $16,000 ÷ 52 ≈ $308 per week.

13. A scale drawing where 1/8" means an actual size of 1 ft. implies that a scale drawing of 1" means an actual size of (1')(8) = 8'

14. (10')(12') = 120 sq.ft. Since each tile is 1 sq.ft., a total of 120 tiles will be used.

15. (30')(4')(1/4') = 30 cu.ft.

16. To convert a given number of cubic feet into an equivalent number of cubic yards, divide by 27.

17. 5800 ÷ 50 = 116 min. = 1 hour 56 minutes

18. $3\frac{1}{6}"+4\frac{1}{4}"+3\frac{5}{8}"+5\frac{7}{16}"+=3\frac{8}{48}"+4\frac{12}{48}"+3\frac{30}{48}"+5\frac{21}{48}"=15\frac{71}{48}"=16\frac{23}{48}"$

19. 2 ÷ 1/8 = 16, so a 2" drawing represents an actual length of 16 feet.

6 (#2)

20. The area of the 4 walls = 2(7 1/2')(8') + 2(9')(8') = 264 sq.ft. Then, 264 ÷ 400 = .66 or about 2/3 gallon of paint.

21. $3750 + $1200 + $3150 = $8100. Then, $3750/$8100 ≈ 46%

22. 2 cu.yds. ÷ 5 cu.ft. = 54 ÷ 5 = 10.8. Now, (10.8)(2 cu.ft.) ≈ 22 cu.ft. Note: 2 cu.yds. = 54 cu.ft.

23. (4)(6) = 24 man-days. Then, 24 ÷ 3 = 8 days

24. 2448 ÷ 144 = 17. Then, (17)($27.50) = $467.50

25. (75')(125') = 9375 sq.ft. The maximum area of the building = (.55)(9375 sq.ft.) * 5156 sq.ft.

TEST 3

DIRECTIONS: Each question or incomplete statement is followed by several suggested answers or completions. Select the one that BEST answers the question or completes the statement. *PRINT THE LETTER OF THE CORRECT ANSWER IN THE SPACE AT THE RIGHT.*

1. A steak weighed 2 pounds, 4 ounces. How much did it cost at $4.60 per pound?

    A. $7.80 B. $8.75 C. $9.90 D. $10.35

2. twenty pints of water just fill a pail. the capacity of the pail, in gallons, is

    A. 2 B. 2 1/4 C. 2 1/2 D. 2 3/4

3. The sum of 5/12 and 1/4 is

    A. 7/12 B. 2/3 C. 3/4 D. 5/6

4. The volume of earth, in cubic yards, excavated from a trench 4'0" wide by 5'6" deep by 18'6" long is MOST NEARLY

    A. 14.7 B. 15.1 C. 15.5 D. 15.9

5. 5/8 written as a decimal is

    A. 62.5 B. 6.25 C. .625 D. .0625

6. The number of cubic feet in a cubic yard is

    A. 9 B. 12 C. 27 D. 36

7. If it costs $16.20 to lay one square yard of asphalt, to lay a patch 15' by 15', it will cost MOST NEARLY

    A. $405.00 B. $3,645.00 C. $134.50 D. $243.00

8. You are assigned thirty (30) asphalt workers to be divided into two crews so that one crew will have 2/3 as many men as the other.
The number of men you would put into the SMALLER crew is

    A. 10 B. 12 C. 14 D. 20

9. It takes 12 asphalt workers, working 6 hours a day, 5 days to complete a certain job. The number of days it will take 10 men, working 8 hours a day, to do the same job, assuming all work at the same rate, is

    A. 2 1/2 B. 3 C. 4 1/2 D. 6

10. A street is laid to a 3% grade. This means that in 150 ft., the street grade will rise

    A. 4 1/2 inches B. 45 inches
    C. 4 1/2 feet D. 45 feet

11. The sum of the following dimensions, 3 4/8, 4 1/8, 5 1/8, and 6 1/4, is

    A. 19	B. 19 1/8	C. 19 1/4	D. 19 1/2

12. A worker is paid $9.30 per hour.
    If he works 8 hours each day on Monday, Tuesday, and Wednesday, 3 1/2 hours on Thursday, and 3 hours on Friday, the TOTAL amount due him is

    A. $283.65	B. $289.15	C. $276.20	D. $285.35

13. The price of metal lath is $395.00 per 100 square yards. The cost of 527 square yards of this lath is MOST NEARLY

    A. $2,076.50	B. $2,079.10	C. $2,081.70	D. $2,084.30

14. The total cost of applying 221 square yards of plaster board is $3,430.
    The cost per square yard is MOST NEARLY

    A. $14.00	B. $14.50	C. $15.00	D. $15.50

15. In a three-coat plaster job, the scratch coat is 1/8 in. thick in front of the lath, the brown coat is 3/16 in. thick, and the finish coat is 1/8 in. thick.
    The TOTAL thickness of this plaster job, measured from the face of the lath, is

    A. 7/16"	B. 1/2"	C. 9/16"	D. 5/8"

16. If an asphalt worker earns $38,070 per year, his wages per month are MOST NEARLY

    A. $380.70	B. $735.00	C. $3,170.00	D. $3,807.00

17. The sum of 4 1/2 inches, 3 1/4 inches, and 7 1/2 inches is 1 foot _____ inches.

    A. 3	B. 3 1/4	C. 3 1/2	D. 4

18. The area of a rectangular asphalt patch, 9 ft. 3 in. by 6 ft. 9 in., is _____ square feet.

    A. 54	B. 54 1/4	C. 54 1/2	D. 62 7/16

19. The number of cubic feet in a cubic yard is

    A. 3	B. 9	C. 16	D. 27

20. A 450 ft. long street with a grade of 2% will have one end of the street higher than the other end by _____ feet.

    A. 2	B. 44	C. 9	D. 20

21. If the drive wheel of a roller is 6 ft. in diameter and the tiller wheel is 4 ft. in diameter, whenever the drive wheel makes a complete revolution on a straight pass, the tiller wheel makes _____ revolution(s).

    A. 1	B. 1 1/4	C. 1 1/2	D. 2

22. A point on the centerline of a street is marked: Station 42 + 51. Another point on the centerline 30 feet from the first is marked Station 42+81.
    A third should be marked Station

    A. 12+51	B. 42+21	C. 45+51	D. 72+51

23. In twenty minutes, a truck moving with a speed of 30 miles an hour will cover a distance 23._____
    of _____ miles.

    A. 3   B. 5   C. 10   D. 30

24. The number of pounds in a ton is   24._____

    A. 500   B. 1,000   C. 2,000   D. 5,000

25. During his summer vacation, a boy earned $45.00 per day and saved 60% of his earn-   25._____
    ings.
    If he worked 45 days, how much did he save during his vacation?

    A. $15.00   B. $18.00   C. $1,215.00   D. $22.50

KEY (CORRECT ANSWERS)

1. D   11. A
2. C   12. A
3. B   13. C
4. B   14. D
5. C   15. A

6. C   16. C
7. A   17. B
8. B   18. D
9. C   19. D
10. C   20. C

21. C
22. B
23. C
24. C
25. C

SOLUTIONS TO PROBLEMS

1. ($4.60)(2 1/4 lbs.) = $10.35

2. 1 gallon = 8 pints, so 20 pints = 20/8 = 2 1/2 gallons

3. $\dfrac{5}{12}+\dfrac{1}{4}=\dfrac{5}{12}+\dfrac{3}{12}=\dfrac{8}{12}=\dfrac{2}{3}$

4. (4')(5 1/2')(18 1/2') = 407 cu.ft. Since 1 cu.yd. = 27 cu.ft., 407 cu.ft. ≈ 15.1 cu.yds.

5. 5/8 = 5 ÷ 8.000 = .625

6. There are (3)(3)(3) = 27 cu.ft. in a cu.yd.

7. (15')(15') = 225 sq.ft. = 25 sq.yds. Then, ($16.20)(25) = $405.00

8. Let 2x = size of smaller crew and 3x = size of larger crew. Then, 2x + 3x = 30. Solving, x = 6. Thus, the smaller crew consists of 12 workers.

9. (12)(6)(5) = 360 worker-days. Then, 360 ÷ [(10)(8)] = 4 1/2 days

10. (.03)(150') = 4 1/2 ft.

11. $3\dfrac{4}{8}+4\dfrac{1}{8}+5\dfrac{1}{8}+6\dfrac{2}{8}=18\dfrac{8}{8}=19$

12. ($9.30)(8+8+8+3 1/2+3) = ($9.30)(30 1/2) = $283.65

13. The cost of 527 sq.yds. = (5.27)($395.00) = $2081.65 ≈ $2081.70

14. $3430 ÷ 221 ≈ $15.50

15. $\dfrac{1}{8}"+\dfrac{3}{16}"+\dfrac{1}{8}"=\dfrac{2}{16}"+\dfrac{3}{16}"+\dfrac{2}{16}"=\dfrac{7}{16}"$

16. $38,070 ÷ 12 = $3172.50 ≈ $3170.00 per month

17. 4 1/2" + 3 1/4" + 7 1/2" = 15 1/4" = 1 ft. 3 1/4 in.

18. 9 ft. 3 in. = 9 1/4 ft., 6 ft. 9 in. = 6 3/4 ft. Area = (9 1/4)(6 3/4) = 62 7/16 sq.ft.

19. A cubic yard = (3)(3)(3) = 27 cubic feet

20. (450')(.02) = 9 ft.

21. 6/4 = 1 1/2 revolutions

22. Station 42 + 51
    30 ft away would be 51 + 30 = 81 OR 51 - 30 = 21
    Station 42 + 81 or 42 + 21 (ANSWER: B.)

5 (#3)

23. 30 miles in 60 minutes means 10 miles in 20 minutes.

24. There are 2000 pounds in a ton.

25. ($45.00)(.60) = $27.00 savings per day. For 45 days, his savings is (45)($27.00) = $1215.00

PHILOSOPHY, PRINCIPLES, PRACTICES, AND TECHNICS OF SUPERVISION, ADMINISTRATION, MANAGEMENT, AND ORGANIZATION

TABLE OF CONTENTS

	Page
MEANING OF SUPERVISION	1
THE OLD AND THE NEW SUPERVISION	1
THE EIGHT (8) BASIC PRINCIPLES OF THE NEW SUPERVISION	1
I. Principle of Responsibility	1
II. Principle of Authority	2
III. Principle of Self-Growth	2
IV. Principle of Individual Worth	2
V. Principle of Creative Leadership	2
VI. Principle of Success and Failure	2
VII. Principle of Science	3
VIII. Principle of Cooperation	3
WHAT IS ADMINISTRATION?	3
I. Practices Commonly Classed as "Supervisory"	3
II. Practices Commonly Classed as "Administrative"	3
III. Practices Commonly Classed as Both "Supervisory" and "Administrative"	4
RESPONSIBILITIES OF THE SUPERVISOR	4
COMPETENCIES OF THE SUPERVISOR	4
THE PROFESSIONAL SUPERVISOR-EMPLOYEE RELATIONSHIP	4
MINI-TEXT IN SUPERVISION, ADMINISTRATION, MANAGEMENT, AND ORGANIZATION	5
I. Brief Highlights	5
A. Levels of Management	6
B. What the Supervisor Must Learn	6
C. A Definition of Supervision	6
D. Elements of the Team Concept	6
E. Principles of Organization	6
F. The Four Important Parts of Every Job	7
G. Principles of Delegation	7
H. Principles of Effective Communications	7
I. Principles of Work Improvement	7
J. Areas of Job Improvement	7
K. Seven Key Points in Making Improvements	8

	L.	Corrective Techniques for Job Improvement	8
	M.	A Planning Checklist	8
	N.	Five Characteristics of Good Directions	9
	O.	Types of Directions	9
	P.	Controls	9
	Q.	Orienting the New Employee	9
	R.	Checklist for Orienting New Employees	9
	S.	Principles of Learning	10
	T.	Causes of Poor Performance	10
	U.	Four Major Steps in On-the-Job Instructions	10
	V.	Employees Want Five Things	10
	W.	Some Don'ts in Regard to Praise	11
	X.	How to Gain Your Workers' Confidence	11
	Y.	Sources of Employee Problems	11
	Z.	The Supervisor's Key to Discipline	11
	AA.	Five Important Processes of Management	12
	BB.	When the Supervisor Fails to Plan	12
	CC.	Fourteen General Principles of Management	12
	DD.	Change	12
II.	Brief Topical Summaries		13
	A.	Who/What is the Supervisor?	13
	B.	The Sociology of Work	13
	C.	Principles and Practices of Supervision	14
	D.	Dynamic Leadership	14
	E.	Processes for Solving Problems	15
	F.	Training for Results	15
	G.	Health, Safety, and Accident Prevention	16
	H.	Equal Employment Opportunity	16
	I.	Improving Communications	16
	J.	Self-Development	17
	K.	Teaching and Training	17
		1. The Teaching Process	17
		a. Preparation	17
		b. Presentation	18
		c. Summary	18
		d. Application	18
		e. Evaluation	18
		2. Teaching Methods	18
		a. Lecture	18
		b. Discussion	18
		c. Demonstration	19
		d. Performance	19
		e. Which Method to Use	19

PHILOSOPHY, PRINCIPLES, PRACTICES, AND TECHNICS
OF
SUPERVISION, ADMINISTRATION, MANAGEMENT, AND ORGANIZATION

MEANING OF SUPERVISION

The extension of the democratic philosophy has been accompanied by an extension in the scope of supervision. Modern leaders and supervisors no longer think of supervision in the narrow sense of being confined chiefly to visiting employees, supplying materials, or rating the staff. They regard supervision as being intimately related to all the concerned agencies of society, they speak of the supervisor's function in terms of "growth," rather than the "improvement" of employees.

This modern concept of supervision may be defined as follows: Supervision is leadership and the development of leadership within groups which are cooperatively engaged in inspection, research, training, guidance, and evaluation.

THE OLD AND THE NEW SUPERVISION

TRADITIONAL
1. Inspection
2. Focused on the employee
3. Visitation
4. Random and haphazard
5. Imposed and authoritarian
6. One person usually

MODERN
1. Study and analysis
2. Focused on aims, materials, methods, supervisors, employees, environment
3. Demonstrations, intervisitation, workshops, directed reading, bulletins, etc.
4. Definitely organized and planned (scientific)
5. Cooperative and democratic
6. Many persons involved (creative)

THE EIGHT (8) BASIC PRINCIPLES OF THE NEW SUPERVISION

I. Principle of Responsibility
   Authority to act and responsibility for acting must be joined.
   A. If you give responsibility, give authority.
   B. Define employee duties clearly.
   C. Protect employees from criticism by others.
   D. Recognize the rights as well as obligations of employees.
   E. Achieve the aims of a democratic society insofar as it is possible within the area of your work.
   F. Establish a situation favorable to training and learning.
   G. Accept ultimate responsibility for everything done in your section, unit, office, division, department.
   H. Good administration and good supervision are inseparable.

II. Principle of Authority
The success of the supervisor is measured by the extent to which the power of authority is not used.
   A. Exercise simplicity and informality in supervision
   B. Use the simplest machinery of supervision
   C. If it is good for the organization as a whole, it is probably justified.
   D. Seldom be arbitrary or authoritative.
   E. Do not base your work on the power of position or of personality.
   F. Permit and encourage the free expression of opinions.

III. Principle of Self-Growth
The success of the supervisor is measured by the extent to which, and the speed with which, he is no longer needed.
   A. Base criticism on principles, not on specifics.
   B. Point out higher activities to employees.
   C. Train for self-thinking by employees to meet new situations.
   D. Stimulate initiative, self-reliance, and individual responsibility
   E. Concentrate on stimulating the growth of employees rather than on removing defects.

IV. Principle of Individual Worth
Respect for the individual is a paramount consideration in supervision.
   A. Be human and sympathetic in dealing with employees.
   B. Don't nag about things to be done.
   C. Recognize the individual differences among employees and seek opportunities to permit best expression of each personality.

V. Principle of Creative Leadership
The best supervision is that which is not apparent to the employee.
   A. Stimulate, don't drive employees to creative action.
   B. Emphasize doing good things.
   C. Encourage employees to do what they do best.
   D. Do not be too greatly concerned with details of subject or method.
   E. Do not be concerned exclusively with immediate problems and activities.
   F. Reveal higher activities and make them both desired and maximally possible.
   G. Determine procedures in the light of each situation but see that these are derived from a sound basic philosophy.
   H. Aid, inspire, and lead so as to liberate the creative spirit latent in all good employees.

VI. Principle of Success and Failure
There are no unsuccessful employees, only unsuccessful supervisors who have failed to give proper leadership.
   A. Adapt suggestions to the capacities, attitudes, and prejudices of employees.
   B. Be gradual, be progressive, be persistent.
   C. Help the employee find the general principle; have the employee apply his own problem to the general principle.
   D. Give adequate appreciation for good work and honest effort.
   E. Anticipate employee difficulties and help to prevent them.
   F. Encourage employees to do the desirable things they will do anyway.
   G. Judge your supervision by the results it secures.

VII. Principle of Science
Successful supervision is scientific, objective, and experimental. It is based on facts, not on prejudices.
  A. Be cumulative in results.
  B. Never divorce your suggestions from the goals of training.
  C. Don't be impatient of results.
  D. Keep all matters on a professional, not a personal, level.
  E. Do not be concerned exclusively with immediate problems and activities.
  F. Use objective means of determining achievement and rating where possible.

VIII. Principle of Cooperation
Supervision is a cooperative enterprise between supervisor and employee.
  A. Begin with conditions as they are.
  B. Ask opinions of all involved when formulating policies.
  C. Organization is as good as its weakest link.
  D. Let employees help to determine policies and department programs.
  E. Be approachable and accessible—physically and mentally.
  F. Develop pleasant social relationships.

WHAT IS ADMINISTRATION

Administration is concerned with providing the environment, the material facilities, and the operational procedures that will promote the maximum growth and development of supervisors and employees. (Organization is an aspect and a concomitant of administration.)

There is no sharp line of demarcation between supervision and administration; these functions are intimately interrelated and, often, overlapping. They are complementary activities.

I. Practices Commonly Classed as "Supervisory"
  A. Conducting employees' conferences
  B. Visiting sections, units, offices, divisions, departments
  C. Arranging for demonstrations
  D. Examining plans
  E. Suggesting professional reading
  F. Interpreting bulletins
  G. Recommending in-service training courses
  H. Encouraging experimentation
  I. Appraising employee morale
  J. Providing for intervisitation

II. Practices Commonly Classified as "Administrative"
  A. Management of the office
  B. Arrangement of schedules for extra duties
  C. Assignment of rooms or areas
  D. Distribution of supplies
  E. Keeping records and reports
  F. Care of audio-visual materials
  G. Keeping inventory records
  H. Checking record cards and books

I. Programming special activities
   J. Checking on the attendance and punctuality of employees

III. Practices Commonly Classified as Both "Supervisory" and "Administrative"
   A. Program construction
   B. Testing or evaluating outcomes
   C. Personnel accounting
   D. Ordering instructional materials

RESPONSIBILITIES OF THE SUPERVISOR

A person employed in a supervisory capacity must constantly be able to improve his own efficiency and ability. He represent the employer to the employees and only continuous self-examination can make him a capable supervisor.

Leadership and training are the supervisor's responsibility. An efficient working unit is one in which the employees work with the supervisor. It is his job to bring out the best in his employees. He must always be relaxed, courteous, and calm in his association with his employees. Their feelings are important, and a harsh attitude does not develop the most efficient employees.

COMPETENCES OF THE SUPERVISOR

   I. Complete knowledge of the duties and responsibilities of his position.
   II. To be able to organize a job, plan ahead, and carry through.
   III. To have self-confidence and initiative.
   IV. To be able to handle the unexpected situation and make quick decisions.
   V. To be able to properly train subordinates in the positions they are best suited for.
   VI. To be able to keep good human relations among his subordinates.
   VII. To be able to keep good human relations between his subordinates and himself and to earn their respect and trust.

THE PROFESSIONAL SUPERVISOR-EMPLOYEE RELATIONSHIP

There are two kinds of efficiency: one kind is only apparent and is produced in organizations through the exercise of mere discipline; this is but a simulation of the second, or true, efficiency which springs from spontaneous cooperation. If you are a manager, no matter how great or small your responsibility, it is your job, in the final analysis, to create and develop this involuntary cooperation among the people whom you supervise. For, no matter how powerful a combination of money, machines, and materials a company may have, this is a dead and sterile thing without a team of willing, thinking, and articulate people to guide it.

The following 21 points are presented as indicative of the exemplary basic relationship that should exist between supervisor and employee:

1. Each person wants to be liked and respected by his fellow employee and wants to be treated with consideration and respect by his superior.
2. The most competent employee will make an error. However, in a unit where good relations exist between the supervisor and his employees, tenseness and fear do not exist. Thus, errors are not hidden or covered up, and the efficiency of a unit is not impaired.

3. Subordinates resent rules, regulations, or orders that are unreasonable or unexplained.
4. Subordinates are quick to resent unfairness, harshness, injustices, and favoritism.
5. An employee will accept responsibility if he knows that he will be complimented for a job well done, and not too harshly chastised for failure; that his supervisor will check the cause of the failure, and, if it was the supervisor's fault, he will assume the blame therefore. If it was the employee's fault, his supervisor will explain the correct method or means of handling the responsibility.
6. An employee wants to receive credit for a suggestion he has made, that is used. If a suggestion cannot be used, the employee is entitled to an explanation. The supervisor should not say "no" and close the subject.
7. Fear and worry slow up a worker's ability. Poor working environment can impair his physical and mental health. A good supervisor avoids forceful methods, threats, and arguments to get a job done.
8. A forceful supervisor is able to train his employees individually and as a team, and is able to motivate them in the proper channels.
9. A mature supervisor is able to properly evaluate his subordinates and to keep them happy and satisfied.
10. A sensitive supervisor will never patronize his subordinates.
11. A worthy supervisor will respect his employees' confidences.
12. Definite and clear-cut responsibilities should be assigned to each executive.
13. Responsibility should always be coupled with corresponding authority.
14. No change should be made in the scope or responsibilities of a position without a definite understanding to that effect on the part of all persons concerned.
15. No executive or employee, occupying a single position in the organization, should be subject to definite orders from more than one source.
16. Orders should never be given to subordinates over the head of a responsible executive. Rather than do this, the officer in question should be supplanted.
17. Criticisms of subordinates should, whoever possible, be made privately, and in no case should a subordinate be criticized in the presence of executives or employees of equal or lower rank.
18. No dispute or difference between executives or employees as to authority or responsibilities should be considered too trivial for prompt and careful adjudication.
19. Promotions, wage changes, and disciplinary action should always be approved by the executive immediately superior to the one directly responsible.
20. No executive or employee should ever be required, or expected, to be at the same time an assistant to, and critic of, another.
21. Any executive whose work is subject to regular inspection should, wherever practicable, be given the assistance and facilities necessary to enable him to maintain an independent check of the quality of his work.

MINI-TEXT IN SUPERVISION, ADMINISTRATION, MANAGEMENT, AND ORGANIZATION

I. Brief Highlights

   Listed concisely and sequentially are major headings and important data in the field for quick recall and review.

A. Levels of Management
Any organization of some size has several levels of management. In terms of a ladder, the levels are:

The first level is very important because it is the beginning point of management leadership.

B. What the Supervisor Must Learn
A supervisor must learn to:
1. Deal with people and their differences
2. Get the job done through people
3. Recognize the problems when they exist
4. Overcome obstacles to good performance
5. Evaluate the performance of people
6. Check his own performance in terms of accomplishment

C. A Definition of Supervisor
The term supervisor means any individual having authority, in the interests of the employer, to hire, transfer, suspend, lay-off, recall, promote, discharge, assign, reward, or discipline other employees or responsibility to direct them, or to adjust their grievances, or effectively to recommend such action, if, in connection with the foregoing, exercise of such authority is not of a merely routine or clerical nature but requires the use of independent judgment.

D. Elements of the Team Concept
What is involved in teamwork? The component parts are:
1. Members
2. A leader
3. Goals
4. Plans
5. Cooperation
6. Spirit

E. Principles of Organization
1. A team member must know what his job is.
2. Be sure that the nature and scope of a job are understood.
3. Authority and responsibility should be carefully spelled out.
4. A supervisor should be permitted to make the maximum number of decisions affecting his employees.
5. Employees should report to only one supervisor.
6. A supervisor should direct only as many employees as he can handle effectively.
7. An organization plan should be flexible.

8. Inspection and performance of work should be separate.
9. Organizational problems should receive immediate attention.
10. Assign work in line with ability and experience.

F. The Four Important Parts of Every Job
1. Inherent in every job is the *accountability* for results.
2. A second set of factors in every job is *responsibilities*.
3. Along with duties and responsibilities one must have the *authority* to act within certain limits without obtaining permission to proceed.
4. No job exists in a vacuum. The supervisor is surrounded by key *relationships*.

G. Principles of Delegation
Where work is delegated for the first time, the supervisor should think in terms of these questions:
1. Who is best qualified to do this?
2. Can an employee improve his abilities by doing this?
3. How long should an employee spend on this?
4. Are there any special problems for which he will need guidance?
5. How broad a delegation can I make?

H. Principles of Effective Communications
1. Determine the media.
2. To whom directed?
3. Identification and source authority.
4. Is communication understood?

I. Principles of Work Improvement
1. Most people usually do only the work which is assigned to them.
2. Workers are likely to fit assigned work into the time available to perform it.
3. A good workload usually stimulates output.
4. People usually do their best work when they know that results will be reviewed or inspected.
5. Employees usually feel that someone else is responsible for conditions of work, workplace layout, job methods, type of tools/equipment, and other such factors.
6. Employees are usually defensive about their job security.
7. Employees have natural resistance to change.
8. Employees can support or destroy a supervisor.
9. A supervisor usually earns the respect of his people through his personal example of diligence and efficiency.

J. Areas of Job Improvement
The areas of job improvement are quite numerous, but the most common ones which a supervisor can identify and utilize are:
1. Departmental layout
2. Flow of work
3. Workplace layout
4. Utilization of manpower
5. Work methods
6. Materials handling

7. Utilization
8. Motion economy

K. Seven Key Points in Making Improvements
1. Select the job to be improved
2. Study how it is being done now
3. Question the present method
4. Determine actions to be taken
5. Chart proposed method
6. Get approval and apply
7. Solicit worker participation

L. Corrective Techniques of Job Improvement
Specific Problems
1. Size of workload
2. Inability to meet schedules
3. Strain and fatigue
4. Improper use of men and skills
5. Waste, poor quality, unsafe conditions
6. Bottleneck conditions that hinder output
7. Poor utilization of equipment and machine
8. Efficiency and productivity of labor

General Improvement
1. Departmental layout
2. Flow of work
3. Work plan layout
4. Utilization of manpower
5. Work methods
6. Materials handling
7. Utilization of equipment
8. Motion economy

Corrective Techniques
1. Study with scale model
2. Flow chart study
3. Motion analysis
4. Comparison of units produced to standard allowance
5. Methods analysis
6. Flow chart and equipment study
7. Down time vs. running time
8. Motion analysis

M. A Planning Checklist
1. Objectives
2. Controls
3. Delegations
4. Communications
5. Resources
6. Manpower

7. Equipment
8. Supplies and materials
9. Utilization of time
10. Safety
11. Money
12. Work
13. Timing of improvements

N. Five Characteristics of Good Directions
In order to get results, directions must be:
1. Possible of accomplishment
2. Agreeable with worker interests
3. Related to mission
4. Planned and complete
5. Unmistakably clear

O. Types of Directions
1. Demands or direct orders
2. Requests
3. Suggestion or implication
4. volunteering

P. Controls
A typical listing of the overall areas in which the supervisor should establish controls might be:
1. Manpower
2. Materials
3. Quality of work
4. Quantity of work
5. Time
6. Space
7. Money
8. Methods

Q. Orienting the New Employee
1. Prepare for him
2. Welcome the new employee
3. Orientation for the job
4. Follow-up

R. Checklist for Orienting New Employees   Yes   No
1. Do you appreciate the feelings of new employees when they first report for work? ___ ___
2. Are you aware of the fact that the new employee must make a big adjustment to his job? ___ ___
3. Have you given him good reasons for liking the job and the organization? ___ ___
4. Have you prepared for his first day on the job? ___ ___
5. Did you welcome him cordially and make him feel needed? ___ ___

                                                                              Yes   No

6. Did you establish rapport with him so that he feels free
   to talk and discuss matters with you?   ___   ___
7. Did you explain his job to him and his relationship to you?   ___   ___
8. Does he know that his work will be evaluated periodically
   on a basis that is fair and objective?   ___   ___
9. Did you introduce him to his fellow workers in such a way
   that they are likely to accept him?   ___   ___
10. Does he know what employee benefits he will receive?   ___   ___
11. Does he understand the importance of being on the job
    and what to do if he must leave his duty station?   ___   ___
12. Has he been impressed with the importance of accident
    prevention and safe practice?   ___   ___
13. Does he generally know his way around the department?   ___   ___
14. Is he under the guidance of a sponsor who will teach
    the right way of doing things?   ___   ___
15. Do you plan to follow-up so that he will continue to adjust
    successfully to his job?   ___   ___

S. Principles of Learning
   1. Motivation
   2. Demonstration or explanation
   3. Practice

T. Causes of Poor Performance
   1. Improper training for job
   2. Wrong tools
   3. Inadequate directions
   4. Lack of supervisory follow-up
   5. Poor communications
   6. Lack of standards of performance
   7. Wrong work habits
   8. Low morale
   9. Other

U. Four Major Steps in On-The-Job Instruction
   1. Prepare the worker
   2. Present the operation
   3. Tryout performance
   4. Follow-up

V. Employees Want Five Things
   1. Security
   2. Opportunity
   3. Recognition
   4. Inclusion
   5. Expression

W. Some Don'ts in Regard to Praise
1. Don't praise a person for something he hasn't done.
2. Don't praise a person unless you can be sincere.
3. Don't be sparing in praise just because your superior withholds it from you.
4. Don't let too much time elapse between good performance and recognition of it

X. How to Gain Your Workers' Confidence
Methods of developing confidence include such things as:
1. Knowing the interests, habits, hobbies of employees
2. Admitting your own inadequacies
3. Sharing and telling of confidence in others
4. Supporting people when they are in trouble
5. Delegating matters that can be well handled
6. Being frank and straightforward about problems and working conditions
7. Encouraging others to bring their problems to you
8. Taking action on problems which impede worker progress

Y. Sources of Employee Problems
On-the-job causes might be such things as:
1. A feeling that favoritism is exercised in assignments
2. Assignment of overtime
3. An undue amount of supervision
4. Changing methods or systems
5. Stealing of ideas or trade secrets
6. Lack of interest in job
7. Threat of reduction in force
8. Ignorance or lack of communications
9. Poor equipment
10. Lack of knowing how supervisor feels toward employee
11. Shift assignments

Off-the-job problems might have to do with:
1. Health
2. Finances
3. Housing
4. Family

Z. The Supervisor's Key to Discipline
There are several key points about discipline which the supervisor should keep in mind:
1. Job discipline is one of the disciplines of life and is directed by the supervisor.
2. It is more important to correct an employee fault than to fix blame for it.
3. Employee performance is affected by problems both on the job and off.
4. Sudden or abrupt changes in behavior can be indications of important employee problems.
5. Problems should be dealt with as soon as possible after they are identified.
6. The attitude of the supervisor may have more to do with solving problems than the techniques of problem solving.
7. Correction of employee behavior should be resorted to only after the supervisor is sure that training or counseling will not be helpful.

8. Be sure to document your disciplinary actions.
9. Make sure that you are disciplining on the basis of facts rather than personal feelings.
10. Take each disciplinary step in order, being careful not to make snap judgments, or decisions based on impatience.

AA. Five Important Processes of Management
1. Planning
2. Organizing
3. Scheduling
4. Controlling
5. Motivating

BB. When the Supervisor Fails to Plan
1. Supervisor creates impression of not knowing his job
2. May lead to excessive overtime
3. Job runs itself—supervisor lacks control
4. Deadlines and appointments missed
5. Parts of the work go undone
6. Work interrupted by emergencies
7. Sets a bad example
8. Uneven workload creates peaks and valleys
9. Too much time on minor details at expense of more important tasks

CC. Fourteen General Principles of Management
1. Division of work
2. Authority and responsibility
3. Discipline
4. Unity of command
5. Unity of direction
6. Subordination of individual interest to general interest
7. Remuneration of personnel
8. Centralization
9. Scalar chain
10. Order
11. Equity
12. Stability of tenure of personnel
13. Initiative
14. Esprit de corps

DD. Change

Bringing about change is perhaps attempted more often, and yet less well understood, than anything else the supervisor does. How do people generally react to change? (People tend to resist change that is imposed upon them by other individuals or circumstances.

Change is characteristic of every situation. It is a part of every real endeavor where the efforts of people are concerned.

1. Why do people resist change?
   People may resist change because of:
   a. Fear of the unknown
   b. Implied criticism
   c. Unpleasant experiences in the past
   d. Fear of loss of status
   e. Threat to the ego
   f. Fear of loss of economic stability

2. How can we best overcome the resistance to change?
   In initiating change, take these steps:
   a. Get ready to sell
   b. Identify sources of help
   c. Anticipate objections
   d. Sell benefits
   e. Listen in depth
   f. Follow up

II. Brief Topical Summaries

   A. Who/What is the Supervisor?
      1. The supervisor is often called the "highest level employee and the lowest level manager."
      2. A supervisor is a member of both management and the work group. He acts as a bridge between the two.
      3. Most problems in supervision are in the area of human relations, or people problems.
      4. Employees expect: Respect, opportunity to learn and to advance, and a sense of belonging, and so forth.
      5. Supervisors are responsible for directing people and organizing work. Planning is of paramount importance.
      6. A position description is a set of duties and responsibilities inherent to a given position.
      7. It is important to keep the position description up-to-date and to provide each employee with his own copy.

   B. The Sociology of Work
      1. People are alike in many ways; however, each individual is unique.
      2. The supervisor is challenged in getting to know employee differences. Acquiring skills in evaluating individuals is an asset.
      3. Maintaining meaningful working relationships in the organization is of great importance.
      4. The supervisor has an obligation to help individuals to develop to their fullest potential.
      5. Job rotation on a planned basis helps to build versatility and to maintain interest and enthusiasm in work groups.
      6. Cross training (job rotation) provides backup skills.

7. The supervisor can help reduce tension by maintaining a sense of humor, providing guidance to employees, and by making reasonable and timely decisions. Employees respond favorably to working under reasonably predictable circumstances.
8. Change is characteristic of all managerial behavior. The supervisor must adjust to changes in procedures, new methods, technological changes, and to a number of new and sometimes challenging situations.
9. To overcome the natural tendency for people to resist change, the supervisor should become more skillful in initiating change.

C. Principles and Practices of Supervision
1. Employees should be required to answer to only one superior.
2. A supervisor can effectively direct only a limited number of employees, depending upon the complexity, variety, and proximity of the jobs involved.
3. The organizational chart presents the organization in graphic form. It reflects lines of authority and responsibility as well as interrelationships of units within the organization.
4. Distribution of work can be improved through an analysis using the "Work Distribution Chart."
5. The "Work Distribution Chart" reflects the division of work within a unit in understandable form.
6. When related tasks are given to an employee, he has a better chance of increasing his skills through training.
7. The individual who is given the responsibility for tasks must also be given the appropriate authority to insure adequate results.
8. The supervisor should delegate repetitive, routine work. Preparation of recurring reports, maintaining leave and attendance records are some examples.
9. Good discipline is essential to good task performance. Discipline is reflected in the actions of employees on the job in the absence of supervision.
10. Disciplinary action may have to be taken when the positive aspects of discipline have failed. Reprimand, warning, and suspension are examples of disciplinary action.
11. If a situation calls for a reprimand, be sure it is deserved and remember it is to be done in private.

D. Dynamic Leadership
1. A style is a personal method or manner of exerting influence.
2. Authoritarian leaders often see themselves as the source of power and authority.
3. The democratic leader often perceives the group as the source of authority and power.
4. Supervisors tend to do better when using the pattern of leadership that is most natural for them.
5. Social scientists suggest that the effective supervisor use the leadership style that best fits the problem or circumstances involved.
6. All four styles—telling, selling, consulting, joining—have their place. Using one does not preclude using the other at another time.

7. The theory X point of view assumes that the average person dislikes work, will avoid it whenever possible, and must be coerced to achieve organizational objectives.
8. The theory Y point of view assumes that the average person considers work to be a natural as play, and, when the individual is committed, he requires little supervision or direction to accomplish desired objectives.
9. The leader's basic assumptions concerning human behavior and human nature affect his actions, decisions, and other managerial practices.
10. Dissatisfaction among employees is often present, but difficult to isolate. The supervisor should seek to weaken dissatisfaction by keeping promises, being sincere and considerate, keeping employees informed, and so forth.
11. Constructive suggestions should be encouraged during the natural progress of the work.

E. Processes for Solving Problems
1. People find their daily tasks more meaningful and satisfying when they can improve them.
2. The causes of problems, or the key factors, are often hidden in the background. Ability to solve problems often involves the ability to isolate them from their backgrounds. There is some substance to the cliché that some persons "can't see the forest for the trees."
3. New procedures are often developed from old ones. Problems should be broken down into manageable parts. New ideas can be adapted from old one.
4. People think differently in problem-solving situations. Using a logical, patterned approach is often useful. One approach found to be useful includes these steps:
   a. Define the problem
   b. Establish objectives
   c. Get the facts
   d. Weigh and decide
   e. Take action
   f. Evaluate action

F. Training for Results
1. Participants respond best when they feel training is important to them.
2. The supervisor has responsibility for the training and development of those who report to him.
3. When training is delegated to others, great care must be exercised to insure the trainer has knowledge, aptitude, and interest for his work as a trainer.
4. Training (learning) of some type goes on continually. The most successful supervisor makes certain the learning contributes in a productive manner to operational goals.
5. New employees are particularly susceptible to training. Older employees facing new job situations require specific training, as well as having need for development and growth opportunities.
6. Training needs require continuous monitoring.
7. The training officer of an agency is a professional with a responsibility to assist supervisors in solving training problems.

8. Many of the self-development steps important to the supervisor's own growth are equally important to the development of peers and subordinates. Knowledge of these is important when the supervisor consults with others on development and growth opportunities.

G. Health, Safety, and Accident Prevention
1. Management-minded supervisors take appropriate measures to assist employees in maintaining health and in assuring safe practices in the work environment.
2. Effective safety training and practices help to avoid injury and accidents.
3. Safety should be a management goal. All infractions of safety which are observed should be corrected without exception.
4. Employees' safety attitude, training and instruction, provision of safe tools and equipment, supervision, and leadership are considered highly important factors which contribute to safety and which can be influenced directly by supervisors.
5. When accidents do occur, they should be investigated promptly for very important reasons, including the fact that information which is gained can be used to prevent accidents in the future.

H. Equal Employment Opportunity
1. The supervisor should endeavor to treat all employees fairly, without regard to religion, race, sex, or national origin.
2. Groups tend to reflect the attitude of the leader. Prejudice can be detected even in very subtle form. Supervisors must strive to create a feeling of mutual respect and confidence in every employee.
3. Complete utilization of all human resources is a national goal. Equitable consideration should be accorded women in the work force, minority-group members, the physically and mentally handicapped, and the older employee. The important question is: "Who can do the job?"
4. Training opportunities, recognition for performance, overtime assignments, promotional opportunities, and all other personnel actions are to be handled on an equitable basis.

I. Improving Communications
1. Communications is achieving understanding between the sender and the receiver of a message. It also means sharing information—the creation of understanding.
2. Communication is basic to all human activity. Words are means of conveying meanings; however, real meanings are in people.
3. There are very practical differences in the effectiveness of one-way, impersonal, and two-way communications. Words spoken face-to-face are better understood. Telephone conversations are effective, but lack the rapport of person-to-person exchanges. The whole person communicates.
4. Cooperation and communication in an organization go hand in hand. When there is a mutual respect between people, spelling out rules and procedures for communicating is unnecessary.
5. There are several barriers to effective communications. These include failure to listen with respect and understanding, lack of skill in feedback, and misinterpreting the meanings of words used by the speaker. It is also common

practice to listen to what we want to hear, and tune out things we do not want to hear.
6. Communication is management's chief problem. The supervisor should accept the challenge to communicate more effectively and to improve interagency and intra-agency communications.
7. The supervisor may often plan for and conduct meetings. The planning phase is critical and may determine the success or the failure of a meeting.
8. Speaking before groups usually requires extra effort. Stage fright may never disappear completely, but it can be controlled.

J. Self-Development
1. Every employee is responsible for his own self-development.
2. Toastmaster and toastmistress clubs offer opportunities to improve skills in oral communications.
3. Planning for one's own self-development is of vital importance. Supervisors know their own strengths and limitations better than anyone else.
4. Many opportunities are open to aid the supervisor in his developmental efforts, including job assignments; training opportunities, both governmental and non-governmental—to include universities and professional conferences and seminars.
5. Programmed instruction offers a means of studying at one's own rate.
6. Where difficulties may arise from a supervisor's being away from his work for training, he may participate in televised home study or correspondence courses to meet his self-development needs.

K. Teaching and Training
1. The Teaching Process
Teaching is encouraging and guiding the learning activities of students toward established goals. In most cases this process consists of five steps: preparation, presentation, summarization, evaluation, and application.

   a. Preparation
   Preparation is two-fold in nature; that of the supervisor and the employee. Preparation by the supervisor is absolutely essential to success. He must know what, when, where, how, and whom he will teach. Some of the factors that should be considered are:
   1) The objectives
   2) The materials needed
   3) The methods to be used
   4) Employee participation
   5) Employee interest
   6) Training aids
   7) Evaluation
   8) Summarization

   Employee preparation consists in preparing the employee to receive the material. Probably the most important single factor in the preparation of the employee is arousing and maintaining his interest. He must know the objectives of the training, why he is there, how the material can be used, and its importance to him.

b. Presentation
   In presentation, have a carefully designed plan and follow it. The plan should be accurate and complete, yet flexible enough to meet situations as they arise. The method of presentation will be determined by the particular situation and objectives.

c. Summary
   A summary should be made at the end of every training unit and program. In addition, there may be internal summaries depending on the nature of the material being taught. The important thing is that the trainee must always be able to understand how each part of the new material relates to the whole.

d. Application
   The supervisor must arrange work so the employee will be given a chance to apply new knowledge or skills while the material is still clear in his mind and interest is high. The trainee does not really know whether he has learned the material until he has been given a chance to apply it. If the material is not applied, it loses most of its value.

e. Evaluation
   The purpose of all training is to promote learning. To determine whether the training has been a success or failure, the supervisor must evaluate this learning.
   In the broadest sense, evaluation includes all the devices, methods, skills, and techniques used by the supervisor to keep himself and the employees informed as to their progress toward the objectives they are pursuing. The extent to which the employee has mastered the knowledge, skills, and abilities, or changed his attitudes, as determined by the program objectives, is the extent to which instruction has succeeded or failed.
   Evaluation should not be confined to the end of the lesson, day, or program but should be used continuously. We shall note later the way this relates to the rest of the teaching process.

2. Teaching Methods
   A teaching method is a pattern of identifiable student and instructor activity used in presenting training material.
   All supervisors are faced with the problem of deciding which method should be used at a given time.

   a. Lecture
      The lecture is direct oral presentation of material by the supervisor. The present trend is to place less emphasis on the trainer's activity and more on that of the trainee.

   b. Discussion
      Teaching by discussion or conference involves using questions and other techniques to arouse interest and focus attention upon certain areas, and by doing so creating a learning situation. This can be one of the most

valuable methods because it gives the employees an opportunity to express their ideas and pool their knowledge.

c. Demonstration
The demonstration is used to teach how something works or how to do something. It can be used to show a principle or what the results of a series of actions will be. A well-staged demonstration is particularly effective because it shows proper methods of performance in a realistic manner.

d. Performance
Performance is one of the most fundamental of all learning techniques or teaching methods. The trainee may be able to tell how a specific operation should be performed but he cannot be sure he knows how to perform the operation until he has done so.
As with all methods, there are certain advantages and disadvantages to each method.

e. Which Method to Use
Moreover, there are other methods and techniques of teaching. It is difficult to use any method without other methods entering into it. In any learning situation, a combination of methods is usually more effective than any one method alone.

Finally, evaluation must be integrated into the other aspects of the teaching-learning process.

It must be used in the motivation of the trainees; it must be used to assist in developing understanding during the training; and it must be related to employee application of the results of training.

This is distinctly the role of the supervisor.

BASIC FUNDAMENTALS OF WATER POLLUTION

TABLE OF CONTENTS

	Page
COLLECTING AND TREATING WASTES	1
Primary Treatment	2
Secondary Treatment	3
Lagoons and Septic Tanks	4
THE NEED FOR FURTHER TREATMENT OF WASTES	4
The Types of Pollutants	5
Oxygen-demanding Wastes	5
Disease-causing Agents	5
Plant Nutrients	5
Synthetic Organic Chemicals	5
Inorganic Chemicals and Mineral Substances	5
Sediments	6
Radioactive Substances	6
Heat	6
ADVANCED METHODS OF TREATING WASTES	6
Coagulation-Sedimentation	7
Adsorption	7
Electrodialysis	8
The Blending of Treated Water	8
NEW CHALLENGES FOR WASTE TREATMENT	9
Chemical Oxidation	9
Polymers and Pollution	10
THE PROBLEM OF WASTE DISPOSAL	10

BASIC FUNDAMENTALS OF WATER POLLUTION

COLLECTING AND TREATING WASTES

The most common form of pollution control in the United States consists of a system of sewers and waste treatment plants. The sewers collect the waste water from homes, businesses, and many industries and deliver it to the plants for treatment to make it fit for discharge into streams or for reuse.

There are two kinds of sewer systems — combined and separate. Combined sewers carry away both water polluted by human use and water polluted as it drains off homes, streets, or land during a storm.

In a separated system, one system of sewers, usually called sanitary, carries only sewage. Another system of storm sewers takes care of the large volumes of water from rain or melting snow.

Each home has a sewer or pipe which connects to the common or lateral sewer beneath a nearby street. Lateral sewers connect with larger sewers called trunk or main sewers. In a combined sewer system, these trunk or main sewers discharge into a larger sewer called an interceptor. The interceptor is designed to carry several times the dry-weather flow of the system feeding into it.

During dry weather when the sewers are handling only the normal amount of waste water, all of it is carried to the waste treatment plant. During a storm when the amount of water in the sewer system is much greater, part of the water, including varying amounts of raw sewage, is allowed to bypass directly into the receiving streams. The rest of the wastes are sent to the treatment plant. If part of the increased load of water were not diverted, the waste treatment plant would be overloaded and the purifying processes would not function properly. (A research, development, and demonstration program is being conducted to solve this urban runoff pollution problem. The aim is to develop technology that will control and/or treat combined sewer overflows, storm water discharges, and general washoff of rainwater polluted by dirt or other contaminants on the land.)

Interceptor sewers are also used in sanitary sewer systems as collectors of flow from main sewers and trunks, but do not normally include provisions for bypassing.

A waste treatment plant's basic function is to speed up the natural processes by which water purifies itself. In many cases, nature's treatment process in streams and lakes was adequate before our population and industry grew to their present size.

When the sewage of previous years was dumped into waterways, the natural process of purification began. First, the sheer volume of clean water in the stream diluted the small amount of wastes. Bacteria and other small organisms in the water consumed the sewage or other organic matter, turning it into new bacterial cells, carbon dioxide, and other products.

But the bacteria normally present in water must have oxygen to do their part in breaking down the sewage. Water acquires this all important oxygen by absorbing it from the air and from plants that grow in the water itself. These plants use sunlight to turn the carbon dioxide present in water into oxygen.

The life and death of any body of water depend mainly upon its ability to maintain a certain amount of dissolved oxygen. This dissolved oxygen — or DO — is what fish breathe. Without it, they suffocate. If only a small amount of sewage is dumped into a stream, fish are not affected, and the bacteria can do their work and the stream can quickly restore its oxygen loss from the atmosphere and from plants. Trouble begins when the sewage load is excessive. The sewage will decay and the water will begin to give off odors. If carried to the extreme, the water could lose all of its oxygen, resulting in the death of fish and beneficial plant life.

Since dissolved oxygen is the key element in the life of water, the demands on it are used as a measure in telling how well a sewage treatment plant is working. This measuring device is called biochemical oxygen demand, or BOD. If the effluent or the end-product from a treatment plant has a high content of organic pollutants, the effluent will have a high BOD. In other words, it will demand more oxygen from the water to break down the sewage and consequently will leave the water with less oxygen (and also dirtier).

With the growth of the nation, the problems of pollution have become more complex. The increased amounts of wastes and the larger demands for water have reduced the capacity of running water to purify itself. Consequently, cities and industry have had to begin thinking about removing as much as possible of the oxygen-demanding pollutants from their sewage.

Adequate treatment of wastes along with providing a sufficient supply of clean water has become a major concern.

Primary Treatment

At present, there are two basic ways of treating wastes. They are called primary and secondary. In primary treatment, solids are allowed to settle and are removed from the water Secondary treatment, a further step in purifying waste water, uses biological processes.

As sewage enters a plant for primary treatment, it flows through a screen. The screen removes large floating objects such as rags and sticks that may clog pumps and small pipes. The screens vary from coarse to fine — from those with parallel steel or iron bars with openings of about half an inch or more to screens with much smaller openings.

Screens are generally placed in a chamber or channel in an inclined position to the flow of the sewage to make cleaning easier. The debris caught on the upstream surface of the screen can be raked off manually or mechanically.

Some plants use a device known as a comminutor which combines the functions of a screen and a grinder. These devices catch and then cut or shred the heavy solid material. In the process, the pulverized matter remains in the sewage flow to be removed later in a settling tank.

After the sewage has been screened, it passes into what is called a grit chamber where sand, grit, cinders, and small stones are allowed to settle to the bottom. A grit chamber is highly important for cities with combined sewer systems because it will remove the grit or gravel that washes off streets or land during a storm and ends up at treatment plants.

The unwanted grit or gravel from this process is usually disposed of by filling land near a treatment plant.

In some plants, another screen is placed after the grit chamber to remove any further material that might damage equipment or interfere with later processes.

With the screening completed and the grit removed, the sewage still contains dissolved organic and inorganic matter along with suspended solids. The latter consist of minute particles of matter that can be removed from the sewage by treatment in a sedimentation tank. When the speed of the flow of sewage through one of these tanks is reduced, the suspended solids will gradually sink to the bottom. This mass of solids is called raw sludge.

Various methods have been devised for removing sludge from the tanks.

In older plants, sludge removal was done by hand. After a tank had been in service for several days or weeks, the sewage flow was diverted to another tank. The sludge in the bottom of the out-of-service tank was pushed or flushed with water to a pit near the tank and then removed, usually by pumping, for further treatment or disposal.

Almost all plants built within the past 30 years have had a mechanical means for removing the sludge from sedimentation tanks. Some plants remove it continuously while others remove it at intervals.

To complete the primary treatment, the effluent from the sedimentation tank is chlorinated before being discharged into a stream or river. Chlorine gas is fed into the water to kill and reduce the number of disease-causing bacteria. Chlorination also helps to reduce objectionable odors.

Although 30 percent of the municipalities in the United States give only primary treatment to their sewage, this process by itself is considered entirely inadequate for most needs.

Today's cities and industry, faced with increased amounts of wastes and wastes that are more difficult to remove from water, have turned to secondary and even advanced waste treatment.

Secondary Treatment

Secondary treatment removes up to 90 percent of the organic matter in sewage by making use of the bacteria in it. The two principal types of secondary treatment are trickling filters and the activated-sludge process.

The trickling filter process or the activated-sludge process is used mostly today. After the effluent leaves the sedimentation tank in the primary stage of treatment, it flows or is pumped to a facility using one or the other of these processes. A trickling filter is simply a bed of stones from three to ten feet deep through which the sewage passes. Bacteria gather and multiply on these stones until they can consume most of the organic matter in the sewage. The cleaner water trickles out through pipes in the bottom of the filter for further treatment.

The sewage is applied to the bed of stones in two principal ways. One method consists of distributing the effluent intermittently through a network of pipes laid on or beneath the surface of the stones.

Attached to these pipes are smaller, vertical pipes which spray the sewage over the stones.

Another much-used method consists of a vertical pipe in the center of the filter connected to rotating horizontal pipes which spray the sewage continuously upon the stones.

The trend today is toward the use of the activated sludge process instead of trickling filters. This process speeds up the work of the bacteria by bringing air and sludge heavily laden with bacteria into close contact with the sewage.

After the sewage leaves the settling tank in primary treatment, it is pumped to an aeration tank where it is mixed with air and sludge loaded with bacteria and allowed to remain for several hours. During this time, the bacteria break down the organic matter.

From the aeration tank, the sewage, now called mixed liquor, flows to another sedimentation tank to remove the solids. Chlorination of the effluent completes the basic secondary treatment.

The sludge, now activated with additional millions of bacteria and other tiny organisms, can be used again by returning it to an aeration tank for mixing with new sewage and ample amounts of air.

The activated sludge process, like most other techniques, has advantages and limitations. The size of the units necessary for this treatment is small, thereby requiring less land space and the process is free of flies and odors. But it is more costly to operate than the filter, and the activated sludge process sometimes loses its effectiveness when faced with difficult industrial wastes.

An adequate supply of oxygen is necessary for the activated sludge process to be effective. Air is mixed with sewage and biologically active sludge in the aeration tanks by three different methods.

The first, mechanical aeration, is accomplished by drawing the sewage from the bottom of the tank and spraying it over the surface, thus causing the sewage to absorb large amounts of oxygen from the atmosphere.

In the second method, large amounts of air under pressure are piped down into the sewage and forced out through openings in the pipe. The third method is a combination of mechanical aeration and the force air method.

The final phase of the secondary treatment consists of the addition of chlorine, as the most common method of disinfection, to the effluent coming from the trickling filter or the activated sludge process. Chlorine is usually purchased in liquid form, converted to a gas, and injected into the effluent 15 to 30 minutes before the treated water is discharged into a watercourse. If done properly, Chlorination will kill more than 99 percent of the harmful bacteria in an effluent.

Lagoons and Septic Tanks

There are many well-populated areas in the United States that are not served by any sewer systems or waste treatment plants. Lagoons and septic tanks may act as less than satisfactory alternatives at such locations.

A septic tank is simply a tank buried in the ground to treat the sewage from an individual home. Waste water from the home flows into the tank where bacteria in the sewage may break down the organic matter and the cleaner water flows out of the tank into the ground through sub-surface drains. Periodically, the sludge or solid matter in the bottom of the tank must be removed and disposed of.

In a rural setting, with the right kind of soil and the proper location, the septic tank may be a reasonable and temporary means of disposing of strictly domestic wastes. Septic tanks should always be located so that none of the effluent can seep into sources used for drinking.

Lagoons, or, as they are sometimes called, stabilization or oxidation ponds, also have several advantages when used correctly.

They can give sewage primary and secondary treatment or they can be used to supplement other processes.

A lagoon is a scientifically constructed pond, usually three to five feet deep, in which sunlight, algae, and oxygen interact to restore water to a quality that is often equal to or better than effluent from secondary treatment. Changes in the weather may change the effectiveness of lagoons.

When used with other waste treatment processes, lagoons can be very effective. A good example of this is the Santee, California, water reclamation project. After conventional primary and secondary treatment by activated sludge, the town's waste water is kept in a lagoon for 30 days. Then the effluent, after chlorination, is pumped to land immediately above a series of lakes and allowed to trickle down through sandy soil into the lakes. The resulting water is of such good quality the residents of the area can swim, boat, and fish in the lake water.

THE NEED FOR FURTHER TREATMENT OF WASTES

In the past, pollution control was concerned primarily with problems caused by domestic and the simpler wastes of industry. Control was aimed principally towards protecting downstream public water supplies and stopping or preventing nuisance conditions.

Pollution problems were principally local in extent and their control a local matter.

This is no longer true. National growth and change have altered this picture. Progress in abating pollution has been outdistanced by population growth, the speed of industrial progress and technological developments, changing land practices, and many other factors.

The increased production of goods has greatly increased the amounts of common industrial wastes. New processes in manufacturing are producing new, complex wastes that sometimes defy present pollution control technology. The increased application of commercial fertilizers and the development and widespread use of a vast array of new pesticides are resulting in a host of new pollution problems from water draining off land.

The growth of the nuclear energy field and the use of radioactive materials foreshadow still another complicating and potentially serious water pollution situation.

Long stretches of both interstate and intrastate streams are subjected to pollution which ruins or reduces the use of the water for many purposes. Conventional biological waste treatment processes are hard-pressed to hold the pollution line, and for a growing number of our larger cities, these processes are no longer adequate.

Our growing population not only is packing our central cities but spreading out farther and farther into suburbia and exurbia. Across the country, new satellite communities are being born almost daily. The construction or extension of sewer lines has not matched either the growth rate or its movements. Sea water intrusion is a growing problem in coastal areas. It is usually caused by the excessive pumping of fresh water from the ground which lowers the water level, allowing salt water to flow into the ground water area.

The Types of Pollutants

Present-day problems that must be met by sewage treatment plants can be summed up in the eight types of pollutants affecting our waters.

The eight general categories are: common sewage and other oxygen-demanding wastes; disease-causing agents; plant nutrients; synthetic organic chemicals; inorganic chemicals and other mineral substances; sediment; radioactive substances; and heat.

Oxygen-demanding wastes — These are the traditional organic waste and ammonia contributed by domestic sewage and industrial wastes of plant and animal origin. Besides human sewage, such wastes result from food processing, paper mill production, tanning, and other manufacturing processes. These wastes are usually destroyed by bacteria if there is sufficient oxygen present in the water. Since fish and other aquatic life depend on oxygen for life, the oxygen-demanding wastes must be controlled, or the fish die.

Disease-causing agents — This category includes infectious organisms which are carried into surface and ground water by sewage from cities and institutions, and by certain kinds of industrial wastes, such as tanning and meat packing plants. Man or animals come in contact with these microbes either by drinking the water or through swimming, fishing, or other activities. Although modern disinfection techniques have greatly reduced the danger of this type of pollutant, the problem must be watched constantly.

Plant nutrients — These are the substances in the food chain of aquatic life, such as algae and water weeds, which support and stimulate their growth. Carbon, nitrogen, and phosphorus are the three chief nutrients present in natural water. Large amounts of these nutrients are produced by sewage, certain industrial wastes, and drainage from fertilized lands. Biological waste treatment processes do not remove the phosphorus and nitrogen to any substantial extent -- in fact, they convert the organic forms of these substances into mineral form, making them more usable by plant life. The problem starts when an excess of these nutrients over-stimulates the growth of water plants which cause unsightly conditions, interfere with treatment processes, and cause unpleasant and disagreeable tastes and odors in the water.

Synthetic organic chemicals — Included in this category are detergents and other household aids, all the new synthetic organic pesticides, synthetic industrial chemicals, and the wastes from their manufacture. Many of these substances are toxic to fish and aquatic life and possibly harmful to humans. They cause taste and odor problems and resist conventional waste treatment. Some are known to be highly poisonous at very low concentrations. What the long-term effects of small doses of toxic substances may be is not yet known.

Inorganic chemicals and mineral substances — A vast array of metal salts, acids, solid matter, and many other chemical compounds are included in this group. They reach our waters from mining and manufacturing processes, oil field operations, agricultural practices, and natural sources. Water used in irrigation picks up large amounts of minerals as it filters down through the soil on its way to the nearest stream. Acids of a wide variety are discharged as wastes by industry, but the largest single source of acid in our water comes from mining operations and mines that have been abandoned. Many of these types of chemicals are being created each year. They interfere with natural stream purification, destroy fish and other aquatic life, cause excessive hardness of water supplies, corrode expensive water treatment equipment, increase commercial and recreational boat maintenance costs, and boost the cost of waste treatment.

Sediments — These are the particles of soils, sands, and minerals washed from the land and paved areas of communities into the water. Construction projects are often large sediment producers. While not as insidious as some other types of pollution, sediments are a major problem because of the sheer magnitude of the amount reaching our waterways. Sediments fill stream channels and harbors, requiring expensive dredging, and they fill reservoirs, reducing their capacities and useful life. They erode power turbines and pumping equipment, and reduce fish and shellfish populations by blanketing fish nests and food supplies. More importantly, sediments reduce the amount of sunlight penetrating the water. The sunlight is required by green aquatic plants which produce the oxygen necessary to normal stream balance. Sediments greatly increase the treatment costs for municipal and industrial water supply and for sewage treatment where combined sewers are in use.

Radioactive substances — Radioactive pollution results from the mining and processing of radioactive ores; from the use of refined radioactive materials in power reactors and for industrial, medical, and research purposes; and from fallout following nuclear weapons testing. Increased use of these substances poses a potential public health problem. Since radiation accumulates in humans, control of this type of pollution must take into consideration total exposure in the human environment -- water, air, food, occupation, and medical treatment.

Heat — Heat reduces the capacity of water to absorb oxygen. Tremendous volumes of water are used by power plants and industry for cooling. Most of the water, with the added heat, is returned to streams, raising their temperatures. With less oxygen, the water is not as efficient in assimilating oxygen-consuming wastes and in supporting fish and aquatic life. Unchecked waste heat discharges can seriously alter the ecology of a lake, a stream, or even part of the sea.

Water in lakes or stored in impoundments can be greatly affected by heat. Summer temperatures heat up the surfaces, causing the water to form into layers, with the cooler water forming the deeper layers. Decomposing vegetative matter from natural and man-made pollutants deplete the oxygen from these cooler lower layers with harmful effects on the aquatic life. When the oxygen-deficient water is discharged from the lower gates of a dam, it may have serious effects on downstream fish life and reduce the ability of the stream to assimilate downstream pollution.

To complicate matters, most of our wastes are a mixture of the eight types of pollution, making the problems of treatment and control that much more difficult.

Municipal wastes usually contain oxygen-consuming pollutants, synthetic organic chemicals such as detergents, sediments, and other types of pollutants. The same is true of many industrial wastes which may contain, in addition, substantial amounts of heat from cooling processes. Water that drains off the land usually contains great amounts of organic matter in addition to sediment. Also, land drainage may contain radioactive substances and pollutants washed from the sky, vegetation, buildings, and streets during rainfall.

ADVANCED METHODS OF TREATING WASTES

These new problems of a modern society have placed additional burden upon our waste treatment systems. Today's pollutants are more difficult to remove from the water. And increased demands upon our water supply aggravate the problem. During the dry season, the flow of rivers decreases to such an extent that they have difficulty in assimilating the effluent from waste treatment plants.

In the future, these problems will be met through better and more complete methods of removing pollutants from water and better means for preventing some wastes from even reaching our streams in the first place.

The best immediate answer to these problems is the widespread application of existing waste treatment methods. Many cities that have only primary treatment need secondary treatment. Many other cities need enlarged or modernized primary and secondary systems.

But this is only a temporary solution. The discharge of oxygen-consuming wastes will increase despite the universal application of the most efficient waste treatment processes now available. And these are the simplest wastes to dispose of. Conventional treatment processes are already losing the battle against the modern-day, tougher wastes.

The increasing need to reuse water now calls for better and better waste treatment. Every use of water — whether in home, in the factory, or on the farm — results in some change in its quality.

To return water of more usable quality to receiving lakes and streams, new methods for removing pollutants are being developed. The advanced waste treatment techniques under investigation range from extensions of biological treatment capable of removing nitrogen and phosphorus nutrients to physical-chemical separation techniques such as adsorption, distillation, and reverse osmosis.

These new processes can achieve any degree of pollution control desired and, as waste effluents are purified to higher and higher degrees by such treatment, the point is reached where effluents become *too good to throw away.*

Such water can be deliberately and directly reused for agricultural, industrial, recreational, or even drinking water supplies. This complete water renovation will mean complete pollution control and, at the same time, more water for the nation.

Coagulation-Sedimentation

The application of advanced techniques for waste treatment, at least in the next several years, will most likely take up where primary and secondary treatment leave off. Ultimately, entirely new systems will no doubt replace the modern facilities of today.

The process known as coagulation-sedimentation may be used to increase the removal of solids from effluent after primary and secondary treatment. Besides removing essentially all of the settleable solids, this method can, with proper control and sufficient addition of chemicals, reduce the concentration of phosphate by over 95 percent.

In this process, alum, lime, or iron salts are added to effluent as it comes from the secondary treatment. The flow then passes through flocculation tanks where the chemicals cause the smaller particles to floc or bunch together into large masses.

The larger masses of particles or lumps will settle faster when the effluent reaches the next step — the sedimentation tank.

Although used for years in the treatment of industrial wastes and in water treatment, coagulation-sedimentation is classified as an advanced process because it is not usually applied to the treatment of municipal wastes. In many cases, the process is a necessary pre-treatment for some of the other advanced techniques.

Adsorption

Technology has also been developed to effect the removal of refractory organic materials. These materials are the stubborn organic matter which persists in water and resists normal biological treatment.

The effects of the organics are not completely understood, but taste and odor problems in water, tainting of fish flesh, foaming of water, and fish kills have been attributed to such materials.

Adsorption consists of passing the effluent through a bed of activated carbon granules which will remove more than 98 percent of the organics. To cut down the cost of the procedure, the carbon granules can be cleaned by heat and used again.

An alternative system utilizing powdered carbon is under study. Rather than pass the effluent through a bed of granules, the powdered carbon is put directly into the stream. The organics stick to the carbon, and then the carbon is removed from the effluent by using coagulating chemicals and allowing the coagulated carbon particles to settle in a tank.

The use of this finely ground carbon will improve the rate at which the refractory organics are removed. The potential widespread use of powdered carbon adsorption depends largely on the effectiveness of regenerating the carbon for use again.

Except for the salts added during the use of water, municipal waste water that has gone through the previous advanced processes will be restored to a chemical quality almost the same as before it was used.

When talking of salts in water, salt is not limited to the common kind that is used in the home for seasoning food. In waste treatment language, salts mean the many minerals dissolved by water as it passes through the air as rainfall, as it trickles through the soil and over rocks, and as it is used in the home and factory.

Electrodialysis

Electrodialysis is a rather complicated process by which electricity and membranes are used to remove salts from an effluent. A membrane is usually made of chemically treated plastic. The salts are forced out of the water by the action of an electric field. When a mineral salt is placed in water, it has a tendency to break down into ions. An ion is an atom or a small group of atoms having an electrical charge.

As an example, the two parts of common table salt are sodium and chlorine. When these two elements separate as salt dissolves in water, the sodium and chlorine particles are called ions. Sodium ions have a positive charge, while chlorine ions have a negative charge.

When the effluent passes through the electrodialysis cell, the positive sodium ions are attracted through a membrane to a pole or electrode that is negatively charged. The negatively charged chlorine ions are pulled out of the water through another membrane toward an electrode with a positive charge.

With the salts removed by the action of the two electrodes, the clean water flows out of the electrodialysis cell for reuse or discharge into a river or stream.

As a city uses its water, the amount of salts in the water increases by 300-400 milligrams per liter. Fortunately, electrodialysis can remove this buildup of salts.

In other words, this process returns the salt content of the water back to where it was or even better than when the city first received the water.

The Blending of Treated Water

Properly designed and applied, the methods that have been explained will be able to supply any quality of water for any reuse.

But none of these processes will stand alone. They must be used in a series or a parallel plan. In a series, all the sewage passes through all the processes, one after another, each process making a particular contribution toward improving the water. For example, the conventional primary treatment removes the material that will readily settle or float; the secondary biological step takes care of the decomposable impurities; coagulation-sedimentation, the third, step, eliminates the suspended solids; carbon adsorption removes the remaining dissolved organic matter; electrodialysis returns the level of the salts to what it was before the water was used; and, finally, chlorination provides the health safety barrier against disease carriers.

Basically, the same result can be achieved by separating the effluent into two streams. In this instance, all of the waste receives the primary and secondary treatment and then passes through the coagulation-sedimentation and adsorption processes which remove the organic matter. Half of the sewage is then treated by evaporation and adsorption to remove all impurities including the minerals. This effluent, when blended with the other half, can provide water with the desired level of minerals. After chlorination, the water can be reused.

Almost any degree of water quality can be achieved by varying the flow of the two streams. This technique reduces the treatment cost, since only a fraction of the flow requires treatment with the more expensive unit processes, such as distillation.

Distillation or evaporation basically consists of bringing the effluent to the boiling point. The steam or vapor produced is piped to another chamber where it is cooled, changing it back to a liquid. Most of the unwanted polluting impurities remain in the original chamber. However, some volatile substances may distill along with the water and carry along foreign materials that contribute objectionable taste.

As most people have discovered, distilled water has a flat, disagreeable taste caused by the absence of minerals and air. But by blending this pure water with water that still contains some minerals, a clean, better tasting water results. And, just as importantly, the more expensive distillation process is used on only part of the effluent, and the rest of the waste water is treated by the less costly procedures.

NEW CHALLENGES FOR WASTE TREATMENT

So far, the most readily available processes that will solve most current pollution problems have been covered. But the future holds many new challenges. Scientists are still looking for the ultimate system that will do the complete job of cleaning up water, simply and at a reasonable cost.

One such possible process under study is reverse osmosis. When liquids with different concentrations of mineral salts are separated by a membrane, molecules of pure water tend to pass by osmosis from the more concentrated to the less concentrated side until both liquids have the same mineral content.

Scientists are now exploring ways to take advantage of the natural phenomena of osmosis, but in reverse. When pressure is exerted on the side with the most minerals, this natural force reverses itself, causing the molecules of pure water to flow out of the compartment containing a high salt concentration.

This means that perfectly pure water is being taken out of the waste rather than taking pollutants out of water as is the traditional way. And this process takes clean water away from everything — bacteria, detergents, nitrates.

Tests have shown that the theory works well, resulting in water good enough to drink. Efforts are now under way to develop large membranes with long life. Also, the process and equipment need to be tested on a large scale.

Many other techniques to improve waste treatment are under development in laboratories and in the field.

For example, special microscopic organisms are being tested for removing nitrates from waste water by reducing the nitrates to elemental nitrogen.

Chemical Oxidation

Municipal waste waters contain many organic materials only partially removed by the conventional treatment methods. Oxidants such as ozone and chlorine have been used for many years to improve the taste and odor qualities or to disinfect municipal drinking water. They improve the quality of water by destroying or altering the structure of the chemicals in the water.

However, the concentration of the organic materials in drinking water supplies is much less than it is in the waste-bearing waters reaching treatment plants. Until recently, the cost of the oxidants has prevented the use of this process in the treating of wastes. Now improvements in the production and application of ozone and pure oxygen may reduce costs sufficiently to make their use practicable. When operated in conjunction with other processes, oxidation could become an effective weapon in eliminating wastes resistant to other processes.

Polymers and Pollution

In discussing the coagulation-sedimentation process, mention was made of the use of alum or lime to force suspended solids into larger masses. The clumping together helps speed up one of the key steps in waste treatment — the separation of solids and liquids.

During the past 25 years, the chemical industry has been working on synthetic organic chemicals, known as polyelectrolytes or polymers, to further improve the separation step.

Formerly, polymers have proved effective when used at a later stage of treatment -- the sludge disposal step. Sludge must be dewatered so that it can be more easily disposed of. By introducing polymers into the sludge, the physical and chemical bonds between the solids are tightened. When this happens, the water can be extracted more rapidly.

Wider use of polymers is now being investigated. By putting polymers into streams or rivers, it may be possible to capture silt at specified locations so that it can be removed in quantity.

If polymers are put into raw sewage, waste treatment plants may be able to combine a chemical process with the standard primary and secondary stages. And this method of removing solids can be applied immediately without lengthy and expensive addition of buildings or new facilities.

The chemicals also hold promise as a means of speeding the flow of waste waters through sewer systems, thus, in effect, increasing the capacity of existing systems.

THE PROBLEM OF WASTE DISPOSAL

No matter how good the treatment of wastes, there is always something left over. It may be the rags and sticks that were caught on the screens at the very beginning of the primary treatment. It could be brine or it could be sludge — that part of the sewage that settles to the bottom in sedimentation tanks. Whatever it is, there is always something that must be burned, buried, or disposed of in some manner.

It is a twofold problem. The sludge or other matter must be disposed of to complete a city's or industry's waste treatment. And it must be disposed of in a manner not to add to or upset the rest of the environment.

If it is burned, it must be done in a way not to add to the pollution of the atmosphere. This would only create an additional burden for our already overburdened air to cope with. And air pollutants by the action of rain and wind have a habit of returning to the water, complicating the waste treatment problem rather than helping it.

There are many methods and processes for dealing with the disposal problem, which is sometimes referred to as the problem of ultimate disposal. The most common method for disposing of sludge and other waste concentrates consists of digestion followed by filtration and incineration.

The digestion of sludge takes place in heated tanks where the material can decompose naturally and the odors can be controlled. As digested sludge consists of 90 to 95 percent water, the next step in disposal must be the removal of as much of the water as possible.

Water can be removed from sludge by use of a rotating filter drum and suction. As the drum rotates in the sludge, the water is pulled through the filter and the residues are peeled off for disposal. For more effective dewatering, the sludge can be first treated with a coagulant chemical such as lime or ferric chloride to produce larger solids before the sludge reaches the filter.

Drying beds which are usually made of layers of sand and gravel can be used to remove water from sludge. The sludge is spread over the bed and allowed to dry. After a week or two of drying, the residue will be reduced in volume and, consequently, will be easier to dispose.

Incineration consists of burning the dried sludge to reduce the residues to a safe, non-burnable ash. The ash can be disposed of by filling unused land or by dumping it well out into the ocean. Since most of the pollutants have been removed by the burning, the ash should cause very little change in the quality of the ocean waters.

A very promising new method of sludge disposal gets rid of the unwanted sludge and helps restore a ravaged countryside. In many areas of the country, tops of hills and mountains were sliced away to get at the coal beneath. This strip mining left ugly gashes and scars in otherwise beautiful valleys of many states. It would take nature many years to restore the denuded areas.

With the new disposal idea, digested sludge in semi-liquid form is piped to the spoiled areas. The slurry containing many nutrients from the wastes, is spread over the land to give nature a hand in returning grass, trees, and flowers to the barren hilltops.

Restoration of the countryside will also help in the control of acids that drain from mines into streams and rivers, endangering the fish and other aquatic life and adding to the difficulty in reusing the water. Acids are formed when pyrite containing iron and sulfur is exposed to the air.

Sludge or other waste concentrates are not always costly burdens. By drying and other processes, some cities have produced fertilizers that are sold to help pay for part of the cost of treating wastes. If not sold to the public, some municipalities use the soil enrichers on parks, road parkways, and other public areas.

Some industries have found they can reclaim certain chemicals during waste treatment and reuse them in manufacturing or refining processes. Other firms have developed saleable by-products from residues in waste treatment.

More studies are going on to find greater use for sludge to help solve the disposal problem and to help offset the cost of waste treatment.

BASIC FUNDAMENTALS OF SEWAGE TREATMENT AND DISPOSAL

CONTENTS

	Page
CHAPTER 1: SEWAGE	1
Sources of Sewage and Wastes	1
Definitions	2
Appearance of Sewage	3
Composition of Sewage	3
Solids in Sewage	3
Definitions of Solids in Sewage	4
Dissolved Gases	5
Biological Composition Sewage	5
Condition of Sewage	8
Chemical Changes in Sewage Composition	8
CHAPTER 2: SEWAGE DISPOSAL	12
Sewage Treatment	12
Sewage Disposal	12
Role of Dissolved Oxygen in Receiving Waters	13
Biochemical Oxygen Demand (BOD)	13
Self-purification	14
Need for Sewage Treatment	15
Legal Aspects of Sewage Disposal	17
CHAPTER 3: SEWAGE TREATMENT METHODS	19
Preliminary Treatment	19
Primary Treatment	20
Secondary Treatment	20
Chlorination	21
Sludge Treatment	21
Package Units	21
CHAPTER 4: PRELIMINARY TREATMENT	22
Racks and Bar Screens	22
Fine Screens	22
Comminuting Devices	22
Grit Chambers	23
Pre-aeration Tanks	24
CHAPTER 5: PRIMARY TREATMENT	25
Septic Tanks	25
Two-story Tanks	26
Plain Sedimentation Tanks	30
Chemical Treatment	34

CHAPTER 6: SECONDARY TREATMENT 37
    Trickling Filters 37
    Second Sedimentation Tanks 45
    Activated Sludge 45
    Modifications of the Conventional Activated Sludge Process 50
    Operation of Activated Sludge Process 52
    Contact Aeration 54
    Intermittent Sand Filters 55
    Stabilization Ponds... 56

CHAPTER 1

SEWAGE

Sewage is largely the water supply of a community after it has been fouled by various uses. From the standpoint of source, it may be a combination of the liquid or water-carried wastes from residences, business buildings, and institutions, together with those from industrial establishments, and with such ground water, surface and storm water as may be present.

Volume. The amount or volume of sewage produced varies in different communities depending on a number of factors. A strictly residential community with well-constructed sewers from which storm waters are excluded might average 40 gallons per person per day while an industrial community or one in which the domestic use of water is unusually high may have 200 gallons or more per person per day requiring disposal. In the United States, a figure of 100 gallons per person per day has been considered a reasonable average, though this figure is tending to increase with the growing use of automatic laundry and dishwashing machines and garbage grinders. Where storm waters are admitted to the sewers carrying domestic and industrial wastes, the average is, of course, much higher.

SOURCES OF SEWAGE AND WASTES

Sewage originates from several different sources:
1. Human and animal wastes
2. Household wastes
3. Storm flows
4. Ground water infiltration
5. Industrial wastes

1. *Human and Animal Wastes*: These consist of the body discharges which become part of sewage through flushing of toilet facilities, and to some extent those of animals which are washed into sewers from soil or streets. These wastes are the most important as affecting public health because they may contain organisms which produce disease in man and their safe and effective treatment constitutes a major problem in conditioning sewage for disposal.

2. *Household Wastes*: These are derived from home laundry operations, bathing, kitchen wastes, from washing and cooking foods and dishwashing. Most of these contain soaps, synthetic detergents usually containing foaming agents now generally used in housekeeping. Kitchen wastes have particles of food and greases which are becoming a more significant and increasing part of household wastes with the growing use of home garbage grinding units.

3. *Street Washings and Storm Flows*: Rains and storms deposit varying amounts of water on the land, much of which drains or washes over the surface and carries with it grit, sand, leaves, and other debris that may be lying on the drained surfaces. In some communities, this storm drainage is allowed to flow into the sewers or collecting devices for the community wastes and becomes an important component of the sewage. In other communities, these flows are collected separately for disposal and do not become a part

of the community sewage. Storm flow volume varies with the intensity of rainfall, topography, and pavements and roof areas. Storm waters from roof areas are of particular significance with respect to the volume of sewage to be treated when they are connected, usually illegally, to sewers from which they are supposedly excluded.

4. *Ground Water Infiltration*: Sewers, the collecting devices for sewage, are buried in the ground and in many instances are laid below ground water levels, particularly when such levels are high because of excessive seasonal rainfall. Since the joints between sections of the pipe forming the sewers are not all tight, an opportunity exists for the flow of ground water, or infiltration, into the sewers. Collecting sewers are usually not under pressure, the flow in them being by gravity only, and consequently such infiltration is not only possible but at times is considerable. The volume of ground water infiltration cannot be determined accurately. It is influenced by soil composition, the type of sewer construction, ground water conditions, and rainfall and other weather conditions.

5. *Industrial Wastes*: The waste products of manufacturing processes are an important part of community sewage and their effective disposal must be provided for. In many areas industrial or manufacturing wastes are collected with other community components of sewage for ultimate treatment and disposal. These wastes vary widely in type and volume, depending on the manufacturing establishments located in the community. In some instances the volume and character of industrial wastes are such that separate collecting and disposal devices must be provided. Many types of industrial wastes contain frothing or foaming agents, detergents, and other chemical substances that interfere with the final disposal of the community sewage or damage sewers and other structures. Thus, they cannot be added directly to the sewage but must be given a preliminary treatment or disposed of by separate and special means.

DEFINITIONS

Descriptive names have been given to the various types of sewage depending on their sources as described above. These are defined as follows:

Domestic sewage is that containing human and animal wastes and household wastes. Ground water infiltration is also included. This sewage is typical of residential areas where there are no or only very minor industrial operations.

Sanitary sewage is commonly considered to be the same as domestic sewage. It includes all of the domestic sewage but may also contain much, if not all, of the industrial wastes of the community.

Storm waters consist of the surface run off from storms, flowing from roofs, pavements, and over natural ground surfaces.

Combined sewage is a mixture of domestic or sanitary sewage and storm waters when both are collected in the same sewers.

Industrial wastes are the waste waters from manufacturing processes. They may be collected and disposed of by themselves or may be added to and become part of sanitary or combined sewage.

APPEARANCE OF SEWAGE

Sewage is a turbid liquid containing solid material in suspension. When fresh it is gray in color, and has a musty and not unpleasant odor. It carries varying amounts and kinds of floating matter; fecal solids, bits of food, garbage, paper, sticks, and other types of material disposed of in the daily life of a community of people. With the passage of time, the color gradually changes from gray to black, foul and unpleasant odors develop and black solids appear floating on the surface or throughout the liquid. In this state, it is termed septic sewage.

COMPOSITION OF SEWAGE

Sewage consists of water plus solids which are dissolved or carried in suspension in the water. The solids are very small in amount, usually less than 0.1 percent by weight, but they are the part of the sewage that presents the major problems in its adequate treatment and disposal. The water provides only the volume and a vehicle for transportation of the solids.

These solids may be dissolved, suspending, or floating. Advertising slogans for a certain brand of soap has established as an acceptable standard the idea of 99.44 percent pure. An average domestic sewage, consisting of over 99.44 percent water meets an even stricter standard of purity. However, the less than 0.1 percent solids portion of sewage is a much more potent and significantly impurity than the 0.56 percent impurity of the soap product.

SOLIDS IN SEWAGE

The solids in sewage may be divided into two general groups, depending on their composition or on their physical condition. Thus, we have the organic and inorganic solids which may in turn be suspended and dissolved solids. These groupings are shown in Figure 1 with definitions following the figure.

FIGURE 1
PHYSICAL CONDITION AND COMPOSITION OF SOLIDS
IN AN AVERAGE DOMESTIC SEWAGE
(Numbers are in parts per million)

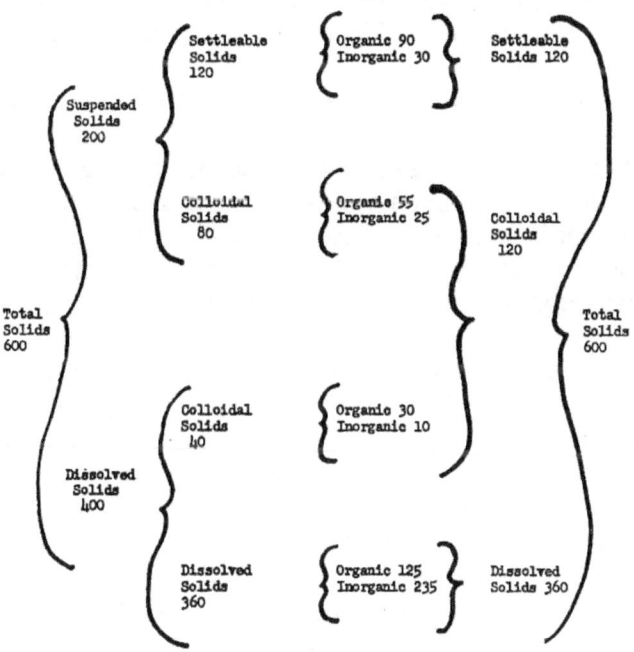

DEFINITIONS OF SOLIDS IN SEWAGE

Organic Solids: These are generally of animal or vegetable origin including the waste products of animal and vegetable life, dead animal matter, plant tissue, or organisms, but may include synthetic organic compounds. They are substances which contain carbon, hydrogen, and oxygen, some of which may be combined with nitrogen, sulphur or phosphorus. The principal groups are proteins, carbohydrates, and fats, together with the products of their decomposition. They are subject to decay or decomposition through the activity of bacteria and other living organisms and are combustible, that is, they can be burned.

Inorganic solids are those substances which are inert and not subject to decay. Exceptions to this characteristic are certain mineral compounds or salts—such as sulfates—which under certain conditions, to be discussed in detail later, can be broken down to simpler substances such as the reduction of sulfates to sulfides. Inorganic solids are frequently designate as mineral substances and include sand, gravel, silt, and the mineral salts in the water supply which produce the hardness and mineral content of the water. In general, they are noncombustible.

The amount of these solids, both organic and inorganic, in sewage, imparts to it what is frequently termed its *strength*. Actually, the amount of concentration of the organic solids and their capacity to undergo decay or decomposition is the principal part of this strength. The greater the concentration of organic solids, the stronger the sewage. A *strong sewage* can be defined as one containing a large amount of solids, particularly organic solids. A *weak sewage* is one containing only a small amount of organic solids.

As already noted, solids can be grouped depending on their physical state as suspended solids, colloidal solids, and dissolved solids, each of which may include both organic and inorganic solids.

Suspended solids are those which are visible and in suspension in the water. They are the solids which can be removed from the sewage by physical or mechanical means, such as sedimentation or filtration. More exactly, they are the solids which are retained on the asbestos mat filter in a Gooch crucible. They include the larger floating particles and consist of sand, grit, clay, fecal solids, paper, sticks of wood, particles of food and garbage, and similar materials. They are about 70 percent organic solids and 30 percent inorganic solids, the latter being principally sand and grit.

Suspended solids are divided into two parts—settleable solids and colloidal solids.

Settleable solids are that portion of the suspended solids which are of sufficient size and weight to settle in a given period of time, usually one hour. As used in this Manual, they are those which will settle in an Imhoff cone in one hour. They are usually reported as millimeters of solids per liter of sewage, but may be reported as parts per million by weight gas given in Figure 1. They are about 75 percent organic and 25 percent inorganic.

Colloidal Suspended Solids: These are somewhat loosely defined as the difference between the total suspended solids and the settleable solids. There is, at present, no simple or standard laboratory tests to specifically determine colloidal matter. Some will settle out if the quiescent period in the Imhoff cone test is longer than one hour, but most will remain in suspension over long periods of several days or more. They constitute that portion of the total suspended solids (about 40 percent) which are not readily removed by physical or mechanical treatment facilities but will not pass the asbestos mat filter in a Gooch crucible. In composition they are about two-thirds organic and one-third inorganic, are subject to rapid decay, and are an important factor in the treatment and disposal of sewage.

Dissolved Solids: The term "dissolved solids as commonly used in discussing sewage is not technically correct. All of these solids are not in true solution but they include some solids in the colloidal state. As used, the term means all of the solids which pass through the asbestos filter in a Gooch crucible. Of the total dissolved solids, about 90 percent are in true solution and about ten percent colloidal. Dissolved solids, as a whole, are about 40 percent organic and 60 percent inorganic. The colloidal portion is higher in percent organic matter than the solids in true solution as the latter includes all of the mineral salts in the water supply.

Total Solids, as the term implies, includes all of the solid constituents of sewage. They are the total of the organic and inorganic solids or the total of the suspended and dissolved solids. In an average domestic sewage, they are about half organic and half inorganic, and about two-thirds in solution and one-third in suspension. It is the organic half of the solids, which are subject to decay, that constitute the main problem in sewage treatment.

As already noted, the weights of the various types of solids as given in Figure 1, and as carried through the definitions, are based on an average domestic sewage, equivalent to approximately 100 gallons per capita per day. Addition of storm water flows or ground water infiltration may change those solids relationships markedly. Similarly, the introduction of industrial wastes may increase the solids content, particularly the organic solids, with very definite variations in the strength of the sewage. Also, sewage varies widely in both composition and volume from hour to hour, depending upon changes in community activities. Obviously, sewage is likely to be at its maximum strength and flow during the daytime and be at a minimum during the night hours. Also, sewage may vary in its composition from day to day with corresponding changes in the industrial and community activities from which the sewage originates. On Sundays and weekends and holidays, flows and strengths are frequently reduced because of the lowered rate of communal activity. Any table of sewage composition can give only an average composition. The amounts of solids indicated cannot be applied equally to all sewages at all times.

DISSOLVED GASES

Sewage contains small and varying concentrations of dissolved gases. Among the most important of these is oxygen, present in the original water supply and also dissolved from air in contact with the surface of flowing sewage. This oxygen, familiarly known as *dissolved oxygen*, is an exceedingly important component of sewage and its functions will be discussed in detail below. In addition to dissolved oxygen, sewage may contain other gases, such as *carbon dioxide*, resulting from the decomposition of organic matter; *nitrogen* dissolved from the atmosphere; *hydrogen sulfide* formed by the decomposition of organic and certain inorganic sulfur compounds. These gases, although small in amount, function importantly in the decomposition and treatment of sewage solids and signify to a major degree the progress of such treatment procedures.

Volatile Liquids. Sewage may contain volatile liquids. These are, in general, liquids which boil at less than 212 degrees Fahrenheit, as, for example, gasoline.

BIOLOGICAL COMPOSITION OF SEWAGE

Sewage also contains countless numbers of living organisms, most of them too small in size to be visible except when viewed under a microscope. They are a natural living part of the organic matter found in sewage and their presence is of utmost importance because they are one of the reasons for sewage treatment and the success of such treatment, involving decay or

decomposition, is dependent upon their activities. It can well be said that they are the workers used by a sewage treatment plant operator and his success may be measured by his knowledge of and attention to their likes and dislikes in their eating habits and environment.
 These microscopic living organisms may be considered to be of two general types: bacteria and other more complex living organisms.

 Bacteria: Bacteria are living organisms, microscopic in size, which consist of a single cell and are similar in functions and life processes to plants. Some bacteria are *motile*, able to move about freely by their own power, and others are *non-motile*. Like all living organisms, bacteria require food, oxygen and water. They can exist only when the environment provides these necessities. In turn, they produce waste products as the result of their life processes.
 Bacteria can be divided into two main groups: Parasitic bacteria and Saprophytic bacteria.

 Parasitic bacteria are those which normally live off of another living organism, known as the host, since they require a food supply already prepared for their consumption, and generally do not develop outside the body of the host. The parasitic bacteria of importance in sewage originate, in general, in the intestinal tract of human beings and animals and reach the sewage by means of body discharges. Included among the parasitic bacteria are certain specific types which, during their growth within the body of the host, produce toxic or poisonous compounds that cause disease in the host. These bacteria are called *pathogenic bacteria*. They may be present in sewage receiving the body discharges of persons ill with such diseases as typhoid fever, cholera, or other intestinal infections. The possible presence of these microorganisms in sewage is one of the principal reasons why sewage must be carefully collected, adequately treated, disposed of safely, to prevent any transfer by sewage flows of these pathogenic or disease-producing bacteria from person to another.

 The *saprophytic bacteria* are those which feed on dead organic matter, thus decomposing organic solids to obtain their needed nourishment, and producing in turn waste substances which consist of both organic and inorganic solids. By this activity they are of utmost importance in sewage treatment methods designed to facilitate or hasten natural decomposition of the organic solids in sewage. Such processes of decomposition will not progress without their activity. In the absence of bacterial life—sterility—decomposition will not take place. Sterile sewage is not subject to the type of decomposition upon which the familiar methods of sewage treatment are based. There are many species of saprophytic bacteria, each of which plays a specific role in the breakdown of the organic solids of sewage. Each species tends to die away following completion of its part in the process of decomposition.

 All of the bacteria, parasitic and saprophytic, require, in addition to food, oxygen for respiration. Certain of them can use only oxygen dissolved in water, termed *dissolved oxygen* and sometimes called *free* or *molecular oxygen*. These organisms are known as *aerobic bacteria* and the process of degradation of organic solids which they carry out is terms *aerobic decomposition*, oxidation or decay. This type of decomposition proceeds in the presence of dissolved oxygen without the production of foul odors or unsightly conditions. Other types o9f bacteria cannot exist in the presence of dissolved oxygen but must obtain the required supply of this element from the oxygen content of organic and some inorganic solids which is made available by their decomposition. Such microorganisms are termed *anaerobic bacteria* and the process of degradation of solids which they bring about is called *anaerobic decomposition* or putrefaction, that is, decomposition in the absence of dissolved oxygen, which results in the production of foul odors and unsightly conditions.
 To complicate the reactions involved in the decay of organic matter, certain aerobic types can adjust themselves to live and function in the absence of dissolved oxygen and are termed

facultative aerobic bacteria. Conversely, some varieties of anaerobic bacteria can become accustomed to live and grow in the presence of dissolved oxygen and are thus termed *facultative anaerobic bacteria.*

Such adaptability of the saprophytic bacteria to various sources of oxygen is of great importance in the decomposition of organic solids in sewage and thus in the various treatment procedures.

In addition to food and oxygen, bacteria require moisture to remain alive. This is adequately provided in sewage by its water component.

In order to function at maximum efficiency, bacteria require a favorable temperature. They are very susceptible to changes in temperature in that their rate of growth and reproduction, which is directly proportional to the amount of work done, is definitely and sharply affected by such variations. The larger proportion of the saprophytic types thrive best at temperatures from 20°C to 40°C, or 68°F to 104°F. These are known as *mesophilic* types. Variations from this temperature range limit the activity of mesophilic bacteria, practically eliminating it at extremely low temperatures and at high temperatures. Mesophilic sludge digestion proceeds most rapidly at 35°C or 95°F. Other bacteria live best at high temperatures, in the range of 55°C to 60°C, or 130°F to 140°F. These are known as *thermophilic* types. Thermophilic bacteria function in sewage treatment, principally in high temperature digestion of sludge solids. A very few types of bacteria find their optimum conditions at low temperatures, 0°C to 5°C, or 32°F to 40°F. These are known as *psychrophilic* bacteria. Temperatures, consequently, are of major importance in the operation of sewage treatment processes.

When all of these environmental conditions of food supply, oxygen, moisture, and temperature are properly maintained at their optimum amounts for the full functioning of the bacteria, decomposition of the sewage solids proceeds in a natural orderly manner.

Other Microscopic Organisms. In addition to the bacteria, other living organisms, usually so small in size as to require microscopic viewing, are found in sewage. They are present in large numbers also, although not in as great densities as the various species of bacteria. These other microorganisms tend to be larger and more complex in structure than the bacteria. Some of them are plants and some are animals. All originate in the soil or in the organic wastes that go to make up sewage. Some are motile (able to move about), others are not. All require food, oxygen, and moisture. They can be either aerobic or anaerobic or facultative in their oxygen requirements. Their growth is affected by the temperature of the environment in much the same degree as the bacteria. These organisms also function in the decomposition and degradation of the organic solids in sewage. They use these solids as food, and produce waste products simpler in chemical structure. These waste products, in turn, frequently serve as food for certain types of saprophytic bacteria. Many of the larger forms are predatory by nature and prey upon other organisms, especially the bacteria.

Macroscopic Organisms: In addition to the two groups of microscopic organisms described above, many larger more complex organisms play a part in the decomposition of organic matter. These are termed *macroscopic*, that is, visible to the naked eye. They include varieties of worms and insects in various stages of development. Some are active in sewage treatment plant facilities and others are prevalent in streams highly polluted by sewage or other organic wastes.

Some forms of all of these organisms, microscopic and macroscopic, are essential to the orderly decomposition of organic matter in nature, and hence are equally essential for the proper functioning of the usual methods of sewage treatment. In fact, biological organisms actually carry on the processes of treatment and the only responsibility of the operator is to provide the environmental condition best suited to them.

Viruses: There is one other form of life found in sewage that is of interest to the sewage treatment plant operator. These are *viruses*. They are smaller than any of the microscopic organisms, too small to be seen under the ordinary microscope used in bacteriological work. They do not play a significant part in sewage treatment processes, but are important in that they are, like pathogenic bacteria, the causative agents of a number of diseases of man. Some, such as the virus of hepatitis, originate in the intestines of man and are carried with intestinal wastes to the sewage.

CONDITION OF SEWAGE

The extent and nature of the bacterial decomposition of solids in sewage has given rise to certain terms descriptive of the condition of the sewage.

Fresh sewage is, as the name indicates, the first stage after waste solids have been added to water to produce sewage. It contains the dissolved oxygen present in the water supply and remains fresh as long as there is sufficient oxygen to maintain aerobic decomposition. Such sewage is turbid with solids in suspension or floating, greyish in color, and has a musty, not unpleasant odor.

Septic sewage describes a sewage in which the dissolved oxygen has been completely exhausted so that anaerobic decomposition of the solids has been established with the production of hydrogen sulfide and other gases. Such sewage is characterized by a blackish color, foul and unpleasant odor, and with black floating and suspended solids.

Stable sewage is sewage in which the solids have decomposed to relative inert solids which are subject to no further decomposition or are only slowly decomposable. Dissolved oxygen is again present by absorption from the atmosphere; there is little or no odor and few suspended solids.

CHEMICAL CHANGES IN SEWAGE COMPOSITION

The activities of biological life in sewage produce many changes in the chemical composition of its solids. These chemical changes or, as they should be called, biochemical changes (since they are brought about by biological growth) not only indicate the activities of the microorganisms but likewise measure the degree of decomposition of the solids and thus the effectiveness of any particular treatment process.

In sewage treatment the physical force of gravity materially reduces the suspended solids in sewage, especially the settleable portion. With the colloidal or non-settleable solids, biochemical changes result in the removal of molecules of water bound in them. This loss of water causes them to stick together or flocculate to form heavier or settleable solids. These settled solids, both organic and inorganic, which are removed are called, respectively, sludge and grit.

Under anaerobic decomposition, oxygen is removed from complex compounds and simpler ones are formed. Such biochemical reactions continue, and step-by-step complex compounds are broken down until the final end product of stable inorganic and organic substances is produced.

The complex organic solids originally added to water to form sewage are compounds of the element *carbon* combined with other elements such as nitrogen, sulfur, phosphorus, hydrogen oxygen, and others, and frequently tightly bound molecules of water. In the process of aerobic decomposition, oxygen is combined with these elements so that the final end products of biochemical change when carried to completion are carbon dioxide, water, nitrates, sulfates, phosphates, and other similar substances usually designated as mineral salts. These are in general quite similar to or the same as the inorganic solids of the sewage and serve as fertilizers or food for the production of new complex organic matter by plant growth.

During the steps of biochemical decomposition, intermediate products are formed. They include organic and inorganic acids, gases such as hydrogen sulfide, methane, carbon dioxide, and in many instances very foul smelling gases resulting from the biochemical changes in organic sulfur compounds. It is these by-products of decomposition which appear in the different stages of sewage treatment, particularly the digestion of sludge solids, and affect, sometimes adversely and sometimes not, the progress of the digestion reactions. The particular compounds produced and the amounts of each are dependent upon the type of microorganisms carrying on the reactions. Thus, the appearance of excessive concentrations of acid in sludge digestion indicates that decomposition of the organic matter is being carried on by organisms that will not produce a rapid and orderly anaerobic destruction of the solids but will cause incomplete digestion and the formation of by-products detrimental to good treatment—such as the production of non-combustible gas which is disagreeably odorous from sludge digestion.

The intermediate products of biochemical decomposition of organic solids provide an excellent indication of the progress of biological activity and the type and degree of treatment resulting.

The process of biochemical changes is well illustrated by the nitrogen, carbon, and sulfur cycles, Figures 2, 3, and 4, which show the steps or stages through which organic matter containing nitrogen, carbon, or sulfur pass from dead organic matter through decomposition to products used by plant life upon which animal life depends. Animal life in turn through waste products, death, and decay ends up as dead organic matter to start the cycles over again.

In all three cycles, the left half of the figures pertain to living matter while the right half of the figures is concerned with dead or waste material. Sewage treatment and disposal lie in the right half.

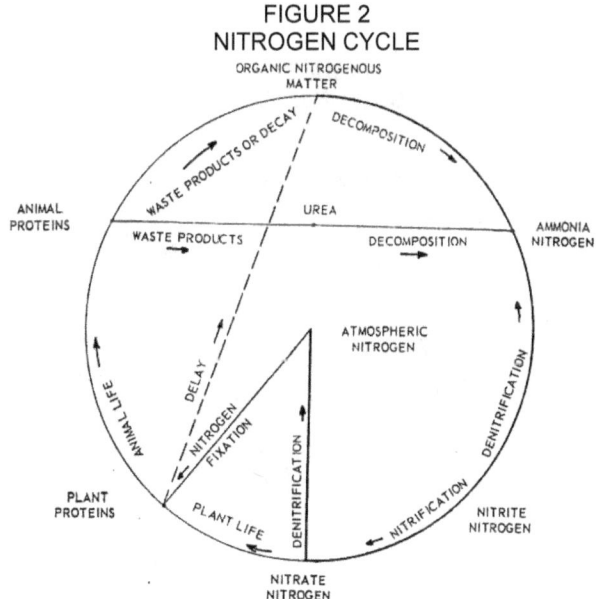

FIGURE 2
NITROGEN CYCLE

9

FIGURE 3
CARBON CYCLE

The three cycles illustrate nature's conservation of matter. The products of death are changed to become the support of plant and animal life. Air and water serve as a huge reservoir in which oxygen, nitrogen, carbon dioxide, and other gases produced in one part of the cycle can be stored till needed in another part.

Sewage treatment does not alter or modify natural processes. A treatment plant is merely a device to localize in a most suitable place a workshop in which the natural processes of decomposition of dead organic matter can be carried on as far as necessary and to some extent be controlled and accelerated.

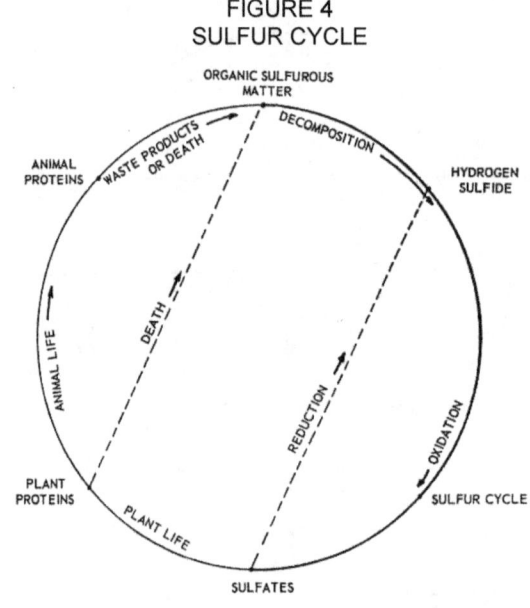

FIGURE 4
SULFUR CYCLE

10

In the biochemical changes in sewage, the dissolved gases play an important role. This is especially true of dissolved oxygen which, when present in the sewage or when added to it by treatment devices, insures the growth and activities of the aerobic microorganisms and thus the progress of aerobic decomposition without the production of putrefactive conditions. When dissolved oxygen is completely exhausted, the aerobic organisms are displaced by anaerobic varieties, and anaerobic decomposition takes place with the rapid development of putrefaction and the accompanying unsightly black appearance of the sewage together with foul odors. Although the other gases dissolved in the water fraction of the sewage do not control biological activities to the extent of the dissolved oxygen, they also play a part. Hydrogen sulfide, a foul-smelling gas, is the result of anaerobic decomposition of sulfur-bearing compounds and produces acid conditions which may affect further biochemical reactions and which will exert corrosive action on the sewage structures. Carbon dioxide, if present in excessive amounts, indicates that acid decomposition of the solids is taking place, with resulting reduction in the rate of decay. In the case of sludge digestion, carbon dioxide production reduces the generation of combustible gas which is a valuable by-product of such operations.

The chemical or biochemical changes in sewage solids are best measured by chemical analyses. Such chemical analyses will:

1. Detect and measure biochemical reactions.
2. Detect and measure the chemical compounds formed during such biochemical reactions.
3. Measure the degree and rate of the decomposition of organic solids.
4. Measure the efficiencies of various methods and devices used in sewage treatment.

CHAPTER 2

SEWAGE DISPOSAL

As discussed in Chapter 1, sewage is the waste water of community life. In composition it includes dissolved and suspended organic solids, which are putrescible and, therefore, will decay. Sewage also contains countless numbers of living organisms—bacteria and other microorganisms whose life activities cause the process of decomposition. When decay proceeds under anaerobic conditions, that is, in the absence of dissolved oxygen in the sewage, offensive conditions result and odors and unsightly appearances are produced. When decay proceeds under aerobic conditions, that is, in the presence of dissolved oxygen, offensive conditions do not result and the process is greatly accelerated.

The promotion of cleanliness by the removal of filth and wastes to an area remote from the center of activity is important. It is only by such practices that the environment can be maintained in an acceptable and safe condition. Among the waste products of life are the disease-producing (pathogenic) bacteria and viruses which can be readily transferred by sewage from sick individuals to well ones. Properly regulated procedures for disposal of sewage are necessary to protect the health of the people and to maintain the cleanliness of the environment and the comfort of the inhabitants.

A sharp distinction must be made between the term "sewage disposal" which is the subject of this chapter and "sewage treatment" which is covered in subsequent chapters. All sewage has to be disposed of. Some sewage is subjected to various types of treatment *before* disposal, but some sewage receives no treatment before disposal.

SEWAGE TREATMENT

Sewage treatment is a process in which the solids in sewage are partially removed and partially changed by decomposition from complex highly putrescible organic solids to mineral or relatively stable organic solids. The extent of this change is dependent on the treatment processes involved. After all treatment processes have been completed, it is still necessary to dispose of the liquid and the solids which have been removed.

SEWAGE DISPOSAL

There are three methods by which final disposal of sewage can be accomplished.

Disposal by Irrigation: This involves spreading the sewage over the surface of the ground, generally by irrigation ditches. There is some evaporation, but most of the sewage soaks into the ground and supplies moisture with small amounts of fertilizing ingredients for plant life. Use of this method is largely restricted to small volumes of sewage from a relatively small population and where land area is available. It has its best use in arid or semi-arid areas where the moisture added to the soil is of special value. If crops are cultivated on the disposal area, industrial wastes which would be toxic or impair the growth of vegetation must be excluded from sewers. Because of the ever present possibility that sewage may contain pathogenic organisms, the production of foods for human consumption which may be eaten without cooking is not desirable.

Subsurface Disposal: By this method sewage is introduced into the ground below its surface through pits or tile fields. It is commonly used for disposal of settled sewage from

12

residences or institutions where there is only a limited volume of sewage. Because it has little application for municipalities, any discussion of the many details involved would be of little value in this manual.

Disposal by Dilution: Disposal by dilution is the simple method of discharging sewage into a surface water such as a river, lake, or ocean. This results in the pollution of the receiving water. The degree of pollution depends on the dilution, the volume, and composition of sewage as compared to the volume of water with which it is mixed. When the volume and organic content of the sewage is small, compared with the volume of the receiving water, the dissolved oxygen present in the receiving water is adequate to provide for aerobic decomposition of the organic solids in the sewage so that nuisance conditions do not develop. However, in spite of the continued aerobic status of the receiving water, the bacterial pollution remains a health menace and floating solids in the sewage, if not previously removed, are visible evidence of the pollution.

Where the dissolved oxygen in the receiving water is inadequate to maintain aerobic decomposition, anaerobic decomposition takes place and putrefaction with objectionable conditions results. It is not so much the volume of sewage that is the critical factor as the amount of readily decomposable organic matter in the sewage. Thus, a volume of sewage that has been treated to remove or reduce this organic matter can be discharged to a natural surface water without creating objectionable conditions, while the same volume of raw or untreated sewage might produce a nuisance. The dissolved oxygen in the receiving water is the determining factor.

ROLE OF DISSOLVED OXYGEN IN RECEIVING WATERS

When sewage solids are discharged into water, decay and decomposition proceed owing to activities of the bacteria and microorganisms present in the sewage and in the receiving water. Oxygen is required for the functioning of all such biological and biochemical reactions. As discussed previously, when dissolved oxygen is present, aerobic organisms carry on the work, and aerobic decomposition of the organic solids proceeds. When oxygen is absent, anaerobic organisms take over and putrefaction results. Thus, when sewage is discharged into a stream, the reactions depend upon the dissolved oxygen present in the water.

Oxygen is dissolved in water from air in contact with the water surface until the point of saturation at a given temperature is reached. At a temperature of 0°C, water contains 14.6 ppm of dissolved oxygen at saturation. This concentration is reduced as the water temperature increases, so that at a temperature of 15°C, the dissolved oxygen concentration at saturation is 10.00 ppm. When the dissolved oxygen concentration is reduced below the saturation value, more is dissolved from the air. Turbulent flow of a stream over stones, riffles, and rapids increase the rate of solution of oxygen, or reaeration. By means of reaeration, additional oxygen is made available for the biochemical decomposition of putrescible organic solids

BIOCHEMICAL OXYGEN DEMAND – BOD

The amount of oxygen required for the aerobic biological oxidation of the organic solids in a sewage or waste is the *biochemical oxygen demand (BOD)*. It is determined by a laboratory test. Since this decomposition extends over a long period of time and is dependent on temperature, BOD values from laboratory tests should state the time and temperature used in making the test. Those most commonly used are 5 days and 20°C (68°F); and unless other time and temperature are specifically mentioned, these are generally assumed to have been the time and temperature used.

SELF-PURIFICATION

When sewage is discharged into a stream, decay and decomposition continue and proceed towards completion. A stream polluted at a given point would, as a result of the decomposition of the polluting organic matter, tend to return to a state similar to that before the pollution occurred. This is generally designated as the process of *self-purification*. It proceeds by physical, chemical, and biological means. The physical reactions are essentially those of sedimentation of suspended solids to form deposits called sludge banks, the bleaching and other effects of sunlight and reaeration.

The chemical and biological reactions are more complex. Here the living organisms feed on the organic solids, producing waste products which may destroy them and at the same time serve as food for succeeding types, which carry on the process of decomposition to a further degree—until finally the complex organic compounds are reduced to stable inorganic salts, such as nitrates, sulfates, phosphates, etc. These, in turn, serve as food for other biological forms, such as the algae, which during the process of their growth and metabolism produce oxygen as a waste product. This then dissolves in the water, adding to that obtained through reaeration. These reactions return the stream or water to a condition of relative cleanliness, and self-purification may be considered complete. The progress of self-purification is dependent upon time, temperature, oxygen supply, and the other environmental factors which regulate biological growths.

Self-purification of a stream is generally considered to take place in four stages with the stream divided into four zones which merge into each other. These are called the zones of degradation, decomposition, recovery, and clean water. As noted below under zone of decomposition, this zone is not always present.

Zone of Degradation: The first of these zones occurs immediately below the point of pollution and is designated as the *Zone of Degradation*. This zone is characterized by visible evidences of pollution. Floating solids, such as bits of garbage, sticks, paper, and possibly fecal solids, are present. The turbidity of the stream is markedly increased by the sewage discharge. Oxygen is reduced but is not immediately exhausted. Fish life decreases and is limited to those species which can survive in water with relatively little dissolved oxygen. Biological life, although not visible, abounds. Bacteria are present in large numbers—including those pathogenic ones that were in the sewage. Fungus organisms also are present and in time long stringy growths of these will be found clinging to rocks and shrubs on the shoreline. Active growth of the microbiological life absorbs and gradually exhausts the dissolved oxygen. If the flow in the stream in this section is slow, sedimentation of the suspended solids takes place to create sludge banks. This accumulation of sewage solids putrefies and further contributes to the degradation of the stream.

Zone of Decomposition: As the dissolved oxygen supply is exhausted, the *Zone of Degradation* passes into the *Zone of Decomposition*, where anaerobic decomposition or putrefaction is initiated.

With a heavy load of pollution this occurs quickly. With a smaller discharge of sewage relative to the volume of the stream, the change to the second zoned proceeds more slowly. When the volume of sewage discharged is relatively very small so that dissolved oxygen is continuously adequate to sustain aerobic life, the stream may not pass into the *Zone of Decomposition*, and the *Zone of Degradation* may pass directly into the *Zone of Recovery*.

The *Zone of Decomposition* is characterized by the development of anaerobic decomposition. Dissolved oxygen is almost or entirely depleted and all fish life disappears. The water turns black, and foul odors are produced as a result of the decomposition of the organic solids by anaerobic organisms which are present in large numbers. Sedimentation of suspended solids continues with sludge deposits appearing which are similar to those occurring in the first zone. As decomposition of organic matter progresses, the putrescible solids are reduced in amount and putrefactive reactions begin to decline in rate. Oxygen from reaeration first equals and then exceeds the rate at which it is being used for biochemical decomposition so that some dissolved oxygen is present at the lower edge of this zone, which merges into the third zone, the *Zone of Recovery*.

Zone of Recovery: In the *Zone of Recovery*, dissolved oxygen appears in gradually increasing amounts, organic solids decrease, and a favorable appearance of the stream is attained. Microorganisms in reduced numbers are present but the anaerobes are dying and aerobic species are present. Fish can again survive, and other higher forms of organisms appear in large numbers. Sedimentation of solids continues, and the organic solids in the sludge banks and bottom deposits are acted on by worms and larvae which are large enough to be visible, to affect further decomposition.

As previously indicated, if aerobic conditions are always present in the stream, the *Zone of Recovery* follows immediately after the *Zone of Degradation*.

Zone of Clean Water: In the *Zone of Recovery*, decomposition of organic solids is largely completed and mineral and stable inorganic solids are found in major concentrations. The stream then flows into the fourth and final zone, the *Zone of Clean Water*. Here the water is similar in appearance to what it was before it received the polluting material. Visible floating solids are absent, the water is clear, free from suspended matter, and has returned to its original color. Oxygen is at or near the point of saturation. Living microscopic organisms, including bacteria, are present but in relatively small numbers. Larger organisms are abundant, principally the algae and other forms which find in clean water their optimum environment and which use as food the stable inorganic compounds resulting from decomposition of the complex organic solids characteristic of the sewage that produced the pollution. Fish are generally more abundant than before the pollution occurred because of the increase in the population of macroscopic organisms which serves to increase the food supply for the fish.

The time required for self-purification of a stream or the distance it must flow to pass through the four zones is dependent upon the strength and relative volumes of pollution and stream flow, on the turbulence of flow, the temperature of the water, and, of major importance, on whether or not additional pollution is discharged into the stream during the progress of self-purification.

Possibility of Residual Pollution: The process of self-purification affects primarily the putrescible matter in the sewage. Some pathogenic organisms and viruses may survive. Other polluting substances, especially metallic and other compounds not completely organic in nature originating from industrial and manufacturing processes, are not changed by the biochemical processes. These substances, if present in sufficient concentration, interfere with and inhibit biological decomposition and may remain as a residual pollution which can impair the quality of the receiving stream to such a degree that the water is not suitable for use for water supply, recreational, industrial, and other purposes.

NEED FOR SEWAGE TREATMENT

The problem of sewage disposal developed with the use of water to pick up and carry away waste products of human life. Prior to that the volume of wastes, without the water vehicle, was small and disposal was largely restricted to the individual's or family's excreta. The earliest method was to leave body waste and garbage on the surface of the ground where it was gradually decayed by bacteria, mostly the saprophytic anaerobic type. This caused the production of foul odors. Later experience showed that if these wastes were promptly buried the development of these odors was prevented. The next step was the development of the earth privy, a method for the disposal of excremental wastes which is still widely used.

With the development of community water supplies and the use of water to flush or transport wastes from habitations, it became necessary to find disposal methods not only for the wastes themselves but for the water which carried them. All of the three possible methods—irrigation, subsurface disposal and dilution—were employed.

As urban communities increased in population, with proportional increase in the volume of sewage and amount of organic waste, all methods of disposal resulted in such unsatisfactory conditions that remedial measures became essential and the development of methods of treatment of sewage prior to ultimate disposal was started.

The objectives sought in sewage treatment include:

1. Maintenance of sources for use as domestic water supplies
2. Prevention of disease
3. Prevention of nuisances
4. Maintenance of clean waters for bathing and other recreational purposes
5. Maintenance of clean waters for the propagation and survival of fish life
6. Conservation of water for industrial and agricultural uses
7. Prevention of silting in navigable channels

A sewage treatment plant is designed to remove from the sewage enough organic and inorganic solids so that it can be disposed of without infringing upon the objectives sought.

The various processes used in sewage treatment parallel closely the processes involved in the self-purification of a polluted stream. Treatment devices merely localize and confine these processes to a restricted, controlled, suitable area and provide favorable conditions for the acceleration of the physical and biochemical reactions.

The extent or degree of treatment needed varies greatly from place to place. Basically there are three determining factors:

1. The character and amount of the solids carried by the sewage
2. The objectives sought
3. The ability or capacity of the land (in disposal by irrigation and subsurface disposal) or the receiving water (in disposal by dilution) to handle by self-purification or dispersal the water and solids in the sewage without infringing on the objectives sought

The removal of floating solids by screens may be adequate for sewage discharged into coastal sea waters. A very high removal of suspended solids, decomposition of dissolved organic solids and destruction of pathogenic organisms may be required, however, before discharge to a river which is used downstream as a source of public water supply. Adequate treatment prior to disposal to attain objectives is becoming a must, but excessive overtreatment is an unwarranted extravagance.

After the disposal of the sewage effluent from a treatment plant, there still remain in the plant the solids and water constituting the sludge which has been removed from the sewage. This, too, must be disposed of safely and without nuisance.

The progress of self-purification of a stream can be measured by appropriate physical, chemical, and biological laboratory tests. Similar tests are used to measure and control the progress of sewage treatment plant processes.

LEGAL ASPECTS OF SEWAGE DISPOSAL

The serious problem involving the disposal of sewage and other wastes by adequate and effective means that will eliminate nuisances and not violate the rights and welfare of individuals and communities has led to the development of laws and regulations governing such disposal.

It is presumed that in ancient times, customs slowly developed which regulated the disposal of the wastes of the individuals and of the group. As time went on, custom took on the force of law, and led, over the years, to the formulation of legal regulations—first as common law and then as statutory law.

Mosaic Law: One of the earliest recorded regulations pertaining to waste disposal can be found in the 23rd chapter of Deuteronomy. Moses, as the leader of a great community of people, found it necessary to establish rules for the conduct of his followers. Verses 12 to 14 of this chapter contain that portion of the Mosaic Law which placed the responsibility for proper disposal of excrement with the individual and required that it be buried. Modern research has not changed the fundamental principles involved. Increased knowledge of the transmission of disease from man to man and the need for personal cleanliness in community life have led to better practices and regulation for disposal of these waste products.

Common Law: Perhaps the earliest regulations related to sewage disposal and water pollution were based on the common law as related to the use of streams by owners of property bordering the stream. These specified (a) that every riparian owner is entitled to reasonable use of the water flowing past his property, and (b) that every riparian owner is entitled to have the waters of the stream reach his property in their natural condition and unimpaired as to quality and quantity.

Modern Legal Practice: The general principles of Common Law have been further clarified and modified by any specific statutory laws and regulations concerned with the disposal of sewage into streams and other bodies of water. Large numbers of lawsuits based on instances of pollution have led to legislation in most states governing the treatment and disposal of community wastes. Such legislation usually applies not only to pollution of waterways but controls the installation of treatment facilities by requiring approval of design and supervision of operation by some government body. Disposal of industrial waste as well as of domestic sewage is included in the legislation.

New York State now has stringent laws relating to this important matter of sewage and wastes disposal. Articles 11 and 12 of the Public Health Law regulate sewage disposal for the prevention and control of water pollution.

Article 11, Title III, prohibits the discharge of sewage into waters of the State unless a permit for such discharge has been granted by the State Commissioner of Health. The legal procedures for the control of pollution and regulations relative to construction of sewers and sewage treatment facilities are included.

Article 12 is concerned with the control of water pollution. Section 1200 outlines the policy of the State in this regard, and Section 1201 states the purpose of these regulations.

"Section 1200. Declaration of Policy. It is declared to be the public policy of the State of New York to maintain reasonable standards of purity of the waters of the state consistent with public health and public enjoyment thereof, the propagation and protection of fish and wild life, including birds, mammals, and other terrestrial and aquatic life, and the industrial development of the State, and to that end require the use of all known available and reasonable methods to prevent and control the pollution of the waters of the State of New York."

"Section 1201. Statement of Purpose. It is the purpose of this article to safeguard the waters of the State from pollution by: (a) preventing any new pollution, and (b) abating polluting existing when this chapter is enacted, under a program consistent with the declaration of policy above stated in the provisions of this article."

The ensuing sections of the New York State Public Health Law delineate the procedures that must be followed to control pollution of the State's water resources. The principle of classification of the surface and ground water resources of the State in accordance with the usage to which a specific water should be put is established. Various degrees of permissible pollution of streams, lakes, and ground waters are recognized.

In 1950, there were established seven classes of standards for fresh surface waters, four for tidal salt waters and two for ground waters. Several others have subsequently been established to meet special local conditions. The classes are based on the best use of the waters. The standards do not specify the character of polluting material discharged but are those which the waters must meet after such material has had an opportunity for reasonable dilution and mixture with the waters. Indirectly, however, this does not indicate the treatment pollutional material must have prior to discharge.

Best usages include use for drinking, culinary, food processing, bathing, fishing, ariculture, production of shellfish for marketing, agriculture and industry, navigation, sewage and wastes disposal.

Laws and regulations governing pollution and sewage disposal have become more and more essential with population increase. Only by such legal procedures and their enforcement can a clean, comfortable, and healthy environment be assured for all people.

CHAPTER 3

SEWAGE TREATMENT METHODS

Satisfactory disposal of sewage, whether by irrigation, subsurface methods or dilution, is dependent on its treatment prior to disposal. For disposal by dilution, adequate treatment is necessary to prevent contamination of receiving waters to a degree which might interfere with their best use, whether it be for water supply, recreation, fishing, or any other required purpose. Even when a body of water has no other use than for the disposal of sewage or liquid industrial wastes, some treatment is necessary to avoid offensive conditions.

Sewage treatment is a means whereby in a limit4ed segregated area, and under controlled conditions, it is possible to carry out the various stages, described in Chapter 2, as taking pace in the self-purification of a stream.

The purpose of sewage treatment prior to disposal is to remove from the sewage enough solids to permit the remainder to be discharged to receiving waters without interfering with its best or proper use, taking into consideration the capacity of the receiving waters to assimilate the added load. The solids which are removed are primarily organic but include also inorganic solids. As the best use of a receiving water may vary from use of the water for drinking and culinary purposes to use, primarily, for the disposal of sewage and industrial wastes, the amount or degree of treatment provided for the sewage or wastes must be varied accordingly. Treatment must be provided for the solids and liquids which are removed as sludge, and treatment to control odors, to retard biological activity or destroy pathogenic organisms may also be needed.

While the devices used in sewage treatment are numerous, they may all be included under five methods:

1. Preliminary treatment
2. Primary treatment
3. Secondary treatment
4. Chlorination
5. Sludge treatment

PRELIMINARY TREATMENT

At most plants preliminary treatment is used to protect pumping equipment and facilitate subsequent treatment processes. Preliminary devices are designed to remove or cut up the larger suspended and floating solids; to remove the heavy inorganic solids; and to remove excessive amounts of oils or greases. In some few instances where, for example, disposal by dilution is into tidal waters, the results accomplished by preliminary treatment may be adequate.

To effect the objectives of preliminary treatment, the following devices are commonly used:

1. Screens—rack, bar or fine
2. Comminuting devices—grinders, cutters, shredders
3. Grit chambers
4. Pre-aeration tanks

In addition to the above, chlorination may be used in preliminary treatment. Since chlorination may be used at all stages in treatment, it is considered to be a method by itself and is covered in a separate section in this Manual.

Preliminary treatment devices require careful design and operation. Detailed discussion of them is contained in Chapter 4.

PRIMARY TREATMENT

By this treatment most of the settleable solids or about 40 to 60 percent of the suspended solids are separated or removed from the sewage by the physical process of sedimentation in settling tanks. When certain chemicals are used with primary tanks, much of the colloidal as well as the settleable solids or a total of 80 to 90 percent of the suspended solids are removed. Biological activity in the sewage is of negligible importance.

The purpose of primary devices is to reduce the velocity of the sewage sufficiently to permit solids to settle. Therefore, primary devices may be called settling tanks. Because of variations in design and operation, settling tanks can be divided into four general groups:

1. Septic tanks
2. Two story tanks—Imhoff and several patented units
3. Plain sedimentation tank with mechanical sludge removal
4. Upward flow clarifiers with mechanical sludge removal

When chemicals are used, other auxiliary units are employed. These are:

1. Chemical feed units
2. Mixing devices
3. Flocculators

The results obtained by primary treatment, together with anaerobic sludge digestion as described later, are such that they can be compared with the zone of degradation in stream self-purification. The use of chlorine with primary treatment is discussed under the section on Chlorination.

In many cases, primary treatment is adequate to permit the discharge of the effluent to the receiving waters without interfering with the proper subsequent uses of the waters.

SECONDARY TREATMENT

This must be used where sewage after primary treatment still contains more organic solids in suspension or solution than the receiving waters can assimilate without infringing upon their normal proper use. Secondary treatment depends primarily upon biological aerobic organisms for the biochemical decomposition of organic solids to inorganic or stable organic solids. It is comparable to the zone of recovery in the self-purification of a stream.

The devices used in secondary treatment may be divided into our groups:

1. Trickling filters with secondary settling tanks
2. Aeration tanks—(a) activated sludge with final settling tanks, and (b) contact aeration
3. Intermittent sand filters
4. Stabilization ponds

The use of chlorine with secondary treatment is discussed under the chapter on Chlorination.

20

CHLORINATION

This is a method of treatment which may be employed for many purposes in all stages in sewage treatment, and even prior to preliminary treatment. It involves the application of chlorine to the sewage for the following purposes:

1. Disinfection or destruction of pathogenic organisms
2. Prevention of sewage decomposition—(a) odor control, (b) protection of plant structures
3. Aid in plant operation—(a) sedimentation, (b) trickling filters, (c) activated sludge bulking
4. Reduction or delay of biochemical oxygen demand

SLUDGE TREATMENT

The solids removed from sewage in both primary and secondary treatment units, together with the water removed with them, constitute sewage sludge. While in some few instances satisfactory disposal without treatment is practical, it is generally necessary to subject sludge to some treatment to prepare or condition it for disposal without creating unsatisfactory conditions. Such treatment has two objectives—the removal of part or all of the water in the sludge to greatly reduce its volume, and the decomposition of the putrescible organic solids to mineral solids or to relatively stable organic solids. This is accomplished by a combination of two or more of the following methods.

1. Thickening
2. Digestion with or without heat
3. Drying on sand bed—open or covered
4. Conditioning with chemicals
5. Elutriation
6. Vacuum filtration
7. Heat drying
8. Incineration
9. Wet oxidation
10. Floatation with chemicals and air
11. Centrifuging

PACKAGE UNITS

The term "package units" has come into quite common use in recent years to describe equipment which has been put on the market by a number of manufacturers. There is no universally accepted definition of the term. One meaning is a complete installation including both mechanisms and pre-fabricated containers. This term is also applied to installations where only the mechanisms are purchased and the containers constructed by the purchaser in accordance with plans and specifications prepared by the manufacturer. The latter appears to be the more generally accepted interpretation.

Though specific limitations have not been established, individual package units have, in general, been small installations serving a limited population.

Package units have been adapted to practically all the treatment devices, either singly or in various combinations, listed in this chapter.

CHAPTER 4

PRELIMINARY TREATMENT

The purpose of preliminary treatment is to remove from the sewage some of its constituents which can clog or damage pumps, or interfere with subsequent treatment processes. Preliminary treatment devices are, therefore, designed to:

1. Remove or reduce in size the large suspended or floating organic solids. These solids consist of pieces of wood, cloth, paper, garbage, together with some fecal matter.
2. Remove heavy inorganic solids such as sand, gravel, and possible metallic objects, all of which are called grit.
3. Remove excessive amounts of oils or greases.

A number of devices or types of equipment are used to obtain these objectives.

RACKS AND BAR SCREENS

These consist of bars usually spaced three-quarter inches to six inches. Those most commonly used provide clear openings of one to two inches. Although large screens are sometimes set vertically, screens are usually set at an angle of 45 to 60 degrees with the vertical. They may be cleaned either manually or by means of automatically operated rakes. It has been recommended that hand-cleaned screens, except those for emergency use, should be placed on slopes of 30 to 45 degrees with the vertical. The solids removed by these units can be disposed of by burial or incineration or they may be reduced in size by grinders or shredding devices and returned to the sewage.

FINE SCREENS

Screens with openings of one-eighth inch or less have been used in sewage treatment. They can be classified as bandscreens, disk screens, and drum screens, and are mentioned here because there are a few in operation at existing sewage treatment plants in New York State. They are commonly used in the treatment of many types of industrial wastes, but are no longer considered for sewage treatment except in special cases, because of the limited results obtained.

COMMINUTING DEVICES

Grinders, Cutters, and Shredders: These are devices to break or cut up solids to such size that they can be returned to the sewage without danger of clogging pumps or piping or affecting subsequent treatment devices. They may be separate devices to grind solids removed by screens or a combination of screen and cutters installed within the sewage flow without actually removing these larger solids from the sewage. These latter devices are made by a number of manufacturers under various trade names and, in most cases, consist of fixed, rotating, or oscillating teeth or blades, acting together to reduce the solids to a size which will pass through fixed or rotating screens or grids having openings of about one-fourth inch. Some of these devices are even designed to operate as a low-lift pump.

GRIT CHAMBERS

Sewage usually contains a relatively large amount of inorganic solids such as sand, cinders, and gravel which are called grit. The amount varies greatly depending on a number of factors, but primarily on whether the collecting sewer system is of the sanitary or combined type. Grit will damage pumps by abrasion and cause serious operation difficulties in sedimentation tanks and with sludge digestion by accumulation around and plugging of outlets. It is, therefore, common practice to remove this material by grit chambers. They are usually located ahead of pumps or comminuting devices, and if mechanically cleaned as described below, should be preceded by coarse bar rack screens. Grit chambers are generally designed as long channels. In these channels, the velocity is reduced sufficiently to deposit heavy inorganic solids but to retain organic material in suspension. Channel type chambers should be designed to provide controlled velocities as close as possible to 1.0 foot per second. The detention period should be based on size of particle to be removed and is usually between 20 seconds and 1.0 minute. This is attained by providing several chambers to accommodate variation in flow or by proportional weirs at the end of the chamber or other flow control devices which permit regulation of flow velocity. There are also patented devices to remove grit. A recent development is the injection of air several feet above the floor of a tank type unit. The rolling action of the air keeps the lighter organic matter in suspension and allows the grit relatively free from organic matter to be deposited in the quiescent zone beneath the zone of air diffusion.

Cleaning: Grit chambers are designed to be cleaned manually or by mechanically operated devices. If cleaned manually, storage space for the deposited grit is usually provided. Grit chambers for plants treating wastes from combined sewers should have at least two hand-cleaned units or a mechanically cleaned unit with by-pass. Mechanically cleaned grit chambers are recommended. Single hand-cleaned chambers with by-pass are acceptable for small sewage treatment plants serving sanitary sewer systems. Chambers other than channel type are acceptable, if provided with adequate and flexible controls for agitation and/or air supply devices and with grit removal equipment.

There are a number of mechanical cleaning units available which remove grit by scrapers or buckets while the grit chamber is in normal operation. These require much less grit storage space than manually operated units.

Washing Grit: Grit always contains some organic matter which decomposes and creates odors. To facilitate economical disposal of grit without causing nuisance, the organic matter is sometimes washed from the grit and returned to the sewage. Special equipment is available to wash grit. Mechanical cleaning equipment generally provides for washing grit with sewage as it is removed from the chamber.

Quantity of Grit: This depends on the type of tributary sewer system, the condition of the sewer lines, and other factors. Strictly domestic sewage collected in well-constructed sewers will contain little grit, while combined sewage will carry large volumes of grit reaching a peak at times of severe storms. In general, 1.0 to 4.0 cu. ft. of grit per million gallons can be expected.

Operation: Manually cleaned grit chambers for combined sewage should be cleaned after every large storm. Under ordinary conditions these grit chambers should be cleaned when the deposited grit has filled 50 to 60 percent of the grit storage space. This should be tested at least every ten days.

When mechanically cleaned chambers are used, they must be cleaned at regular intervals to prevent undue load on the cleaning mechanism. Recommendations of the manufacturer should be rigidly observed. This plus experience will determine the cleaning schedule.

A grit in which marked odors develop indicates that too much organic matter is being removed in the grit chamber. If sludge from settling tank is excessively high in inorganic matter, or if there is excessive wear in pumps, comminutors, sludge collectors, or other mechanical equipment, the reason is likely to be inefficient functioning of the grit chamber in removing grit and a study of this unit should be made.

Disposal of Screenings and Grit: Screenings decompose rapidly with foul odors. They should be kept covered in cans at the screens and removed at least daily or oftener for disposal by burial, incineration or through grinders. The walls and platforms of the screen chamber and screen itself should be hosed down and kept clean. Grit containing much organic matter may have to be buried to prevent odor nuisances.

PRE-AERATION TANKS

Pre-aeration of sewage, that is aeration before primary treatment, is sometimes provided for the following purposes:

1. To obtain a greater removal of suspended solids in sedimentation tanks
2. To assist in the removal of grease and oil carried in the sewage
3. To freshen up septic sewage prior to further treatment
4. BOD Reduction

Pre-aeration is accomplished by introducing air into the sewage for a period of 20 to 30 minutes at the design flow. This may be accomplished by forcing compressed air into the sewage at a rate usually taken as 0.10 cu. ft. per gallon of sewage when 30 minutes of aeration is provided or by mechanical agitation whereby the sewage is stirred or agitated so that new surfaces are continually brought into contact with the atmosphere for absorption of air. To insure proper agitation when compressed air is forced into the sewage, air is usually supplied at the rate of 1.0 to 4.0 cubic feet per minute per linear foot of tank or channel. When air for mechanical agitation (either with or without the use of chemicals) is used for additional purpose of obtaining increased reduction in BOD, the detention period should be at least 45 minutes at design flow. The agitation of sewage in the presence of air tends to collect or flocculate lighter suspended solids into heavier masses which settle more readily in the sedimentation tanks. It also helps to separate grease and oil from the sewage and sewage solids and to carry them to the surface. By the addition of air, aerobic conditions are also restored in septic sewage to improve subsequent treatment.

The devices and equipment for introducing the air into the sewage are the same or similar to those used in the activated sludge process and are described under that heading in Chapter 6.

CHAPTER 5

PRIMARY TREATMENT

Primary treatment devices are designed to remove from the sewage organic and inorganic settleable solids by the physical process of sedimentation. This is effected by reducing the velocity of flow. Sewers are designed to maintain a velocity of about two feet per second, which is adequate to carry all solids with the sewage flow and prevent their deposition in the sewers. In preliminary treatment this velocity is lowered to about one foot per second for a very brief period during which the heavier inorganic solids are settled out as grit. In primary treatment the velocity of flow is reduced to a fraction of an inch per second in a settling or sedimentation tank for sufficient time to allow the major portion of the settleable solids, which are largely organic, to settle out of the sewage flow.

Principle primary treatment devices are sedimentation tanks, some of which have the further function of providing for the decomposition of the settled organic solids, known as sludge digestion. There are a number of types of tanks used.

SEPTIC TANKS

The septic tank was one of the earliest primary treatment devices developed. It is designed to hold the sewage at a very low velocity under anaerobic conditions for a period of 12 to 24 hours during which a high removal of the settleable solids in the sewage is effected. These solids decompose in the bottom of the tank with the formation of gas which, entrained in the solids, causes them to rise through the sewage to the surface and lie as a scum layer until the gas has escaped, after which they again settle. This continual floatation and resettling of solids carry them in the current of the sewage toward the outlet, with some eventually passing out with the effluent, thus partially defeating the purpose of the tank. Due to the long holding period and the mixing with decomposing solids, the sewage itself leaves the tank in a septic condition difficult to treat in secondary units.

Septic tanks are no longer used except for very small installations. They do, however, have common use for individual residences, small institutions or schools where the tank effluent can be disposed of by sub-surface methods or where the dilution factor in the receiving waters is high. In such situations, they have the value of requiring a minimum of attention to operation which involves only occasional cleaning of the tank of sludge and scum accumulations.

FIGURE 5
SEPTIC TANK

TWO-STORY TANKS

The two-story tank was developed to correct the two main defects of the septic tank.

1. It prevents the solids once removed from the sewage from again being mixed with it though still providing for decomposition of these solids in the same unit, and
2. It provides an effluent amenable to further treatment

Contact between the sewage and the anaerobic digesting sludge is practically eliminated and the holding period in the tank is reduced.

The best known and most used two-story tank was originally designed by Dr. Karl Imhoff and is known as the Imhoff tank. It may be either circular or rectangular and is divided into three compartments or chambers—(1) the upper section, called the flowing through chamber or sedimentation compartment; (2) the lower section known as sludge digestion chamber; and (3) the gas vent and scum chamber. Figure 6 shows a typical plan and cross-section of an Imhoff tank. It is desirable to be able to reverse the direction of flow to prevent excessive deposition of solids at one end of the flowing-through chamber. Reversing the flow every month will result in an even accumulation of sludge across the bottom of the tank.

FIGURE 6
IMHOFF TANK

In operation, all of the sewage flows through the upper compartment. Solids settle to the bottom of this compartment, which has slopes of about 1.4 vertical to one horizontal, slide down and pass through an opening or slot at the bottom. One of the bottom slopes extends at least six inches beyond the slot. This forms a trap to prevent gas or digesting sludge particles in the lower section from entering the sewage in the upper section. The gas and any rising sludge

26

particles are diverted to the gas vent and scum chamber. This eliminates the main disadvantage of the septic tank. The gas vents should have a surface area of at least 20 percent of the total area of the tank.

It is desirable to start the operation of an Imhoff tank in the spring or early summer when the temperature in the sludge compartment is high enough to promote rapid digestion. Seeding the tank with actively digesting sludge from a nearby Imhoff tank or separate sludge digester is advisable if it can be done conveniently. Otherwise the pH of the sludge in the sludge compartment should be controlled and maintained above 6.8 to prevent an acid condition unfavorable for proper digestion. This can be done by the addition of milk of lime gradually to the influent or by adding lime in the scum chamber. Care should be taken to prevent the addition of a large quantity of lime over a very short period of time as such sudden shocks of lime tend to upset digestion.

Imhoff Tank Operation: There are no mechanical parts in an Imhoff tank. Attention should, however, be given to the following:

1. Daily removal of grease, scum, and floating solids from the sedimentation compartment.

2. Weekly scraping of the sides and sloping bottoms of the sedimentation compartment by a rubber squeegee to remove adhering solids which may decompose.

3. Weekly cleaning the slot at the bottom of the sedimentation compartment. This can be done by use of a chain drag.

4. At least monthly reversal of flow where this is provided for in the design of the tank.

5. Control of the scum in the scum chamber by breaking it up, hosing with water under pressure, keeping it wet with sewage from the sedimentation compartment and removal if the depth approaches two to three feet.

6. Removal of sludge should be done before the sludge depth approaches within 18 inches of the slot in the sedimentation compartment. It is better to remove small amounts frequently than large amounts at long intervals. Sludge should be removed at a slow regular rate to avoid the formation of a channel through the sludge which would permit partially digested sludge and liquid held in storage above the digested sludge to be withdrawn from the tank. Before winter temperatures are expected, most of the digested sludge except that necessary for seeding (about 20 percent) should be removed to provide space for winter accumulations when digestion is very slow. The height of the sludge in the sludge compartment should be determine at inlet and outlet ends of the tank at least once a month. The use of a pump for this purpose is the most desirable and satisfactory. The use of the plate or disc method is not usually satisfactory. The following are suitable methods for measuring the depth of sludge:

    a. One method involves the use of a pitcher pump provided with a rubber suction hose, weighted on the end and the length marked on the hose at intervals of two feet, measuring from the weighted end toward the pump. The hose is gradually lowered through the slot in the sedimentation compartment, meanwhile constantly pumping, and the length of immersed hose, when sludge first comes through the pump is determined. When the sludge elevation is reached, the pump will usually "choke" before sludge appears.

27

    b. A pitcher pump may also be used with a rubber suction hose, weighted on the end by a four foot length of steel pipe as an integral part of the pump suction line. This suction hose may be graduated and marked as above and the determination of sludge depth made in the same manner except that the hose is lowered through the gas vent instead of the sedimentation compartment slot.

    c. The sludge depth may also be determined by use of an iron plate or weighted wooden block, about 12-18 inches square, attached to a wire or chain lowered through the gas vent. The plate or block will stop when the sludge is reached and the distance from the surface to the sludge level is determined from the graduated wire or chain by which the device is lowered.

    d. Where the condition of gas vents will permit the use of a lighter implement, a modification of the above may be used. This consists of a wire loop, 12 or 15 inches in diameter, covered with a disc of a quarter inch mesh wire. A very light chain should be used with this disc suspended at three points.

7. After each time that sludge is removed, the sludge pipes should be flushed and filled with water or sewage to prevent sludge from hardening in and clogging the pipes.

8. Prevention of "Foaming": Every effort should be made to prevent "foaming" because correction after the condition arises is sometimes difficult. "Foaming" is usually associated with an acid condition of the sludge and in such cases may be prevented or corrected by treatment with lime to counteract the acidity of the sludge. When foaming occurs, it is usually desirable to seek the advice of an expert sanitary engineer. There are, however, a few simple measures which may under certain circumstances remedy or improve the condition.

    a. The use of hydrated lime added to the gas vents of Imhoff tanks or to the sludge added to separate digesters will usually aid in correction. The pH value of the resulting sludge and lime mixture in the digestion compartment should not exceed 7.6.

    b. Removing the tank from service where possible for a few days and allowing it to rest will sometimes improve conditions.

    c. In case of Imhoff tanks, agitation of the gas vent area with a water hose or paddles will sometimes help.

    d. When foaming occurs in separate digestion tanks, the gas line should be shut off or disconnected until the tank becomes normal again in order to protect the gas lines and gas control equipment from the foam solids.

    e. Lowering the temperature of the sludge in separate digesters for several days will reduce the foaming activity.

FIGURE 7
IMHOFF TANK – USEFUL EQUIPMENT

The Imhoff tank has no mechanical problems and is relatively easy and economical to operate. It provides sedimentation and sludge digestion in one unit and should produce a satisfactory primary effluent with a suspended solids removal of 40 to 60 percent and a BOD reduction of 25 to 35 percent. The two-story design requires a deep overall tank. Other more recently developed types of tanks have largely replaced the Imhoff tank for large municipal installations. The Imhoff tank is best suited to small municipalities and large institutions where the tributary population is 5,000 or less.

Operators interested in operation and maintenance of Imhoff tanks will find an excellent article by L.W. VanKleeck in the February 1956 issue4 of *Wastes Engineering*, entitled, "Operation of Imhoff Tanks."

Other Two-story Tanks: A number of manufacturers have put on the market prefabricated parts to be installed in tanks constructed according to their designs to produce two-story tanks embodying the Imhoff tank principle. These are patented units with trade names and are classed as "package units".

They provide separate compartments for sedimentation and sludge digestion in one tank. Facilities for heating the digestion compartment can be installed, if desired. The units are circular in shape and made in sizes to serve populations up to 5,000.

Provision is made for the collection and utilization of digestion gas and there are special features such as radial, tangential, and upward flow of the sewage. Some units have mechanical equipment for moving settled solids and sludge to outlets over relatively flat surfaces. This permits reduction in depth of the sedimentation and digestion compartments and lowers the cost of tank construction.

PLAIN SEDIMENTATION TANKS

These are tanks whose major function is to remove settleable solids from the sewage b the process of sedimentation. The settled solids are taken from the tanks continuously or at frequent intervals so that decomposition with gas formation does not have time to develop. The solids are then handled by other units. The solids may flow by gravity to a hopper or to a low point in the bottom of the tank from which they are pumped or removed by hydrostatic pressure. This method, however, has been replaced by the use of mechanical equipment for the collection of the solids in a hopper from which they are removed by pumps. Tanks with mechanical equipment for the collection of solids are known as mechanically cleaned plain sedimentation tanks.

Mechanically Cleaned Plain Sedimentation Tanks: These tanks may be rectangular, circular, or square, but all operate on the same principle of collecting the settled solids by slow moving scrapers to the point of removal.

In the rectangular tanks the scrapers are attached near their ends to two endless chains which pass over sprockets driven by motors. The scrapers are dragged slowly along the tank floor pushing the settled solids to a sludge hopper located at the inlet end of the tank. The scrapers are then lifted by the chains to the surface of the tank where, partially submerged, they serve to push floating solids, grease, and oil to a scum collector at the outlet end of the tank. Another type of mechanism consists of a traveling bridge spanning the tank from which is suspended a blade to push solids to the point of removal and a skimmer blade for floating solids, grease, and oil. These blades operate when traveling in one direction and idle when traveling in the return direction.

FIGURE 8
RECTANGULAR-PLAIN SEDIMENTATION TANK

FIGURE 9
CIRCULAR-PLAIN SEDIMENTATION TANK

The circular tanks have scrapper arms attached to a central motor-driven shaft. The bottom of the tanks are sloped toward the center and the scrappers move the settled solids to a sludge hopper at the center. Skimmer arms are attached to the central shaft at the surface for the collection of floating solids, greases, and oil.

In the square tanks the mechanism is similar to that in the circular tanks. The major difference is that one or both of the rigid arms of the mechanism are equipped with pivoted corner blades which reach out into the four corners of the tank and move the solids in these areas to the path of the circular mechanism.

In the rectangular tanks the sewer enters at one end and flows horizontally to the other end. In the circular tanks sewage enters at the center and flows radially and generally horizontally to the periphery. In the square tanks the sewage may enter at the center and flow to the four sides or at one side and flow across the tank.

Several manufacturers have designed equipment to carry the incoming sewage close to the bottom of the tank from which it flows upward and radially through a sludge blanket to the outlet on the periphery. These are known as upward flow clarifiers and have the value of introducing the solids at the bottom where they are wanted instead of settling them from the upper layers.

31

FIGURE 10
PRIMARY TREATMENT

Manufacturers of mechanical equipment have given trade names to tanks using equipment manufactured by them. This Manual cannot detail the different equipment or comment on the claims made by the manufacturers for their specific designs. There are, however, general features common to all primary settling tanks. New York State has adopted the standards of the Upper Mississippi River Board of Public Health Engineers and Great Lakes Board of Public Health Engineers which are commonly referred to as the Ten States Standards.

Inlets: Inlets should be designed to dissipate the inlet velocity, diffuse the flow equally across the entire cross-section of the tank and prevent short-circuiting. They may be of the weir type but are more commonly a channel with spaced port openings.

Baffles: These are usually found at the inlet and outlet of a tank, the former to assist in diffusing the flow and the latter to hold back floating material from the tank effluent. Mechanically cleaned tanks usually have a scum trough which serves the purpose of the outlet baffle and to which scum is brought by the skimmer. Scum baffles should be provided ahead of outlet weirs on all primary settling tanks, on all final settling tanks in plants not having primary settling facilities and on all non-mechanical final settling tanks.

Outlet Weirs: These vary greatly in design. They are for the purpose of removing the settled sewage as a thin sheet from the surface of the tank and are usually adjustable. It is important that they be kept level for uniform surface removal. The term "*weir loading*" is used to express the gallons per day passing over one foot of the weir. In plants of one mgd or less capacity, this should not exceed 10,000 gallons per linear foot per day, which may be increased to 15,000 for larger plants.

Surface Settling Rate: This is expressed in terms of gallons per square foot of tank area based on the sewage flow per day. For primary tanks not followed by secondary treatment, this rate should not exceed 600 gallons per square foot per day for plants of one mgd or less capacity but may be higher for larger plants. This rate is an important factor and appears to affect directly the percent removal of settleable solids and BOD.

Detention Period: This is the time in hours any sewage is held in the tank based on the sewage flow and tank volume, assuming total displacement and uniform flow through the settling compartment. This was at one time the commonly used factor of design. It has, however, been largely replaced by weir loading and surface settling rate. Based on design flow, detention periods should be at least 2.0 hours.

Overall Dimensions: Recent accepted standards are a minimum of 10.0 feet in length and a liquid depth (mechanically cleaned) of not less than 7.0 feet. The amount of sewage to be treated, the general layout of the sewage treatment plant, the surface settling rate, and manufacturer's equipment determine the tank dimensions. Recent studies have indicated advantages in not making tanks too deep.

The following examples illustrate the use of the foregoing factors to evaluate the operating features of a sedimentation tank. Assume that one million gallons per day is being treated in a rectangular tank 70 feet long, 24 feet wide, and 7 feet deep. The outlet weirs are "H" shaped with four approaches 24 feet long, and two approaches 2 feet long.

Weir Loading
  4 x 24 + 2 x 2 = 100 ft. total weir length

  $$\frac{1,000,000 \text{ gal.}}{100 \text{ ft.}} = 10,000 \text{ gal./ft.}$$

Surface Settling Rate
  24 x 70 = 1,680 sq. ft. surface area

  $$\frac{1,000,000 \text{ gal.}}{1,680 \text{ sq. ft.}} = 595, \text{ gal./sq. ft./day}$$

Detention Period
  1,680 x 7 x 7.5 = 88,200 gal. tank volume

  $$\frac{88,200 \times 24 \text{ gal.}}{000,000 \text{ ft.}} = 2.12, \text{ or about two hours detention}$$

Efficiency of Plain Sedimentation Tanks: Since the process of settling solids in plain sedimentation tanks is the same as in the sedimentation compartment of two-story tanks, similar results may be expected in their operation. About 90 to 95 percent of the settleable solids, and 40 to 60 percent of the total suspended solids, should be removed from the sewage. The BOD should be reduced by about 25 to 35 percent. Such figures are, of course, general and may not apply to specific cases. Sewage with high suspended solids may have a higher percentage removed by sedimentation than sewage with a low suspended solids content, but the suspended solids in the tank effluent may still be greater in the former. A higher percent removal can be expected in a tank treating fresh sewage than in one treating the same sewage after it has become septic because the solids in the septic sewage have been broken up or disintegrated by bacterial decomposition during their long travel in the sewer system. The amount and composition of industrial wastes are also an important factor affecting the percentage removal of suspended solids and BOD by primary settling tanks.

Operation of Mechanically Cleaned Sedimentation Tanks: The establishment and maintenance of proper time schedules for operation of the mechanical cleaning equipment and for removal of sludge from the tank are most important factors in tank operation. They must be determined for each plant. At most plants the collecting mechanisms are run from two to eight hours a day, depending on the size of the plant and the quantity of sludge produced. Very often circular tank mechanisms are run continuously. They should be run often enough to prevent a

33

build-up of solids on the tank bottom. If the solids are allowed to build up in the tank, an undue load may be placed on the mechanism and cause damage to the equ9ipment. Solids may also be decomposed with the resultant production of gas in the settling tank and some floating sludge. Before sludge is removed from the tank, the mechanism should be run for a sufficient time to assure satisfactory collection of bottom solids in the sludge hopper.

Sludge should be removed from the tank at least daily. It is not good practice to remove sludge with an excessive amount of water as this water wastes storage space and heat in digestion tanks. Maintaining a sludge blanket of 12 to 18 inches in the sludge hopper and pumping small amounts at frequent intervals and at a low rate helps to obtain sludge of a higher solids concentration. The sludge pump should have a sampling tap. As a guide, if a sample of sludge in a test jar after setting for ten minutes shows more than a 50 percent volume of sludge, pumping should be continued. If it shows less than 50 percent, removal may be considered reasonably complete. A vacuum gauge on the suction side of the pump and a pressure gauge on the discharge line are valuable. Should either gauge show zero, the operator will know that the line is plugged. A decreasing reading on the pressure gauge shows that the sludge is getting thinner. The sludge removal schedule must be worked out for each plant by observation and tests, keeping in mind that the objective is not to see how fast sludge can be removed but to remove a concentrated sludge while it is still fresh and to have the floor of the tank clean after a removal cycle. Seasonal revision of the schedule will probably be necessary.

Scum and grease should be removed daily from the surface of the tank. Most mechanical collectors direct such material to a grease trough from which it flows to a grease well for disposal by pumping to the digestion tank or by other means.

Where there is more than one tank, poor flow distribution often accounts for poor operation. The operator should check his particular installation to be sure that each tank is receiving its share of the load. When it is found that one tank is receiving more or less than its share, the inlet arrangements should be checked to ascertain whether a manipulation can be made to equalize the flow to each tank. The elevation of all effluent weirs should be checked as uneven weirs can do a great deal to increase short circuiting and unequal flow distribution. When it is necessary to pump to a sedimentation tank, the flow should be at as even a rate as possible to obtain the best possible results.

At all times the operator must be conscious that mechanical equipment requires attention and maintenance. Moving parts must be kept lubricated and weak or worn parts replaced. The best rule is to rigidly follow the instruction manual provided by the manufacturer of the equipment.

Advantages and Disadvantages of Mechanically Cleaned Plain Sedimentation Tanks with Separate Sludge Digestion: Except for relatively small installations, this type of tank has almost universal use in this country and it is being used more and more in the smaller municipal and larger institutional plants.

There are two main reasons for this: (1) the treatment of sludge in separate tanks, especially heated tanks, provides more complete control of the digestion process, and (2) the cost of construction especially for large units is less.

These tanks do, however, require more time and competency in operation than the Imhoff tank, because of the operational requirement and the care and maintenance of mechanical equipment.

CHEMICAL TREATMENT

Chemical treatment has been conventionally classed as intermediate treatment, in that the results obtained by it are greater than with standard primary treatment but less than with secondary treatment. It is included in this Manual under primary treatment because it involves chemical and physical processes as distinct from the biological processes which are the basis of secondary treatment.

Chemical treatment is one of the older methods of sewage treatment which fell into discard but was reintroduced in the decade 1930-40. However, developments in secondary treatment methods, the supervision needed, the cost of chemicals, and the excessive amounts of sludge requiring disposal have caused this method of treatment to be restricted to special conditions. It still has application in the treatment of industrial wastes which are not easily attacked biologically and where conditions in the receiving waters periodically require a higher degree of treatment than standard primary treatment, but do not warrant secondary treatment.

Chemical treatment involves the addition of one or more chemicals to sewage to produce a floc which is an insoluble chemical compound that absorbs colloidal matter, enmeshes non-settleable suspended solids and settles readily. The precipitating chemical also dissociates or ionizes in the sewage and neutralizes the electric charges held by colloidal particles causing them to coalesce to form larger readily settleable solids. The chemicals most widely used are aluminum sulfate or alum, ferrous sulfate with lime, ferric sulfate and ferric chloride with or without lime.

A chemical treatment plant usually has the following features:

1. Preliminary devices—screens, grit chambers, etc. as described in Chapter 4
2. Chemical feeders
3. Mixing units
4. Flocculation tanks
5. Sedimentation tanks such as have already been described
6. Increased facilities for the treatment and disposal of sludge

Chemical Feeders: A large variety of units to feed chemicals, either dry or in solution, in controlled amounts are made by a number of manufacturers. Details are not warranted in this Manual.

Mixing Units: The chemicals when added to sewage must be thoroughly and quickly mixed with it to provide complete and uniform reactions. This is accomplished by violent agitation for a short period of time either by mechanical or hydraulic methods. This agitation is carried on in special tanks, in sections of other tanks, or in the piping system. Mixing devices are made by a number of manufacturers.

Flocculators: After the chemical is mixed with sewage, it is gently agitated for 15 to 30 minutes to foster the coagulation of particles. If BOD reduction is desired, the agitation time may be increased to 45 minutes. The colloidal and suspended solids meet and adhere together in large flocculant masses which settle readily in the sedimentation tank. Different types of equipment to accomplish this purpose are made by a number of manufacturers.

Sludge: The volume of sludge obtained by chemical treatment is greater than with standard primary treatment, necessitating a comparable increase in sludge handling facilities and cost of sludge treatment and disposal.

Efficiency: Chemical treatment can effect a reduction up to 90 percent in suspended solids and up to 70 percent in the BOD. It is well adapted to intermittent operation and has value in sewage treatment to reduce pollution of streams during periods of low flow or to lessen pollution of bathing beaches and recreational waters during months when these facilities are in use. It is of value also for the treatment of sewage containing high concentrations of industrial wastes which will inhibit biological life and interfere with secondary treatment processes.

Operation costs are high due to increase in operators' time, chemicals, and greater quantities of sludge to be treated and disposed of.

Operation: Because of its limited use in sewage treatment operation, details regarding the usage of chemicals in chemical precipitation are not included in this Manual.

CHAPTER 6

SECONDARY TREATMENT

In many situations, primary treatment with the resulting removal of 40 to 60 percent of the suspended solids and approximately 25 to 35 percent of the BOD, together with the removal of floating material from the sewage, is adequate to meet requirements of the receiving water. However, if the accomplishment of primary treatment is not sufficient, there are two basic methods of secondary treatment available, trickling filters and activated sludge. Sand filters can be used when a high degree of treatment or a polishing effect is required. There are several other methods which are used to a limited extent. These types of treatment employ biological growths to effect aerobic decomposition or oxidation of organic material into more stable compounds and provide for a higher degree of treatment that accomplished by primary sedimentation alone.

While trickling filters and activated sludge both depend on aerobic biological organisms to effect decomposition, there is an operational difference. In filters the organisms are attached to the filter medium and the organic material on which they do their work is brought to them. With activated sludge, however, the organisms are migrant and are carried to the organic matter in the sewage. In either case, successful operation involves the maintenance of aerobic environmental conditions favorable for the life cycle of the organisms, and control over the amount of organic matter which they decompose. The organic matter is the food upon which these organisms live. If they are either over-fed or under-fed, their efficiency is reduced.

TRICKLING FILTERS

The word "filter" in this case is not correctly used, for there is no straining of filtering action involved. Actually, a trickling filter is a device for bring settled sewage into contact with biological growths. A more applicable name would be "biological oxidizing bed," but time and usage have made the term trickling filter a popular one and it is used universally to describe this type of unit.

Trickling filters are sturdy work units, not easily upset by shock loads, noted for their consistent performance, and capable of taking considerable abuse. Like all biological units they are affected by temperature; therefore, cold weather slows down biological activity in the filter. They occupy large areas and are expensive to construct.

For economy the filters should be preceded by primary sedimentation tanks equipped with scum collecting devices. Primary treatment ahead of filters makes available the full capacity of the filters for use in the conversion of non-settleable, colloidal, and dissolved solids, to readily settleable solids. These solids which are largely organic, are not removed from the sewage but are converted to living microscopic organisms or stable organic matter temporarily attached to the filter medium and to inorganic matter carried off with the effluent. The attached material eventually sloughs off and is carried away in the filter effluent. For this reason, trickling filters should be followed by secondary sedimentation tanks to remove permanently the solids from the sewage.

Construction: A typical trickling filter consists of three parts: (a) the bed of filter medium, (2) an underdrainage system, and (c) mechanism for distribution the sewage evenly over the surface of the filter.

1. The choice of filter media is often governed by the material locally available or the cost of bring material in. Field stone, gravel, broken stone, blast furnace slag, and anthracite coal have been used for this purpose. Redwood blocks and inert materials molded into appropriate shapes have also been employed. Whatever material is chosen, it is usually specified that it be sound, hard, clean, and free of dust and insoluble in sewage constituents. The material should be approximately cubical in shape to prevent compacting, and of a size to pass a four and one-half inch square screen, but be retained by a two inch square screen. The filter media should have a minimum depth of five feet and should not exceed seven feet in depth. The bed may be rectangular to circular. The former is common where distribution of sewage is by fixed spray nozzles, and the latter where rotating distributors are used as described under (3) below. The filter medium serves the dual purpose of providing a large surface area on which the slimes and gelatinous films produced by bacteria can develop yet leaving sufficient voids to permit free circulation of air throughout the filter.

2. *Underdrain System*: The underdrains serve two purposes: (1) to carry the sewage passing through the filter away from it for subsequent treatment and disposal, an (2) to provide for ventilation of the filter and the maintenance of aerobic condition. The direction of air flow through the filter depends on the difference in temperature between the filter and the sewage being applied. When the filter stone is warmer than the sewage, the direction of air will generally be upwards through the filter. When the temperature of the filter is colder, the direction of the air will be downward. The underdrain system consisting of precast filter blocks which are manufactured from vitrified clay or concrete, covers the entire bottom of the filter and leads to effluent channels. The blocks are usually rectangular in shape and have openings in the upper face equal to at least 20 percent of the surface of the block.

3. *Distributors*: Sewage is applied to the surface of the bed by fixed spray nozzles or rotary distributors. The fixed spray nozzles were used when trickling filters were first developed. The nozzles are attached to pipes laid in the filter medium and are fed intermittently from a siphon controlled dosing tank. By this method sewage is applied to the filter for short periods of time. Between applications, the filter has rest periods while the dosing tank is filling. Many types and shapes of nozzles have been developed and the siphon dosing tank is designed to attain the best possible even distribution of sewage over the entire surface of the filter. At best, the distribution is not even and there are areas of the filter on which very little sewage is sprayed.

Figure 11 shows diagrammatically a siphon controlled dosing tank. When the dosing tank has finished discharging, the level of the sewage is at the lower bend of the vent pipe. The sewage now stands at the level B_1 in both legs of the main trap. The blowoff trap is filled with sewage up to D_1 and the vent pipe is empty. As sewage rises in the dosing tank, it seals the open end of the vent pipe at "A" and prevents the escape of air from the bell. As the sewage continues to rise, the liquid level in the bell also rises. The air in the long leg of the main trap and of the blowoff trap is compressed and the surfaces of the sewage in these two legs are forced downward. When the dosing tank is filled to a point just below the discharge level, the surfaces of the sewage in the main trap and in the blowoff trap are at B_2 and D_2. A further rise of sewage level in the dosing tank causes the air in the bell to escape through the blowoff trap. The release of air causes an inrush of sewage from the dosing tank into the bell and down through the main trap, resulting in the dosing apparatus going into full operation. The discharge continues until the surface of the sewage reaches the lower elbow of the vent pipe. At this point air enters the bell through the vent pipe and the siphonic action is broken. The main trap and the blowoff trap remain filled with sewage. The vent pipe is empty and the cycle of filling and discharge commences again. The air vent in the discharge pipe allows escape of the air forced out of the bell and traps. Twin dosing tanks are often so interlocked that one may be filling while the other is discharging. There are many variations in design of dosing tanks. Some use mechanical devices to replace the main trap shown here.

FIGURE 11
SEWAGE DOSING TANK WITH DEEP SEAL SIPHON
(COURTESY OF PACIFIC FLUSH TANK CO)

The fixed spray nozzles have been largely supplanted by rotary distributors which effect a more even dosage over the entire area of the bed. With the rotary distributors, sewage is fed through a hollow vertical center column to which are attached two or more arms. Each arm contains a number of nozzle openings, all of which point at right angles to the arms and through which sewage is applied to the surface of the filter. The central feed column and arms which revolve slowly over the surface of the circular filter are usually driven by jet action of the sewage as it discharges through the nozzles. Positive drive mechanisms also are available.

Loading: Filter loadings are commonly expressed in terms of hydraulic loading and organic load. The hydraulic load is the number of gallons of sewage applied per acre of filter surface per day, or more accurately, because of different depths of filters, per acre foot per day. The organic loading is the number of pounds of BOD per 1,000 cubic feet of filter medium. Pounds per acre foot or per cubic yard of filter medium also are used.

Based on hydraulic and BOD loadings, trickling filters are classified as "Standard" and "High Rate."

FIGURE 12
TRICKLING FILTER

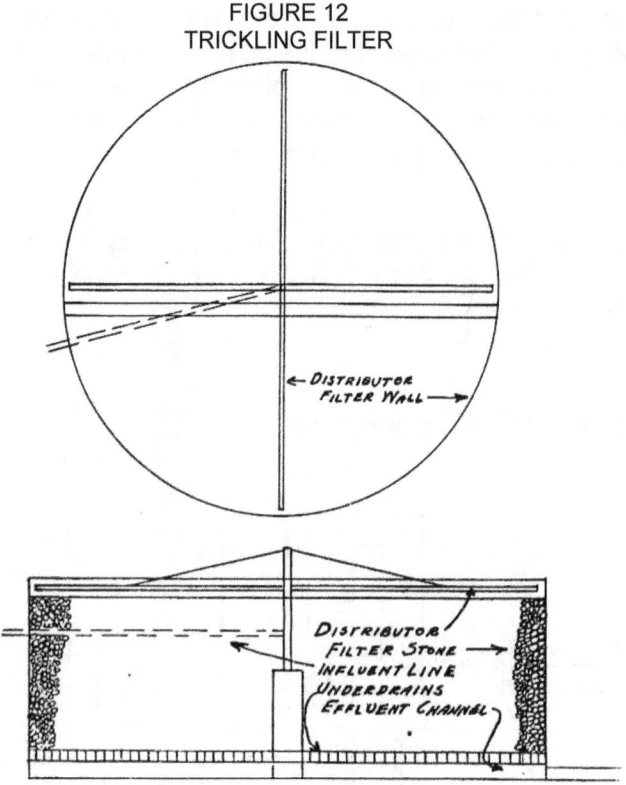

Standard Trickling Filters: These are operated at a hydraulic loading of 1.1 to 4.4 million gallons per acre per day with an organic loading of 5.0 to 25.0 pounds per 1,000 cubic feet of filter medium per day. The following example illustrates how the loadings of an operating filter are obtained:

Suppose a filter 100 feet in diameter and six feet deep is receiving 0.5 mgd of primary tank effluent with a BOD of 150 ppm.

Area of filter (acres) = $\dfrac{\pi d^2}{4 \times 43,560}$ = 0.18 acres

The hydraulic loading = $\dfrac{0.5}{.18}$ = 2.8 mgad (million gallons per acre per day)

The pounds of BOD applied = 0.5 × 8.34 × 150 = 625 pounds per day.

The volume of filter medium $\dfrac{\pi d^2}{4}$ × 6 = 47,124 cubic feet

The BOD loading = $\dfrac{625}{47,124}$ × 1,000 = 13.3 pounds of BOD per 1,000 cubic feet of filter medium per day

Sewage is applied intermittently with rest periods which generally do not exceed five minutes at the designed rate of sewage flow. With proper loadings, the standard trickling filter, including primary and secondary sedimentation units, should under normal operation remove from 80 to 85 percent of the applied BOD. While there is some unloading of solids at all times, which has accumulated on the filter medium, the major unloading occurs several times a year for comparatively short periods of time.

FIGURE 13
STANDARD RATE FILTER

High Rate Trickling Filters: These units are operated with hydraulic loadings of 8.7 to 44.0 million gallons per acre per day and organic loadings of 25.0 to 50.0 pounds per cubic feet of filter medium per day.

When trickling filters were first developed, it was believed that their successful operation required rest periods between dosing. The application of sewage was, therefore, intermittent. It later developed that the rest periods between doses were not essential and had some detrimental effects. This enabled a major increase in the hydraulic loadings and some, though not a proportional, increase in the BOD loadings. The higher hydraulic rate was attained by mixing filter effluent with the normal sewage flow in proportions of up to ten to one and recirculating it through the filter. The higher BOD load is attained by applying a larger volume per acre of the normal sewage flow to the filter. This effects a reduction in the BOD concentration of the sewage as applied to the filter, even though the total BOD load per day is higher. The various ways by which this recirculation is accomplished are patented processes and are identified by trade names, some of which are as follows:

Biofilter: In the biofilter, a process is used involving recirculation and a high rate of application to a shallow trickling filter. The recirculation in this case involves brining the effluent of the filter or of the secondary sedimentation tank back through the primary settling tank. The secondary settling tank sludge is usually very light and can be continually fed back to the primary settling tank where the two types of sludges are collected together and pumped to the digester. See Figure 14a.

FIGURE 14a
BIO-FILTER

41

"Accelo" Filter. The accelo filter, another sewage treatment process, involves the recirculation of filter effluent directly back to the filter as shown in Figure 14b.

FIGURE 14b
ACCELO-FILTER

Aero-Filter. The aero-filter (Figure 14c) is still another process which distributes the sewage by maintaining a continuous rain-like application of the sewage over the filter bed. For small beds, distribution is accomplished by a disk distributor revolving at a high speed of 260 to 369 rpm set 20" above the surface of the filter to give a continuous rain-like distribution over the entire bed. For large beds, a large number of revolving distributor arms, 10 or more, tend to give more uniform distribution. These filters are always operated at a rate in excess of 10 million gallons per acre of surface per day.

FIGURE 14c
AERO-FILTER

A typical combination for loadings of a high rate filter is as follows:

A filter 100 feet in diameter and six feet deep is receiving 1.0 mgd of normal settled sewage with a BOD of 150 ppm with recirculation at a rate of four to one or a total of 5 mg.

Area of filter (acres) = $\dfrac{\Pi d^2}{4 \times 43,560}$ = 0.18 acres

Hydraulic loading = $\dfrac{5.0}{.18}$ = 27.7 mgad (million gallons per acre per day)

Pounds of BOD applied = $1 \times 8.34 \times 150$ = 1,250 pounds per day.

Volume of filter medium = $\dfrac{\Pi d^2}{4} \times 6$ = 47,124 cubic feet

BOD loading = $\dfrac{1,250}{625} \times 1,000$ = 26.6 pounds of BOD per 1,000 cubic feet of filter medium per day

42

High rate trickling filters, including primary and secondary sedimentation, should, under normal operation, remove from 65 to 80 percent of the BOD of the sewage. Recirculation should be adequate to provide continuous dosage at a rate equal to or in excess of 10 million gallons per acre per day with rest periods not more than 15 seconds. As a result of continuous dosing at such high rates, some of the solids accumulated on the filter medium are washed off and carried away with the effluent continuously, and there are no intermittent unloading periods.

High rate trickling filters have been used advantageously for pre-treatment of industrial wastes and unusually strong sewage. When so used, they are called "*roughing filters.*" With these, the BOD loading is usually in excess of 110 pounds of BOD per 1,000 cubic feet of filter medium.

Two high rate filters in series have been used to effect a higher degree of treatment and produce a final settled effluent of less than 30 ppm of BOD.

The following table contains comparative data on a number of features of standard and high rate trickling filters.

TABLE 1

	Hydraulic Loading Mil. Gal. Per Acre Per Day	BOD Loading Pounds BOD per 1,000 Cu. Ft. Filter Medium	Operation	Unloading	Percent BOD Removal Including Primary and Secondary Sedimentation
Standard	1-4	Less than 15	Intermittent	Largely Periodic	80-85
High Rate	10-30	30-110	Continuous	Continuous	65-80

Operation: As both standard and high rate trickling filters are biological workshops, the principles of operation are the same, and the troubles encountered with their maintenance are similar.

The nozzles, whether fixed spray or on rotators, should be inspected daily and all those found clogged or damaged should be cleaned or repaired.

During winter months careful attention is required to prevent freezing, especially with standard rate filters where intermittent operation causes periods of quiescence which are more conducive to freezing than with the continuous operation and constant motion of liquid in high rate filters. There is a tendency of some operators to by-pass the filters during the winter months. This practice should not be a general procedure. A trickling filter should be continued in operation except for brief periods when ice formation is sufficient to cause damage to the distribution system.

The distribution system, whether fixed or moving, should be flushed periodically, preferably daily, to remove any material which might cause clogging. If possible, the underdrains also should be hosed out occasionally.

Where the distribution system involves mechanical equipment with moving parts, the only safe rule is to know well and follow rigidly the instructions in the service manual which the manufacturer supplies for his particular equipment. It should be used, not filed or lost.

The surface of the filter must be kept free from weed growths and accumulation of leaves or other debris. Trees or shrubs in close proximity to a filter should be removed.

A number of chemicals may be received by a sewer system, generally in industrial wastes, which in appreciable concentration are toxic or poisonous to biological life. When the normal efficiency of a filter shows a somewhat sudden drop, immediate checks should be made at industrial plants tributary to the sewer system to determine if there has been a discharge of toxic material into the sewers and to arrange for its elimination or pre-treatment by the industry.

To provide uniform distribution of sewage over the bed practically all rotary distributors require periodic adjustment of the turnbuckles on the guy rods to the arms. This is needed in order to maintain the proper level of the arms and their distance from the surface of the filter. In hot weather the rods become longer and the turnbuckles should be taken up slightly to compensate for the metal expansion due to heat. In cold weather the condition is reversed and the turnbuckles should be let out.

Ponding of filters will occur if the voids in the filter medium become clogged and the free passage of liquid is prevented. This may be due to the use of too small filter medium or disintegrated filter medium. The only way to permanently correct this difficulty is to replace the filter medium with material of proper size and quality. It, however, the voids become filled by prolific growths of organisms and slimes on the surface of the filter medium, there are corrective measures available to the operation which should be employed as soon as ponding is evident. These measures include:

1. Flushing the surface of the ponded area with a fire hose.
2. Applying heavy doses of chlorine for short periods, either directly to the ponding area or to the sewage influent. The latter can best be done at night when the chlorine demand of the sewage is lowest. Chlorine doses up to 5 ppm will kill the excessive growth in the filter.
3. Flooding the entire filter and allowing it to stand full for 24 hours.
4. Cutting the filter out of service and allowing it to stand unused for several days.
5. Temporarily increasing the rate of recirculation. This can be done only where the filters are so designed to permit this method of operation.

Ponding is always an indication that something is wrong, and indicates to the operator not only to use the corrective measures outlined above, but to check the operation of the entire treatment plant for possible cause. If primary units are not properly removing grease or oils, the biological film on the filter medium will be coated, and the organisms will be deprived of oxygen and the sewage kept from contact with the organisms. It may be that the filter installation is inadequate for the plant load. This, of course, calls for the installation of additional units which should be constructed as soon as possible.

Another troublesome condition which frequently develops at trickling filter installations is the excessive production of the filter fly—the psychoda. These flies are so small that they can pass through an ordinary window screen and are very bothersome to the plant operator and nearby neighbors.

The larvae of the flies prefer a breeding place which is damp but not too wet and are, therefore, more prevalent in standard rate filters with intermittent dosages than in high rate filters with continuous dosing. Some of these insects may be present in a normal filter unit which is functioning properly, as the filter fly is one of the natural biological organisms which feeds on the sludge and film growth and assists in the decomposition of organic matter. However, excessive numbers indicate that the biological life in the filter is unbalanced, probably due to organic overloading.

The control of filter flies has proven to be very difficult. Keeping all parts of the filter wet, especially the edges, will discourage their breeding. Numerous insecticides such as D.D.T., chordane, lindane, and others have been tried to rid an infested filter of these pests. None have been completely satisfactory except to give temporary relief. The use of any one insecticide seems to result in the development of resistant strains of the insect. It has been found that it is better to use several in rotation. This treatment is expensive and extreme caution is necessary as too heavy a dose may kill all the desirable and necessary biological life in the filter.

If duplicate filter units are available, one can be taken out of service for a day or two and either flooded or allowed to dry out to create conditions in the filter unfavorable for the fly development.

Although any one of the above may give temporary relief, the only permanent solution to the psychoda nuisance is, as in ponding control, to determine its cause and then to provide corrective action.

Since the operation of the trickling filter depends on biological life, it is evident that when one is first put into service it takes time to build up an adequate population of organisms on the filter medium. This is true not only of a new unit but also of one which has been idle long enough to have the organisms die for want of food and water. Bypassing a unit for any prolonged period should, if possible, be avoided.

Every trickling filter installation has its own particular characteristics. There appears to be no one method of operation best suited to all plants. Advantage should be taken of any provisions for flexible operation which are available, and different methods of operation such as parallel or series flow should be tried to determine the best conditions for the particular plant.

SECONDARY SEDIMENTATION TANKS

Since trickling filters merely alter the character but do not remove solids from the sewage, the effluent contains suspended solids which should be removed before disposal by discharge to receiving waters.

For this purpose, secondary sedimentation tanks or final settling tanks are used. These tanks are similar in design to those described in Chapter 5 on Primary Treatment and should provide a surface settling rate not in excess of 800 gallons per square foot per day based on design flow.

ACTIVATED SLUDGE

The development of the activated sludge process marked an important advance in the secondary treatment of sewage. Like the trickling filter, it is a biological contact process where living aerobic organisms and the organic solids in the sewage are brought together in an environment favorable for the aerobic decomposition of the solids. Since the environment is the sewage itself, efficient operation of the process is dependent on the continual maintenance of dissolved oxygen at all times throughout the sewage being treated. The environment itself, however, accomplishes little unless it is inhabited by enough living workers.

Normal sewage contains some of these biological workers but the number is far too small to do the work at hand. It is necessary, therefore, to add many more organisms and to distribute them throughout the sewage before the activated sludge process can begin to function with any efficiency.

The activated sludge process is usually employed following plain sedimentation. The sewage contains some suspended and colloidal solids and, when agitated in the presence of air, the suspended solids form nuclei on which biological life develop and gradually build up to larger solids which are known as activated sludge.

Activated sludge is a brownish floc-like substance consisting largely of organic matter obtained from the sewage, and inhabited b myriads of bacteria and other forms of biological life. Activated sludge with its living organisms has the property of absorbing or adsorbing colloidal and dissolved organic matter including ammonia from sewage so that the suspended solids are reduced. The biologic organisms utilize the absorbed material as food and convert it into insoluble non-putrescible solids. Much of this conversion is a step-by-step process. Some bacteria attack the original complex substances to produce simpler compounds as their waste products. Other bacteria use these waste products to produce still simpler compounds and the process continues until the final waste products can no longer be used as food for bacteria.

The generation of activated sludge or floc in sewage is a slow process, and the amount so formed from any volume of sewage during its period of treatment is small and inadequate for the rapid and effective treatment of the sewage which requires large concentrations of activated sludge. Such concentration is built up by collecting the sludge produced from each volume of sewage treated and re-using it in the treatment of subsequent sewage flows. The sludge so re-used is known as *return sludge*. This is a cumulative process so that eventually more sludge has been produced and is available for re-use than is needed. The surplus or *excess activated sludge*, is then permanently removed from the treatment process and conditioned for ultimate disposal.

The activated sludge must be kept in suspension during its period of contact with the sewage being treated by some method of agitation. This activated sludge process, therefore, consists of the following steps:

1. Mixing the activated sludge with the sewage to be treated.
2. Aeration and agitation of this mixed liquor for the required length of time.
3. Separation of the activated sludge from the mixed liquor.
4. Return of the proper amount of activated sludge for mixture with the sewage.
5. Disposal of the excess activated sludge.

A number of variations in carrying out the steps given above have been developed to meet different conditions. This has resulted in using the term "conventional activated sludge" for the original activated sludge process and giving specific names to the variations of the original process.

Before considering these variations, it is desirable to define two terms which are commonly used, and to consider the basic steps involved in the activated sludge process.

Sludge Volume Index is the volume in ml of one gram of activated sludge in the mixed liquor which has settled for thirty minutes. The best sludge volume index must be determined for each plant and slight variations from day to day are to be expected, but a rising sludge volume index indicates that the volume occupied by one gram of sludge is increasing, causing a loss in density and a tendency towards bulking which is discussed later.

Sludge Age is the average time in days a particle of suspended solids remains under aeration in the activated sludge sewage treatment process. It is calculated from the weight of activated sludge in the aeration tank and the suspended solids in the sewage entering the aeration tank using the formula:

$$\text{Sludge age} = \frac{V \times A}{Q \times C}$$

V = volume of aeration tank in mg
A = concentration of suspended solids in the aeration tank in ppm
Q = sewage flow in mgd
C = concentration of suspended solids in the sewage entering the aeration tank in ppm exclusive of returned sludge

The sludge age must be kept within certain limits for satisfactory operation, depending on the character of the sewage being treated and must be determined for each plant. For an average domestic sewage a sludge age of three to four days is generally satisfactory.

Mixing the Activated Sludge With the Sewage to be Treated: It is very important that the returned activated sludge be thoroughly mixed with the sewage. This is generally accomplished by adding the return sludge to the settled sewage at the inlet end of the aeration tank in which the agitation provides rapid and satisfactory mixing. In some cases small mixing chambers with agitation are provided, but this is not common practice.

Aeration and Agitation of Mixed Liquor: Aeration accomplishes three objects: mixing the returned activated sludge with the sewage, keeping the sludge in suspension by agitation of the mixture, and supplying the oxygen required for biological oxidation. Air is generally added by one of two methods known as "diffused air" or "pressure aeration" system or by mechanical aeration.

In the *diffused air system*, air under low pressure, generally not more than eight to ten pounds, is supplied by blowers and forced through various types of porous material in plates or tubes which break up the air into fine bubbles. These plates or tubes are so located in the aeration tank that a rotary motion is imparted to the sewage mixture resulting in a considerable amount of air being absorbed from the atmosphere. Diffuser plates are composed of fused crystalline alumina or a high-silica sand. They are set in containers usually made of reinforced concrete. Diffuser tubes are made of similar material or, more recently, of corrugated stainless steel pipe with multiple outlets and wrapped with saran twisted cord. These are suspended in the aeration tank in sections and can be disconnected above the sewage surface and removed for cleaning or renewal. When installed on swing joint connections so that they may be brought to the surface of the tank, they are known as "Swing Diffuser."

To prevent clogging of the diffuser plates or tubes, the air to them should be filtered to remove dust, oil, or other impurities, and the piping should be of non-corrosive material. There are a number of types of filters available based on different principles which may be used alone or in combination.

Mechanical Aerators ae of two general types—paddle and vertical draft tube. The paddle type consists of a paddle wheel or brush partly submerged in the sewage revolving on a horizontal axis. Air is absorbed by surface contact and by droplets thrown through the air by the paddle mechanism. With the vertical draft tube sewage is drawn up or down through a central vertical tube by a revolving impeller. There are a number of types of the vertical draft tube aerator made by different manufacturers, each with special patented features.

In addition to the above two methods, there are several other types of aerators on the market using different devices to introduce or entrain air and provide agitation.

Air Requirements are governed by:

1. The BOD loading
2. The quality of the activated sludge
3. The solids concentration
4. The desired efficiency in BOD removal

The basic air requirement is that there shall be sufficient air added to the sewage to maintain in it at least two ppm of dissolved oxygen under all conditions of loading in all parts of the aeration tanks except immediately beyond the inlets. Tests for dissolved oxygen should be made in different sections of the tank to assure that this value is maintained.

In the diffused air systems, the amount of air added is often stated in terms of the cubic feet of air per gallon of sewage, usually ranging from one-half to one and one-half. A preferable method of expression, now more commonly used, is in terms of cubic feet of air per pound of BOD to be removed from the primary tank effluent. Normal requirements are assumed to be 1,000 cu. ft. per pound of BOD, and the air system should be capable of delivering 150 percent of this figure.

The above figures apply generally to a normal domestic sewage in a conventional type activated sludge plant as defined later. Where industrial wastes are involved or the plant is one of the modified types (also defined later), major variation from these figures may occur and must be determined by operating experience at each plant. Insufficient air will result in a deterioration of the quality of the activated sludge and a serious breakdown of plant efficiency. The use of excessive amounts of air is not only wasteful but may result in a sludge so finely dispersed that it becomes difficult to settle.

Aeration Time: In the activated sludge process, the sludge accomplishes the major part of the removal of BOD and solids from the sewage being treated in a relatively short period of aeration. It takes, however, a much longer time for the sludge to assimilate the organic matter which it has absorbed. During this time an aerobic environment must be maintained. To effect the most complete treatment of sewage and most economical operation in the conventional activated sludge process, an aeration time of six to eight hours has been found to be adequate for diffused air aeration and nine to twelve hours for mechanical aeration. Materially shorter periods are used in some of the modifications of the conventional process. These shorter aeration periods generally result in a lowering of the quality of the plant effluents. This is described later under the various types of activated sludge plants.

Separation of Activated Sludge from the Mixed Liquor: Before the sewage treated in the aeration tank can be disposed of by discharging into receiving waters, the activated sludge must be removed. This is done in secondary or final settling tanks. These tanks are similar in design to the mechanically cleaned primary sedimentation tanks described in Chapter 5. Surface settling rates should not exceed 800 gallons per square foot per day.

The cycle of sludge removal from the secondary tanks is much more important than with primary tanks. Some sludge is being removed continuously to be used as returned sludge in the aeration tanks. The excess sludge must be removed before it loses its activity because of the death of the aerobic organism resulting from lack of oxygen at the bottom of the tank. It is possible, where facilities are available, to reactivate return sludge in separate reaeration tanks before addition to the sewage. However, it is much wiser to retain the activity of the sludge by prompt withdrawal from the tank.

Return of the Proper Amount of Activated Sludge for Mixture with the Sewage: The amount of sludge returned to the aeration tank must be sufficient to produce the desired purification in the available aeration time and yet low enough to give economical air utilization. Because of variations in the character and concentration of the sewage and the type of plant, the amount of returned sludge may range from 10 to 15 percent of the volume of sewage being treated. This will be further discussed in connection with the various types of plants. For a conventional plant, the percentage is usually between 20 and 30 percent. This will result in a concentration of solids in the mixed liquor of from 1,000 to 2,500 ppm in diffused air plants, and 500 to 1,500 ppm in mechanical aeration plants. The best concentration must be determined for each plant by trial operator and should be carefully maintained by controlling the proportion of return sludge. The maximum concentration is limited by the air supply and sewage load. If solids are allowed to build up, the air and food requirements will exceed those available and an upset will occur.

Treatment and Disposal of Excess Activated Sludge: Ultimately, excess activated sludge is treated and disposed of with the sludge from primary sedimentation tanks. There are several methods by which excess activated sludge is combined with sludge from primary devices.

Probably the most common practice is to pump excess sludge to the influent end of the primary sedimentation tank where it is settled with the solids in the raw sewage. The activated sludge settles readily and, because of the large flocculent character of the sludge particles, it tends to strain out some of the non-settleable solids in the sewage, thus reducing the organic and solids load on the aeration tank.

Where the above procedure is not followed, the excess activated sludge is transferred to the sludge digestion tanks either directly or through thickeners.

FIGURE 15a
CONVENTIONAL ACTIVATED SLUDGE

FIGURE 15b
STEP AERATION

FIGURE 15c
MODIFIED AERATION

FIGURE 15d
ACTIVATED AERATION

Conventional Activated Sludge Process: The flow diagram of a conventional activated sludge plant for domestic sewage using the diffused air system is shown in Figure 15a. All of the settled sewage is mixed with the returned activated sludge at the head of the aeration tank. With average domestic sewage, the volume of returned sludge is 20 to 30 percent of the volume of the sewage to be treated. The aeration tanks are designed to provide an aeration time of six to eight hours with diffused air aeration and nine to twelve hours for mechanical aeration. The longer times are used for the lower sewage flows. Air is applied at the rate of one to one and one-half cubic feet per gallon of sewage or 900 to 1100 cubic feet per pound of BOD to be removed. Activated sludge is returned at a rate to maintain a solids content in the mixed liquor of 1,000 to 2,500 ppm. Sludge index and sludge age, as determined for each plant, will usually fall within the range of 200 to 300 and three to four days, respectively. An overall plant efficiency, as measured by reduction in BOD and suspended solids, of 80 to 90 percent can be expected with efficiencies in the upper part of this range predominating.

The conventional activated sludge process is capable of effecting the highest degree of purification yet attained by sewage treatment methods that are in general use with the exception of that obtained by intermittent sand filtration. Although the activated sludge is similar in composition and biochemical reactions to the slime formed on trickling filter medium, it is somewhat more effective. The activated sludge floc moves through the sewage flow and, in effect, goes searching for food. Consequently, the decomposition of the organic matter in the sewage can be more complete than that which can be attained by trickling filters. Since the biological contact process takes place under water, fly breeding is eliminated and odors can be greatly reduced. The space required for activated sludge units is much less than needed for trickling filters used to treat the same volume of flow.

The activated sludge process is not as rugged, however, as the trickling filter process. It is complex and presents many technical problems requiring more operating skill and time. While the activated sludge process can be adapted to treat sewage and wastes of widely varying strengths and composition, it is sensitive to shock loads and toxic substances which may be discharged into sewers, especially from industrial plants. These industrial wastes may destroy or inhibit the activity of the microorganism essential for the decomposition of organic matter.

MODIFICATIONS OF THE CONVENTIONAL ACTIVATED SLUDGE PROCESS

Mention has already been made of modifications of the conventional activated sludge plant. These have been developed to meet local conditions or to effect economies in construction and operation. Several of these modifications are described below.

Step Aeration: In this process, Figure 15b, sewage enters the aeration tank at a number of different points but all of the return sludge is introduced at the first point of entry with, or without, a portion of the sewage. The sludge solids concentration in the mixed liquor is, therefore, greatest at the first step or point of entry and decreases as more sewage is introduced at subsequent steps. This provides a means of ready regulation of the total amount of solids held under aeration. In this process, treatment practically equivalent to the conventional activates sludge process can be attained in about half the aeration time while maintaining the sludge age within proper limits of three to four days.

By using an aeration tank of only half the capacity needed in the conventional process, construction costs and the area required for step aeration are less. Operation costs are about the same for the conventional and step processes.

Tapered Aeration: This process was developed on the theory that the greatest amount of air is needed during the early part of the aeration period. Air is, therefore, introduced into the sewage at a higher rate in the inlet section of the aeration tank than in subsequent sections to roughly approximate the oxygen utilization in the various sections or stages of aeration in the tank.

The advantages claimed for his modification of the conventional activated sludge process are a better control of the process in meeting shock loads and a reduction in the cost of operation.

Modified Aeration: This modification of the conventional activated sludge process, Figure 15c, is also known as high-rate activated sludge treatment. It is applicable where the receiving waters require a degree of treatment greater than that obtained by primary treatment but not the suspended solids and BOD removals that can be obtained by the conventional activated sludge process.

In modified aeration either raw or settled sewage mixed with about 10 percent of return sludge is aerated for a period of only one or two hours. The suspended solids of the mixed liquor are reduced to below 1,000 ppm resulting in a reduction in air requirements. By controlling the air supply, the aeration period, and the percent of return sludge, almost any degree of treatment between primary sedimentation and the conventional activated sludge process can be effected.

This process effects savings in construction and operating costs and takes less area than the conventional plant. The sludge produced is dense, more nearly resembling primary tank sludge than activated sludge, and is not subject to bulking as described later.

Activated Aeration: This process was recently developed in New York City, Figure 15d, and is a conventional or step-activated sludge treatment with a reduced aeration period. The culture which is produced in the activated sludge section and which is ordinarily wasted as excess sludge, is transferred to an activated aeration section which also receives a portion of the settled sewage flow. In the activated aeration section, that portion of settled sewage sent to it is aerated with a low solids concentration of 200 to 400 ppm. Final settling tanks are provided for both sections with effluents to the receiving waters.

By varying the proportion of the total sewage flow between the two sections of the plant and other operating factors, the activated aeration process affords great flexibility and a wide range of treatment efficiency, depending on the requirement of the receiving waters. Reductions in BOD of 80 to 85 percent can be attained along with savings in air costs as compared with the conventional process.

Contact Stabilization is another modification of the conventional activated sludge process. In this method, the biologically active sludge is brought into intimate contact with the sewage for only 15 to 30 minutes, during which time the activated sludge absorbs and adsorbs a high percentage of the suspended, colloidal, and dissolved pollutional matter from the sewage. The mixture then flows to the settling tank from which the sludge is removed to a regenerating tank where it is stabilized and regenerated by aeration. This modification is especially applicable in treating industrial wastes as the entire supply of seed sludge is not vulnerable to shock loads because the majority of the seed is kept under separate aeration. A slug of wastes would only affect that small portion of the sludge being mixed with the sewage.

Aerobic Digestion (Total Oxidation): In this process, a continuous flow of raw sewage or wastes and its macerated solids are aerated vigorously in a tank designed to detain an entire day's flow. The aerated sewage then passes to a conventional settling tank where two functions occur—clarified effluent overflows to the receiving waters and settled sludge is recirculated back to the aeration compartment at a high rate.

This relatively simple process depends upon practically complete stabilization of the putrescible fraction of the sewage by biological oxidation in a single compartment. Experience indicates that this process is sensitive to sudden changes in volume and/or character of the waste. Sludge should be wasted periodically from the system in order to maintain equilibrium and consistently produce a high quality effluent.

This process has been applied at moderately small installations thus far, and experience indicates that the resultant degree of treatment realized compares favorably with other highly efficient secondary processes.

OPERATION OF ACTIVATED SLUDGE PROCESS

Details of operating procedure will vary at different activated sludge plants, depending on a number of factors, such as the type of facilities available, strength and character of the sewage, temperatures, requirements of receiving waters, and others. Best operating procedure for each plant must be determined by experience. With this qualification, the following will generally apply for a conventional type of plant treating an average domestic sewage. For modified type plants, see the sections on these various units.

1. There must be sufficient aeration to maintain a dissolved oxygen content of at least two ppm at all times throughout the aeration tanks, except immediately beyond the inlet. This can be expected when an aeration time of six to eight hours for diffused air and nine to twelve hours with mechanical aeration is provided and when about 1,000 cubic feet of air is supplied for each pound of BOD to be removed.

2. Dissolved oxygen should be present at all times in the treated sewage in the final settling tanks.

3. Activated sludge must be returned continuously from the final settling tanks to the aeration tanks.

4. Optimum rate of returning activated sludge will vary with each installation and with different load factors. In general, it will range from 20 to 30 percent of the sewage flow for diffused air and 10 to 20 percent for mechanical aeration units.

5. The optimum suspended solids content in the aeration tanks may vary considerably but usually in the range of 1,000 to 2,500 ppm with diffused air and 600 to 1,200 ppm with mechanical aeration.

6. A sludge volume index of about 100 and a sludge age of three to four days are normal for most plants. When the optimum sludge volume index is established for a plant, it should be maintained within a reasonably narrow range. A material increase is a warning of trouble ahead as discussed below under sludge bulking.

7. The suspended solids content in the aeration tanks may be controlled by the amount of sludge returned to them. All sludge in excess of that needed in the aeration tanks must be removed from the system. It should be removed in small amounts continuously or at frequent intervals rather than in large amounts at any one time. Sludge held too long in the final settling tank will become septic, lose its activity, and deplete the necessary dissolved oxygen content in the tank. (See 2 above.)

8. Septic conditions in the primary sedimentation tanks will adversely affect the functioning of the activated sludge process. Pre-chlorination or pre-aeration as described under preliminary treatment in Chapter 4 may be used to forestall septic conditions in the sewage

entering the aeration tanks.

9. Periodic or sudden organic overloads, such as may result from large amounts of sludge digester overflow to the primary tanks or from doses of industrial wastes having an excessive BOD or containing toxic chemicals, will usually cause operating difficulties. Whenever possible, overloading should be minimized by controlling the discharge or by pretreatment of such deleterious wastes. It may even be preferable to bypass the activated sludge units at the plant than to knock out the whole activated sludge process. This procedure must be used with caution and if it must become a frequent practice or involves large volumes, the plant facilities are probably inadequate and additional units must be installed.

Sludge Bulking: The most common problem encountered in the operation of activated sludge plants is sludge bulking. A desirable activated sludge is one which settles rapidly leaving a clear, odorless, and stable supernatant. The floc is granular in appearance, with sharp defined edges, is golden brown in color, and has a musty odor. When the character of the activated sludge changes so that its settleability decreases, as measured by a significant rise in the sludge volume index, a condition known as sludge bulking develops in the final settling tank. As a portion of the sludge does not settle in the tank, it is carried away in the effluent. This results in a serious impairment in the quality of the plant effluent and places an added organic load on the receiving waters.

As always, it is better, where possible, to prevent trouble than to correct it, and knowledge of its possible source is the first step in prevention. There are a number of causes for sludge bulking, some of which are given below.

1. Excessive or storm flow resulting in shortened aeration periods

2. Short circuiting of aeration tanks

3. Industrial wastes with high organic content or containing chemicals having toxic effects on bacteria development.

4. Solids content in aeration tanks either too high or too low.

5. Insufficient aeration with failure to maintain dissolved oxygen throughout the system or possibly the use of too much air tending to break up the floc

6. Septic sewage in the primary sedimentation

7. Interruption in the continuity of returning of sludge to the aeration tank or too long intervals in removing excess sludge from the process units.

8. A preponderance of fungi forming thread-like filaments in the sludge.

All of these can be pretty well summed up by saying that sludge bulking results from overloading or the improper balance between the three variable—BOD loading, suspended solids concentration of the mixed liquor, and the amount of air used in aeration.

There are no infallible rules for either the prevention or control of sludge bulking. If the condition does develop, the ultimate solution is to determine the cause and then either correct or eliminate it or take compensatory steps in operation control. There are some remedial steps which can be taken where facilities are available, and which may help to bring the process back to normal operation. Among these are:

1. Addition of hydrated lime to the aeration tanks to raise the pH value to not exceeding 7.1. This was formerly used more than at present. It has been largely replaced by the use of chlorine as noted under 4 below.

2. Reduction of the solids content carried in aeration tanks by removal of some of the activated sludge as excess.

3. Re-aeration of returned activated sludge before entering aeration tanks.

4. Chlorination of returned activated sludge. This must be carefully controlled to avoid killing the organisms in the sludge.

5. Increase aeration in time and rate.

It is sometimes desirable or necessary to remove as much of the sludge as possible from the system and then develop fresh and properly activated sludge.

Frothing: The formation of a thick layer of froth over the surface of aeration tanks is becoming a more common and more serious problem for the operators of activates sludge plants. The cause (or causes) are not definitely known, though it is frequently attributed to the increasing use in industry and homes of synthetic detergent compounds. Whatever the cause, there are several methods of control available. One method is the use of defoamants which tend to reduce surface tension and are quite effective. These materials are expensive and cost may prevent their use when large quantities are required. Another method is the application to the foam of fine sprays of water or plant effluent. The installation and operation of a satisfactory spray system may also involve considerable expenditures. At some plants a combination of these two methods has been used by adding a defoamant to the spray. The necessity for foam control and the control method used depend on the seriousness of the problem and the relative costs of the various control methods at any specific plant.

CONTACT AERATION

The contact aeration process is covered by several patents. Like all secondary treatment processes, it depends on aerobic biological organisms to break down the complex putrescible organic material in sewage into simpler, more stable forms. The organisms are, like those in a trickling filter, stationary and attached to a fixed medium. They are, however, continually submerged and supplied with air by means similar to the diffused air system in the activated sludge process.

A typical contact aeration plant consists of five tanks in series to provide for primary settling, first stage aeration, intermediate settling, second stage aeration, and final settling. In addition, facilities for sludge treatment and disposal must be provided.

The aeration units consist of tanks which contain a number of thin plates made of a variety of materials such as corrugated aluminum sheets or corrugated asbestos sheets. These are suspended vertically and spaced about one and one-half inch center to center. The necessary biological life develops on these sheets. Sewage is carried to the bottom of the tank and passes upward between the plates mixed with air from a diffuser system at the bottom. Aerobic conditions are thus maintained for the biological life on the submerged plates. Growths with organic solids are continually breaking away from the plates. Those from first stage aeration are removed in the intermediate settling tanks and those from second stage aeration in the final settling tank.

The process is quite rugged and can, like the trickling filter, withstand shock loads. The units are adaptable to manufacture and installation as "package" units with automatic controls to reduce, but not eliminate, the time and attention given to operation. A removal of BOD and suspended solids of 90 percent or more can be attained with plants correctly designed and operated. To date, the use of this process has been restricted to plants serving small villages, realty developments or similar small groups. However, with multiple units, larger installations would appear to be practical.

INTERMITTENT SAND FILTERS

The intermittent sand filter is a specially prepared bed of sand on which effluents from primary treatment or from trickling filters or secondary settling tanks may be applied intermittently by using troughs or perforated pipe distributors. The effluent from the filter is removed by an underdrainage system.

Bed Construction: The filter bed should have a depth of clean sand of at least 24 inches overlying clean, graded gravel. The gravel should be placed in at least three layers around the underdrains and to a depth of at least six inches over the top of the underdrains. The sand itself should have an effective size of 0.3 to 0.6 millimeters and have a uniformity coefficient of not more than 3.5. The center to center spacing of underdrains should not be more than 10 feet.

Capacity: When treating a primary effluent from normal sewage, the rate of application on the filter should not exceed 125,000 gallons per acre per day, which should be reduced if the sewage is strong. With trickling filter and secondary settling tank effluent, the loading should not exceed 500,000 gallons per acre per day.

The intermittent sand filter is a true filter which strains out and retains fine suspended solids and also acts as an oxidizing unit. The major portion of the straining and oxidation is effected at or near the surface of the sand. Straining results from the fine nature of the sand medium with small voids and from a biological slime growth of organisms which develops on the surface of the sand. Oxidation is effected, as in all secondary treatment devices, by the living aerobic microorganisms which develop primarily at the surface, forming a slime layer, but also extending into the sane medium.

Operation: It is important that the filter be allowed to empty itself and obtain a fresh air supply at intervals. This is accomplished by intermittent dosing of the sewage onto the filter. Sewage is applied from two to six times a day in quantities sufficient to cover the surface of the filter to a depth of two to three inches; and as the sewage passes down through the sand, air is drawn in from the surface. Sand filters are constructed in two or more units which are used in rotation. Eventually, the slime layer on the surface causes the top layer of sand to become clogged and necessitates the removal of the top layer of sand in order to put the unit back into efficient operation.

Pooling should not be allowed to develop on the beds as this tends to produce septic action, obnoxious odors, and an effluent of poor quality. Pooling indicates that cleaning is necessary. The surface of the beds should be kept level to afford uniform distribution of the sewage and weeds, grass, etc. and should not be allowed to grow on the beds.

For winter use, the open air beds in the northern part of the state should be ridged every two feet in order to hold the ice off the main body of sand. An alternate method is that of raking up small four to six inch piles of the top surface every three feet over the surface of the bed. The bed should be cleaned and leveled as early as possible in the spring. Where natural sand percolation beds are used, it is sometimes advisable to shallow harrow the beds after careful removal of all organic deposits. Such harrowing is not advisable with underdrained beds because of possible damage to the underdraining system.

Efficiency and Use: A well operated intermittent sand filter plant will give a clear, sparkling stable effluent almost completely oxidized and nitrified. Overall plant removals of 95 percent or more of the BOD and suspended solids in the raw sewage can be expected. This exceeds other accepted secondary treatment processes.

When compared with other sewage treatment processes, large areas of land are needed, construction costs per unit of sewage treated are high, and maintenance in keeping filters clean is considerable. The use of filters of this type is restricted to situations where the volume of sewage to be treated is small, or where an exceptionally high grade of plant effluent is necessary. They have been used effectively for the additional treatment of secondary treatment effluents. Modification of the sand filters have been proposed in the past but, in general, have not proven practical for treatment of large volumes of sewage.

STABILIZATION PONDS

In recent years there has developed a system of sewage treatment which depends on the use of specially prepared ponds which are termed *stabilization ponds*. These ponds were first used in areas where warm climates and sunny days are prevalent, but have been found to operate with satisfactory results in colder climates and where there is considerable cloudiness. Stabilization ponds might be used most anywhere. The rate at which they could be operated would vary with temperature, light energy, and other local conditions.

The process involves two steps in the decomposition of organic matter in sewage. The carbonaceous matter in sewage is first broken down by the aerobic organisms with the formation of carbon dioxide. The carbon dioxide so formed is used by algae in their photosynthesis. *Photosynthesis* is a natural process carried on in green plant tissue under the influence of light and in the presence of chlorophyll which is the green coloring substance of plant life. In this process, the oxygen in the carbon dioxide is liberated and dissolved by the liquid in which the algae grow. As a result, the organic matter in sewage is converted into algae and the sewage is supplied with oxygen to support further aerobic decomposition. The sewage solids enter the pond in a highly putrescible state and leave in the form of highly stable algae cells which, within certain limitations, can be discharged to receiving waters without deleterious effect.

Oxidation ponds can be used as a complete treatment receiving raw sewage, or as a secondary treatment for settled sewage, or as a further treatment for effluents from secondary processes. They have been used most commonly as a secondary treatment for primary effluents.

Most stabilization ponds are two to four feet in depth with continuous flow through the pond. They have been designed for loadings of one acre per 400 persons, 50 pounds of BOD per acre per day or 15 pounds of BOD per acre foot per day with detention periods generally greater than 30 days. The natural soil in which they are located should be fairly impervious, so that seepage will not materially affect the surface level of the sewage in the pond.

These ponds are low cost in construction, and require a minimum of operation. The requirement that large, fairly isolated areas be provided limits their use to relatively small populations in areas where land is available.

GLOSSARY OF SEWAGE TREATMENT TERMS
CONTENTS

	Page
Activated Sludge Process....................Arrester, Flame	1
Bacteria................................Burner, Waste Gas	2
Centrifuge....................................Chlorine	3
Clarifier.....................................Digestion	4
Dilution......................................Effluent	5
Ejector, Pneumatic................................Floc	6
Flocculator....................................Grease	7
Grinder, Screenings...........................Impeller	8
Index, Sludge Volume.............................Mold	9
Most Probable Number, (MPN)....................Period	10
pH...Pump	11
Purification....................................Rate	12
Reaeration...............................Sedimentation	13
Seeding, Sludge.................................Sewer	14
Sewerage.....................................Solids	15
Squeegee...................................Treatment	16
Trap, Flame...................................Zooglea	17

GLOSSARY OF SEWAGE TREATMENT TERMS

A

Activated Sludge Process.—See **Process, Activated Sludge.**

Acre-Foot.—A unit of volume used to express the amount of material in a trickling filter. A depth of one foot on an area of one acre is an acre-foot. Regardless of shape, 43,560 cubic feet is equivalent to one acre foot.

Adsorption.—The adherence of dissolved, colloidal, or finely divided solids on the surfaces of solid bodies with which they are brought into contact.

Aeration.—The bringing about of intimate contact between air and a liquid by one of the following methods: Spraying the liquid in the air; or by agitation of the liquid to promote surface absorption of air.

    Diffused Air.—Aeration produced in a liquid by air passed through a diffuser.

    Mechanical.— (1) The mixing, by mechanical means, of sewage and activated sludge, in the aeration tank of the activated sludge process, to bring fresh surfaces of liquid into contact with the atmosphere. (2) The introduction of atmospheric oxygen into a liquid by the mechanical action of paddle or spray mechanisms.

    Modified.—A modification of the activated sludge process in which a shortened period of aeration is employed with a reduced quantity of suspended solids in the mixed liquor.

    Paddle-Wheel.—The mechanical agitation of sewage in the aeration tanks of the activated sludge process by means of paddle wheels.

    Spiral Flow.—A method of diffusing air in an aeration tank of the activated sludge process, where, by means of properly designed baffles, and the proper location of diffusers, a spiral or helical movement is given to the air and the tank liquor.

    Stage.—Division of activated sludge treatment into stages with intermediate settling tanks and return of sludge in each stage.

    Step.—A procedure for adding increments of sewage along the line of flow in the aeration tanks of an activated sludge plant.

    Tapered.—The method of supplying varying amounts of air into the different parts of an aeration tank in the activated sludge process, more at the inlet, less near the outlet, and approximately proportional to the oxygen demand of the mixed liquor under aeration.

Algae.—Primitive plants, one or many-celled, usually aquatic and capable of elaborating their foodstuffs by photosynthesis.

Algicide.—Any substance which kills algae.

Alkaline.—Water or soils containing sufficient amounts of alkaline substances to raise the pH above 7.0, or to harm the growth of crops.

Alkalinity.—A term used to represent the content of carbonates, bicarbonates, hydroxides, and occasionally borates, silicates, and phosphates in water. It is expressed in parts per million of calcium carbonate.

Alum.—A common name for aluminum sulfate.

Arrester, Flame.—A safety device on a gas line which allows gas, but not a flame, to pass through.

B

Bacteria.—Primitive plants, generally free of pigment, which reproduce by dividing in one, two, or three planes. They occur as single cells, groups, chains, or filaments, and do not require light for their life processes. They may be grown by special culturing out of their native habitat.

    Aerobic.—Bacteria which require free (elementary) oxygen for their growth.

    Anaerobic.—Bacteria which grow in the absence of free oxygen and derive oxygen from breaking down complex substances.

    Coli-Aerogenes.—See Bacteria, Coliform Group.

    Coliform Group.—A group of bacteria, predominantly inhabitants of the intestine of man but also found on vegetation, including all aerobic and facultative anaerobic grain-negative, non-spore-forming bacilli that ferment lactose with gas formation. This group includes five tribes of which the very great majority are Eschericheae. The Eschericheae tribe comprises three genera and ten species, of which *Escherichia Coli* and *Aerobacter Aerogenes* are dominant. *The Escherichia Coli* are normal inhabitants of the intestine of man and all vertebrates whereas Aerobacter Aerogenes normally are found on grain and plants, and only to a varying degree in the intestine of man and animals. Formerly referred to as *B.Coli*, B.Coli group, *ColiAerogenes Group.*

    Facultative Anaerobic.—Bacteria which can adapt themselves to growth in the presence, as well as in the absence, of uncombined oxygen.

    Parasitic.—Bacteria which thrive on other living organisms.

    Pathogenic.—Bacteria which can cause disease.

    Saprophytic.—Bacteria which thrive upon dead organic matter.

Bacterial Count.—A measure of the concentration of bacteria.

    Most Probable Number.—See Page 10.

    Plate.—Number of colonies of bacteria grown on selected solid media at a given temperature and incubation period, usually expressed as the number of bacteria per milliliter of sample.

Bed, Sludge.—An area comprising natural or artificial layers of porous material upon which digested sewage sludge is dried by drainage and evaporation. A sludge bed may be opened to the atmosphere or covered usually with a greenhouse-type superstructure. Also called Sludge Drying Bed.

Biochemical.—Resulting from biologic growth or activity, and measured by or expressed in terms of the ensuing chemical change.

Biochemical Action.—Chemical changes resulting from the metabolism of living organisms.

Biochemical Oxygen Demand (BOD).—The quantity of oxygen utilized in the biochemical oxidation of organic matter in a specified time and at a specified temperature. It is not related to the oxygen requirements in chemical combustion, being determined entirely by the availability of the material as a biological food and by the amount of oxygen utilized by the microorganisms during oxidation.

Biochemical Oxygen Demand, Standard.—Biochemical oxygen demand as determined under standard laboratory procedure for five days at 20°C, usually expressed in parts per million.

Buffer.—The action of certain solutions in opposing a change of composition, especially of hydrogen-ion concentration.

Burner, Waste Gas.—A device in a sewage treatment plant for burning the waste gas from a sludge-digestion tank.

C

Centrifuge.—A mechanical device utilizing centrifugal force to separate solids from liquids or for separating liquid emulsions.

Chamber.—A general term applied to a space enclosed by walls or to a compartment, often prefixed by a descriptive word, such as "grit chamber," "screen chamber," "discharge chamber," or "flushing chamber," indicating its function.

Chloramines.—Compounds of organic amines or inorganic ammonia with chlorine.

Chloride of Lime.—Obsolete term; see Chlorinated Lime.

Chlorinated Lime.—A combination of slaked lime and chlorine gas (also termed Bleaching Powder, Chloride of Lime, Hypochlorite of Lime, etc.). When dissolved in water, it serves as a source of chlorine.

Chlorination.—The application of chlorine.

    Break-Point.—The application of chlorine to water, sewage or industrial wastes containing free ammonia to provide free residual chlorination.

    Post.—The application of chlorine to water, sewage, or industrial wastes subsequent to any treatment. The term refers only to a point of application.

    Pre.—The application of chlorine to water, sewage, or industrial wastes prior to any treatment. This term refers only to a point of application.

Chlorine.—An element, when uncombined, exists as a greenish yellow gas about 2.5 times as heavy as air. Under atmospheric pressure and at a temperature of —30.1°F the gas becomes an amber liquid about 1.5 times as heavy as water. The chemical symbol of chlorine is Cl, UP atomic weight is 35.457, and its molecular weight is 70.914.

    Available.—A term used in rating chlorinated lime and hypochlorites as to their total oxidizing power.

    Combined Available Residual.—That portion of the total residual chlorine remaining in water, sewage, or industrial wastes at the end of a specified contact period, which will react chemically and biologically as chloramines, or organic chloramines.

    Demand.—The difference between the amount of chlorine added to water, sewage, or industrial wastes and the amount of residual chlorine remaining at the end of a specified contact period. The demand for any given water varies with the amount of chlorine applied, time of contact, and temperas pure.

    Dose.—The amount of chlorine applied to a liquid, usually expressed in parts per million, or pounds per million gallons.

    Free Available Residual.—That portion of the total residual chlorine remaining in water. sewage, or industrial wastes at the end of a specified contact period. which will react chemically and biologically as hypochlorous acid, hypochlorite ion, or molecular chlorine.

    Liquid.—An article of commerce. Chlorine gas is generally manufactured by the electrolysis of a solution of common salt. The gas is dried and purified and is then liquefied by a combination of compression and refrigeration. Liquid chlorine is shipped under pressure in steel containers.

    Residual.--The total amount of chlorine (combined and free available chlorine) remaining in water, sewage, or industrial wastes at the end of a specified contact period following chlorination.

    Test, Iodometric.—The determination of residual chlorine in water, sewage, or industrial wastes by adding potassium iodide and titrating the liberated iodine with a standard solution of sodium thiosulfate, using starch solution as a colorimetric indicator.

Test, Ortho-Tolidine.—The determination of residual chlorine in water, sewage, or industrial wastes, using ortho-tolidine reagent and colorimetric standards.
Clarifier.—See Tank, Sedimentation.
Coagulation.—(1) The agglomeration of colloidal or finely divided suspended matter by the addition to the liquid of an appropriate chemical coagulant, by biological processes, or by other means. (2) The process of adding a coagulant and the necessary reacting chemicals.
Coils, Digester.—A system of pipes for hot water or steam installed in a sludge-digestion tank for the purpose of heating the sludge.
Coli-Aerogenes, or Coliform Group.—See Bacteria, Coliform Group.
Collector, Grit.—A device placed in a grit chamber to convey deposited grit to one end of the chamber for removal.
    Scum.—A mechanical device for skimming and removing scum from the surface of settling tanks.
    Sludge.—A mechanical device for scraping the sludge on the bottom of a settling tank to a sump, from which it can be drawn by hydrostatic or mechanical action.
Colloids.—Finely divided solids which will not settle but may be removed by coagulation or biochemical action.
Comminution.—The process of screening sewage and cutting the screenings into particles sufficiently fine to pass through the screen openings.
Concentration, Hydrogen-Ion.—See pH.
Copperas.—A common name for ferrous sulfate.
Copperas, Chlorinated.—A solution of ferrous sulfate and ferric chloride produced by chlorinating a solution of ferrous sulfate.
Cross Connection.—In plumbing, a physical connection through which a supply of potable water could be contaminated, polluted, or infected. A physical connection between water supplies from different systems.
Cubic Foot per Second.—A unit of discharge for measurement of flowing liquid, equal to a flow of one cubic foot per second past a given section. Also called Second-Foot.

D

Decomposition of Sewage.—The breakdown of the organic matter in sewage through aerobic and anaerobic processes.
Denitrification.—The reduction of nitrates in solution by biochemical action.
Deoxygenation.—The depletion of the dissolved oxygen in a liquid. Under natural conditions associated with the biochemical oxidation of organic matter present.
Detritus.—The sand, grit, and other coarse material removed by differential sedimentation in a relatively short period of detention.
Diffuser.—A porous plate or tube through which air is forced and divided into minute bubbles for diffusion in liquids. Commonly made of carborundum, alundum, or silica sand.
Digester.—A tank in which the solids resulting from the sedimentation of sewage are stored for the purpose of permitting anaerobic decomposition to the point of rendering the product nonputrescible and inoffensive. Erroneously termed digestor.
Digestion.—The processes occurring in a digester.
    Mesophilic.—Digestion by biological action at or below 113°F.
    Separate Sludge.—The digestion of sludge in separate tanks in which it is placed after it has been allowed to settle in other tanks.

Single-Stage Sludge.—Sludge digestion limited to a single tank for the entire digestion period.

Stage.—The digestion of sludge progressively in several tanks arranged in series.

Thermophilic.—Digestion carried on at a temperature generally between 113°F and 145°F.

Dilution. — (1) A method of disposing of sewage, industrial waste, or sewage treatment plant effluent by discharging it into a stream or body of water. (2) The ratio of volume of flow of a stream to the total volume of sewage or sewage treatment, ant effluent discharged into it.

Disinfection.—The killing of the larger portion (but not necessarily all) of the harmful and objectional microorganisms in, or on, a medium by means of chemicals, heat, ultraviolet light, etc.

Distributor.—A device used to apply liquid to the surface of a filter or contact bed, of two general types, fixed o movable. The fixed type may consist of perforated pipes or notched troughs, sloping boards, or sprinkler nozzles. The movable type may consist of rotating disks or rotating, reciprocating, or traveling perforated pipes or troughs applying a spray, or a thin sheet of liquid.

Dosing Tank.—A tank into which raw or partly treated sewage is introduced and held until the desired quantity has been accumulated, after which it is discharged at such a rate as may be necessary for the subsequent treatment.

Dryer.—A device utilizing heat to remove water.

Flash.—A device for vaporizing water from partly dewatered and finely divided sludge through contact with a current of hot gas or superheated vapor. Included is a squirrel cage mill for separating the sludge cake into fine particles.

Rotary.—A long steel cylinder, slowly revolving, with its long axis slightly inclined, through which passes the material to be dried in hot air. The material passes through from inlet to outlet, tumbling about.

E

E. Coli.—(Escherichia Coli).—A species of genus Escherichia bacteria, normal inhabitant of the intestine of man and all vertebrates. This species is classified among the Coliform Group. See Bacteria, Coliform Group.

Efficiency.—The ratio of the actual performance of a device to the theoretically perfect performance usually expressed as a percentage.

Average.—The efficiency of a machine or mechanical device over the range of load through which the machine operates.

Filter.—The operating results from a filter as measured by various criteria such as percentage reduction in suspended matter, total solids, biochemical oxygen demand, bacteria, color, etc.

Pump.—The ratio of energy converted into useful work to the energy applied to the pump shaft, or the energy difference in the water at the discharge and suction nozzles divided by the energy input at the pump shaft.

Wire-to-Water.—The ratio of the mechanical output of a pump, to the electrical input at the meter.

Effluent.—(1) A liquid which flows out of a containing space. (2) Sewage, water, or other liquid, partially or completely treated, or in its natural state, as the case may be, flowing out of a reservoir, basin, or treatment plant, or part thereof.

Final.—The effluent from the final unit of a sewage treatment plant.

Stable.—A treated sewage which contains enough oxygen to satisfy its oxygen demand.

Ejector, Pneumatic.—A device for raising sewage, sludge, or other liquid by alternately admitting such through an inward swinging check valve into the bottom of an airtight pot and then discharging it through an outward swinging check valve by admitting compressed air to the pot above the liquid.

Elutriation.—A process of sludge conditioning in which certain constituents are removed by successive decantations with fresh water or plant effluent, thereby reducing the demand for conditioning chemicals.

F

Factor.—Frequently a ratio used to express operating conditions.
    Load.—The ratio of the average load carried by any operation to the maximum load carried, during a given period of time, expressed as a percentage. The load may consist of almost anything, such as electrical power, number of persons served, amount of water carried by a conduit, etc.
    Power.—An electrical term describing the ratio of the true power passing through an electric circuit to the product of the volts times the amperes in the circuit. It is a measure of the lag or lead of the current in respect to the voltage. While the power of a current is the product of the voltage times the amperes in the circuit, in alternating current the voltage and amperes are not always in phase, hence the true power may be less than that determined by the product of volts times amperes.

Filter.—A term meaning (1) an oxidizing bed (2) a device for removing solids from a liquid by some type of strainer.
    Biological.—A bed of sand, gravel, broken stone, or other media through which sewage flows or trickles, which depends on biological action for its effectiveness.
    High-Rate.—A trickling filter operated at a high average daily dosing rate usually between 10-30 mgd per acre, sometimes including recirculation of effluent.
    Low-Rate.—A trickling filter designed to receive a small load of BOD per unit volume of filtering material and to have a low dosage rate per unit of surface area (usually 1 to 4 mgd per acre). Also called Standard Rate Filter.
    Roughing.—A sewage filter of relatively coarse material operated at a high rate as a preliminary treatment.
    Sand.—A filter in which sand is used as a filtering medium.
    Sand Sludge.—A bed of sand used to dewater sludge by drainage and evaporation.
    Sludge.—The solid matter in sewage that is removed by settling in primary and secondary settling tanks.
    Trickling.—A treatment unit consisting of a material such as broken stone, clinkers, slate, slats, or brush, over which sewage is distributed and applied in drops, films, or spray, from troughs, drippers, moving distributors, or fixed nozzles, and through which it trickles to the underdrains, giving opportunity for the formation of zoological slimes which clarify and oxidize the sewage.
    Vacuum.—A filter consisting of a cylindrical drum mounted on a horizontal axis, covered with filtering material made of wool, felt, cotton, saran, nylon, dacron, polyethylene or similar substance, by stainless steel coil springs or metal screen, revolving with a partial submergence in the liquid. A vacuum is maintained under the cloth for the larger part of a revolution to extract moisture. The cake is scraped off continuously.

Filtrate.—The effluent of a Filter.

Floc.—Small gelatinous masses, formed in a liquid by the addition of coagulants thereto or through biochemical processes or by agglomeration.

Flocculator.—An apparatus for the formation of floc in water or sewage.

Flotation.—A method of raising suspended matter to the surface of the liquid in a tank as scum—by aeration, by the evolution of gas, chemicals, electrolysis, heat, or bacterial decomposition—and the subsequent removal of the scum by skimming.

Freeboard.—The vertical distance between the normal maximum level of the surface of the liquid in a conduit, reservoir, tank, canal, etc., and the top of the sides of an open conduit, the top of a dam or levee, etc., which is provided so that waves and other movements of the liquid will not overtop the confining structure.

Fungi.—Small nonchlorophyll-bearing plants which lack roots, stems, or leaves and which occur (among other places) in water, sewage, or sewage effluents, growing best in the absence of light. Their decomposition after death may cause disagreeable tastes and odors in water; in some sewage treatment processes they are helpful and in others they are detrimental.

G

Gage.—A device for measuring any physical magnitude.

    Float.—A device for measuring the elevation of the surface of a liquid, the actuation element being a buoyant float which rests upon the surface of the liquid.

    Indicator.—A gage that shows by means of an index, pointer, dial, etc., the instantaneous value of such characteristics as depth, pressure, velocity, stage, discharge, or the movements or positions of water-controlling devices.

    Mercury.—A gage wherein pressure of a fluid is measured by the height of a column of mercury which the fluid pressure will sustain. The mercury is usually contained in a tube, attached to the vessel or pipe containing the fluid.

    Pressure.—A device for registering the pressure of solids, liquids, or gases. It may be graduated to the register pressure in any units desired.

Garbage, Ground.—Garbage shredded or ground by apparatus installed in sinks and discharged to the sewerage system; or garbage collected and hauled to a central grinding station, shredded preliminary to disposal, usually, by digestion with sewage sludge.

Gas.—One of the three states of matter.

    Sewage.—(1) The gas produced by the septicization of sewage. (2) The gas produced during the digestion of sewage sludge, usually collected and utilized.

    Sewer.—Gas evolved in sewers from the decomposition of the organic matter in the sewage. Also any gas present in the sewerage system, even though it is from gas mains, gasoline, cleaning fluid, etc.

Gasification.—The transformation of sewage solids into gas in the decomposition of sewage.

Go Devil.—A scraper with self-adjusting spring blades, inserted in a pipe line, and carried forward by the fluid pressure for clearing away accumulations, tuberculations, etc.

Grade.—(1) The inclination or slope of a stream channel, conduit, or natural ground surface, usually expressed in terms of the ratio or percentage of number of units of vertical rise or fall per unit of horizontal distance. (2) The elevation of the invert of the bottom of a pipe line, canal, culvert, sewer, etc. (3) The finished surface of a canal bed, road bed, top of an embankment. or bottom of an excavation. (4) In plumbing, the fall in inches per foot of length of pipe.

Grease.—In sewage, grease including fats, waxes, free fatty acids, calcium and magnesium soaps, mineral oils, and other non-fatty materials. The type of solvent used for its extraction should be stated.

Grinder, Screenings.—A device for grinding, shredding, or comminuting material removed from sewage by screens.

Grit.—The heavy mineral matter in water or sewage, such as gravel, cinders, etc.

H

Head.—Energy per unit weight of liquid at a specified point. It is expressed in feet.
    Dynamic.—The head against which a pump works.
    Friction.—The head lost by water flowing in a stream or conduit as the result of the disturbances set up by the contact between the moving water and its containing conduit, and by intermolecular friction. In laminar flow the head lost is approximately proportional to the first power of the velocity; in turbulent flow to a higher power, approximately the square of the velocity. While strictly speaking, head losses due to bends, expansions, obstructions, impact, etc., are not included in this term, the usual practice is to include all such head losses under this term.
    Loss of.—The decrease in head between two points.
    Static.—The vertical distance between the free level of the source of supply, and the point of free discharge, or the level of the free surface.
    Total Dynamic.—The difference between the elevation corresponding to the pressure at the discharge flange of a pump and the elevation corresponding to the vacuum or pressure at the suction flange of the pump, corrected to the same datum plane, plus the velocity head at the discharge flange of the pump, minus the velocity head at the suction flange of the pump. It includes the friction head.
    Velocity.—The theoretical vertical height through which a liquid body may be raised due to its kinetic energy. It is equal to the square of the velocity divided by twice the acceleration due to gravity.

Humus.—The dark or black carboniferous residue in the soil resulting from the decomposition of vegetable tissues of plants originally growing therein. Residues similar in appearance and behavior are found in well-digested sludges and in activated sludge.

Hypochlorite.—Compounds of chlorine in which the radical (OC1) is present. They are usually inorganic.
    High Test.—A solid triple salt containing Ca (OC1) 2 to the extent that the fresh solid has approximately 70 percent available chlorine. It is not the same as chlorinated lime.
    Sodium.—A solution containing NaOC1, prepared by passing chlorine into solutions of soda ash, or reacting soda ash solutions with high-test hypochlorites and decanting from the precipitated sludge.

I

Imhoff Cone.—A conically shaped graduated glass vessel used to measure approximately the volume of settleable solids in various liquids of sewage origin.

Imhoff Tank.—See Tank, Imhoff

Impeller.—The rotating part of a centrifugal pump, containing the curved vanes.
    Closed.—An impeller having the side walls extended from the outer circumference of the suction opening to the vane tips.
    Nonclogging.—An impeller of the open, closed, or semi-closed type designed with large passages for passing large solids.

Open.—An impeller without attached side walls.
Screw.—The helical impeller of a screw pump.
Index, Sludge Volume.—The volume is milliliters occupied by one gram of dry solids after the aerated mixed liquor settles 30 minutes, commonly referred to as the Mohlman index.
Influent.—Sewage, water, or other liquid, raw or partly treated, flowing into a reservoir, basin, or treatment plant, or part thereof.

L

Lagoon, Sludge.—A relatively shallow basin, or natural depression, used for the storage or digestion of sludge, and sometimes for its ultimate detention or dewatering.
Lift, Air.—A device for raising liquid by injecting air in and near the bottom of a riser pipe submerged in the liquid to be raised.
Liquefaction.—The changing of the organic matter in sewage from an insoluble to a soluble state, and effecting a reduction in its solid contents.
Liquor.—Any liquid.
Mixed.—A mixture of activated sludge and sewage in the aeration tank undergoing activated sludge treatment.
Supernatant. — (1) The liquor overlying deposited solids. (2) The liquid in a sludge-digestion tank which lies between the sludge at the bottom and the floating scum at the top.
Loading.—The time rate at which material is applied to a treatment device involving length, area, or volume or other design factor.
BOD, Filter.—The pounds of oxygen demand in the applied liquid per unit of filter bed area, or volume of stone per day.
Weir.—Gallons overflow per day per foot of weir length.

M

Main, Force.—A pipe line on the discharge side of a water or sewage pumping station, usually under pressure.
Manometer.—An instrument for measuring pressure; usually it consists of a U-shaped tube containing a liquid, the surface of which in one end of the tube moves proportionally with changes in pressure upon the liquid in the other end. The term is also applied to a tube type of differential pressure gage.
Matter.—Solids, liquids, and gases.
Inorganic.—Chemical substances of mineral origin. They are not usually volatile with heat.
Organic.—Chemical substances of animal, vegetable and industrial origin. They include most carbon compounds, combustible and volatile with heat.
Suspended.—(1) Solids in suspension in sewage or effluent. (2) Commonly used for solids in suspension in sewage or effluent which can readily be removed by filtering in a laboratory.
Microorganism.—Minute organisms either plant or animal, invisible or barely visible to the naked eye.
Moisture, Percentage.—The water content of sludge expressed as the ratio of the loss in weight after drying at 103°C, to the original weight of the sample, multiplied by one hundred.
Mold.—See Fungi.

Most Probable Number, (MPN).—In the testing of bacterial density by the dilution method, that number of organisms per unit volume which, in accordance with statistical theory, would be more likely than any other possible number to yield the observed test result or which would yield the observed test result with the greatest frequency. Expressed as density of organisms per 100 ml.

N

Nitrification.—The oxidation of ammonia nitrogen into nitrates through biochemical action.

O

Overflow Rate.—One of the criteria for the design of settling tanks in treatment plants; expressed in gallons per day per square foot of surface area in the settling tank. See Surface Settling Rate.
Oxidation.—The addition of oxygen, removal of hydrogen, or the increase in the valence of an element.
    Biochemical.—See Oxidation, Sewage.
    Biological.—See Oxidation, Sewage.
    Direct.—Oxidation of substances in sewage without the benefit of living organisms, by the direct application of air or oxidizing agents such as chlorine.
    Sewage.—The process whereby, through the agency of living organisms in the presence of oxygen, the organic matter contained in sewage is converted into a more stable form.
Oxygen.—A chemical element.
    Available.—The quantity of uncombined or free oxygen dissolved in the water of a stream.
    Balance.—The relation between the biochemical oxygen demand of a sewage or treatment plant effluent and the oxygen available in the diluting water.
    Consumed.—The quantity of oxygen taken from potassium permanganate in solution by a liquid containing organic matter. Commonly regarded as an index of the carbonaceous matter present. Time and temperature must be specified. The chemical oxygen demand (COD) uses potassium dichromate.
    Deficiency.—The additional quantity of oxygen required to satisfy the biochemical oxygen demand in a given liquid. Usually expressed in parts per million.
    Dissolved.—Usually designated as DO. The oxygen dissolved in sewage, water or other liquid usually expressed in parts per million or percent of saturation.
    Residual.—The dissolved oxygen content of a stream after deoxygenation has begun.
    Sag.—A curve that represents the profile of dissolved oxygen content along the course of a stream, resulting from deoxygenation associated with biochemical oxidation of organic matter, and reoxygenation through the absorption of atmospheric oxygen and through biological photosynthesis.

P

Parts Per Million.—Milligrams per liter expressing the concentration of a specified component in a dilute sewage. A ratio of pounds per million pounds, grams per million grams, etc.
Percolation.—The flow or trickling of a liquid downward through a contact or filtering medium. The liquid may or may not fill the pores of the medium.
Period.—A time interval.

Aeration.—(1) The theoretical time, usually expressed in hours that the mixed liquor is subjected to aeration in an aeration tank undergoing activated sludge treatment; is equal to (a) the volume of the tank divided by (b) the volumetric rate of flow of the sewage and return sludge. (2) The theoretical time that water is subjected to aeration.

Detention.—The theoretical time required to displace the contents of a tank or unit at a given rate of discharge (volume divided by rate of discharge).

Flowing-Through.—The average time required for a small unit volume of liquid to pass through a basin from inlet to outlet. In a tank where there is no short-circuiting, and no spaces, the detention period and the flowing-through period are the same.

pH.—The logarithm of the reciprocal of the hydrogen-ion concentration. It is not the same as the alkalinity and cannot be calculated therefrom.

Plankton.—Drifting organisms, usually microscopic.

Pollution.—The addition of sewage, industrial wastes, or other harmful or objectionable material to water.

Ponding, Filter.—See Pooling, Filter.

Pooling, Filter.—The formation of pools of sewage on the surface of filters caused by clogging.

Population Equivalent.—(1) The calculated population which would normally contribute the same amount of biochemical oxygen demand (BOD) per day. A common base is 0.167 lb. of 5-day BOD per capita per day. (2) For an industrial waste, the estimated number of people contributing sewage equal in strength to a unit volume of the waste or to some other unit involved in producing or manufacturing a particular commodity.

Pre-Aeration.—A preparatory treatment of sewage comprising aeration to remove gases, add oxygen, or promote flotation of grease, and aid coagulation.

Precipitation, Chemical.—Precipitation induced by addition of chemicals.

Pressure.—Pounds per square inch or square foot.

    Atmospheric.—The pressure exerted by the atmosphere at any point. Such pressure decreases the elevation of the point above sea level increases. One atmosphere is equal to 14.7 lb. per sq. in., 29.92 in. or 760 mm of mercury column or 33.90 ft. of water column at average sea level under standard conditions.

    Hydrostatic.—The pressure, expressed as a total force per unit of area, exerted by a body of water at rest.

    Negative.—A pressure less than the local atmospheric pressure at a given point.

Process.—A sequence of operations.

    Activated Sludge.—A biological sewage treatment process in which a mixture of sewage and activated sludge is agitated and aerated. The activated sludge is subsequently separated from the treated sewage (mixed liquor) by sedimentation, and wasted or returned to the process as needed. The treated sewage overflows the weir of the settling tank in which separation from the sludge takes place.

    Biological.—The process by which the life activities of bacteria, and other microorganisms in the search for food, break down complex organic materials into simple, more stable substances. Self-purification of sewage-polluted streams, sludge digestion, and all so-called secondary sewage treatments result from this process. Also called Biochemical Process.

Pump.—A device used to increase the head on a liquid.

    Booster.—A pump installed on a pipe line to raise the pressure of the water on the discharge side of the pump.

Centrifugal, Fluid.—A pump consisting of an impeller fixed on a rotating shaft and enclosed in a casing, having an inlet and a discharge connection. The rotating impeller creates pressure in the liquid by the velocity derived from centrifugal force.

Centrifugal, Screw.—A centrifugal pump having a screw-type impeller; may be axial-flow, or combined axial and radial-flow, type.

Centrifugal, Closed.—A centrifugal pump where the impeller is built with the vanes enclosed within circular disks.

Diaphragm.—A pump in which a flexible diaphragm, generally of rubber, is the operating part; it is fastened at the outer rim; when the diaphragm is moved in one direction, suction is exerted and when it is moved in the opposite direction, the liquid is forced through a discharge valve.

Double-Suction.—A centrifugal pump with suction pipes connected to the casing from both sides.

Duplex.—A reciprocating pump consisting of two cylinders placed side by side and connected to the same suction and discharge pipe, the pistons moving so that one exerts suction while the other exerts pressure, with the result that the discharge from the pump is continuous.

Horizontal Screw.—A pump with a horizontal cylindrical casing, in which operates a runner with radial blades, like those of a ship's propeller. The pump has a high efficiency at low heads and high discharges, and is used extensively in drainage work.

Mixed Flow.—A centrifugal pump in which the head is developed partly by centrifugal force and partly by the lift of the vanes on the liquid.

Open Centrifugal.—A centrifugal pump where the impeller is built with a set of independent vanes.

Propeller.—A centrifugal pump which develops most of its head by the propelling or lifting action of the vanes on the liquids.

Purification.—The removal, by natural or artificial methods, or objectionable matter from water.

Putrefaction.—Biological decomposition of organic matter with the production of ill-smelling products associated with anaerobic conditions.

Putrescibility. — (1) The relative tendency of organic matter to undergo decomposition in the absence of oxygen. (2) The susceptibility of waste waters, sewage, effluent, or sludge to putrefaction. (3) Term used in water or sewage analysis to define stability of a polluted water or raw or partially treated sewage.

Q

Quicklime.—A calcined material, the major part of which is calcium oxide or calcium oxide in natural association with a lesser amount of magnesium oxide, capable of slaking with water.

R

Rack.—An arrangement of parallel bars.

Bar.—A screen composed of parallel bars, either vertical or inclined, placed in a waterway to catch floating debris, and from which the screenings may be raked. Also called rack.

Coarse.—A rack with 3/4 inch to 6 inch spaces between bars.

Fine.—Generally used for a screen or rack which has openings of 3/32 to 3/16 inches. Some screens have less than 3/32 inch openings.

Radius, Hydraulic.—The cross-sectional area of a stream of water divided by the length of that part of its periphery in contact with its containing conduit; the ratio of area to wetted perimeter.

Rate.—The result of dividing one concrete number by another.

Filtration.—The rate of application of water or sewage to a filter, usually expressed in million gallons per acre per day, or gallons per minute per square foot.

Infiltration.—The rate, usually expressed in cubic feet per second, or million gallons per day per mile of waterway, at which ground water enters an infiltration ditch or gallery, drain, sewer, or other underground conduit.

Surface Settling.—Gallons per day per square foot of free horizontal water surface. Used in design of sedimentation tanks.

Reaeration.—The absorption of oxygen by a liquid, the dissolved oxygen content of which has been depleted.

Reaeration, Sludge.—The continuous aeration of sludge after its initial aeration in the activated sludge process.

Recirculation. — (1) The refiltration of all or a portion of the effluent in a high-rate trickling filter for the purpose of maintaining a uniform high rate through the filter. (2) The return of effluent to the incoming flow to reduce its strength.

Reduction.—The decrease in a specific variable.

Over-All.—The percentage reduction in the final effluent as compared to the raw sewage.

Percentage.—The ratio of material removed from water or sewage by treatment, to the material originally present (expressed as a percentage).

Sludge.—The reduction in the quantity and change in character of sewage sludge as the result of digestion.

Regulator.—A device or apparatus for controlling the quantity of sewage admitted to an intercepting sewer or a unit of a sewage treatment plant.

Reoxygenation.—The replenishment of oxygen in a stream from (1) dilution water entering stream, (2) biological reoxygenation through the activities of certain oxygen-producing plants, and (3) atmospheric reaction.

Residual, Chlorine.—See Chlorine, residual.

Rotor.—The member of an electric generator or water wheel which rotates.

S

Screen.—A device with openings, generally of uniform size, used to retain or remove suspended or floating solids in flowing water or sewage, and to prevent them from entering an intake or passing a given point in a conduit. The screening element may consist of parallel bars, rods, wires, grating, wire mesh, or perforated plate, and the openings may be of any shape, although they are generally circular or rectangular. The device may also be used to segregate granular material, such as sand, crushed rock, and soil, into various sizes.

Scum.—A mass of sewage matter which floats on the surface of sewage.

Second-Foot.—An abbreviated expression for cubic foot per second.

Sedimentation.—The process of subsidence and deposition of suspended matter carried by water, sewage, or other liquids, by gravity. It is usually accomplished by reducing the velocity of the liquid below the point where it can transport the suspended material. Also called Settling. See Precipitation, Chemical.

Final.—Settling of partly settled, flocculated or oxidized sewage in a final tank.

Plain.—The sedimentation of suspended matter in a liquid unaided by chemicals or other special means, and without provision for the decomposition of deposited solids in contact with the sewage.

Seeding, Sludge.—The inoculation of undigested sewage solids with sludge that has undergone decomposition, for the purpose of introducing favorable organisms, thereby accelerating the initial stages of digestion.

Self-Purification.—The natural processes of purification in a moving or still body of water whereby the bacterial content is reduced, the BOD is largely satisfied, the organic content is stabilized, and the dissolved oxygen returned to normal.

Sewage.—Largely the water supply of a community after it has been fouled by various uses. From the standpoint of source it may be a combination of the liquid or water-carried wastes from residences, business buildings, and institutions, together with those from industrial establishments, and with such ground water, surface water, and storm water as may be present.

    Domestic.—Sewage derived principally from dwellings, business buildings, institutions, and the like. (It may or may not contain ground water, surface water, or storm water.)

    Fresh.—Sewage of recent origin containing dissolved oxygen at the point of examination.

    Industrial.—Sewage in which industrial wastes predominate.

    Stable.—Sewage in which the organic matter has been stabilized.

    Raw.—Sewage prior to receiving any treatment.

    Sanitary.—(1) Domestic sewage with storm and surface water excluded. (2) Sewage discharging from the sanitary conveniences of dwellings (including apartment houses and hotels), office buildings, factories, or institutions. (3) The water supply of a community after it has been used and discharged into a sewer.

    Septic.—Sewage undergoing putrefaction under anaerobic conditions.

    Settled.—Sewage from which most of the settleable solids have been removed by sedimentation.

    Stale.—A sewage containing little or no oxygen, but as yet free from putrefaction.

Sewer.—A pipe or conduit. generally closed, but normally not flowing full, for carrying sewage and other waste liquids.

    Branch.—A sewer which receives sewage from a relatively small area, and discharges into a main sewer.

    Combined.—A sewer receiving both surface runoff and sewage.

    House.—A pipe conveying sewage from a single building to a common sewer or point of immediate disposal.

    Intercepting.—A sewer which receives dry-weather flow from a number of transverse sewers or outlets and frequently additional predetermined quantities of storm water (if from a combined system), and conducts such waters to a point for treatment or disposal.

    Lateral.—A sewer which discharges into a branch or other sewer and has no other common sewer tributary to it.

    Main. — (1) A sewer to which one or more branch sewers are tributary. Also called Trunk Sewer. (2) In plumbing, the public sewer in a street, alley, or other premises under the jurisdiction of a municipality.

    Sanitary.—A sewer which carries sewage and to which storm, surface, and ground waters are not intentionally admitted.

    Separate.—See Sewer, Sanitary.

    Storm.—A sewer which carries storm water and surface water, street wash and other wash waters, or drainage, but excludes sewage and industrial wastes. Also called Storm Drain.

    Trunk—A sewer which receives many tributary branches and serves a large territory. See Sewer, Main.

    Outfall.—A sewer which receives the sewage from a collecting system and carries it to a point of final discharge.

Outlet.—The point of final discharge of sewage or treatment plant effluent.

Sewerage.—A comprehensive term which includes facilities for collecting, pumping, treating, and disposing of sewage; the sewerage system and the sewage treatment works.

Shredder.—A device for size reduction.

    Screenings.—A device which disintegrates screenings.

    Sludge.—An apparatus to break down lumps in air-dried digested sludge.

Siphon.—A closed conduit, a portion of which lies above the hydraulic grade line. This results in a pressure less than atmospheric in that portion, and hence requires that a vacuum be created to start flow.

Skimmer, Grease.—A device for removing floating grease or scum from the surface of sewage in a tank.

Skimming.—The process of removing floating grease or scum from the surface of sewage in a tank.

Sleek.—The thin oily film usually present which gives characteristic appearance to the surface of water into which sewage or oily waste has discharged. Also termed slick.

Sloughing.—The phenomenon associated with trickling filters and contact aerators. whereby slime and solids accumulated in the media are discharged with the effluent.

Sludge.—The accumulated settled solids deposited from sewage or industrial wastes, raw or treated. in tanks or basins, and containing more or less water to form a semiliquid mass.

    Activated.—Sludge floc produced in raw or settled sewage by the growth of zoogleal bacteria and other organisms in the presence of dissolved oxygen, and accumulated in sufficient concentration by returning floc previously formed.

    Bulking.—A phenomenon that occurs in activated sludge plants whereby the sludge occupies excessive volumes and will not concentrate readily.

    Conditioning.—Treatment of liquid sludge preliminary to dewatering and drainability, usually by the addition of chemicals.

    Dewatering.—The process of removing a part of the water in sludge by any method, such as draining, evaporation, pressing, centrifuging, exhausting, passing between rollers, or acid flotation, with or without heat. It involves reducing from a liquid to a spadable condition rather than merely changing the density of the liquid (concentration) on the one hand or drying (as in a kiln) on the other.

    Digestion.—The process by which organic or volatile matter in sludge is gasified, liquefied, mineralized. or converted into more stable organic matter, through the activities of living organisms.

    Humus.—See **Humus**.

Solids.—Material in the solid state.

    Dissolved.—Solids which are present in solution.

    Nonsettleable.—Finely divided suspended solids which will not subside in quiescent water, sewage, or other liquid in a reasonable period. Such period is commonly, though arbitrarily, taken as two hours.

    Settleable.—Suspended solids which will subside in quiescent water, sewage, or other liquid in a reasonable period. Such period is commonly, though arbitrarily, taken as one hour. Also called Settling Solids.

    Suspended.—The quantity of material deposited when a quantity of water, sewage, or other liquid is filtered through an asbestos mat in a Gooch crucible.

    Total.—The solids in water, sewage, or other liquids; it includes the suspended solids (largely removable by filter paper) and the filterable solids (those which pass through filter paper).

Volatile.—The quantity of solids in water, sewage, or other liquid, lost on ignition of the total solids.

Squeegee.—(1) A device, generally with a soft rubber edge, used for dislodging and removing deposited sewage solids from the walls and bottoms of sedimentation tanks. (2) The metal blades attached to the lower arms of a clarifier mechanism to move the sludge along the tank bottom.

Stability.—The ability of any substance, such as sewage, effluent, or digested sludge, to resist putrefaction. It is the antonym of putrescibility.

Standard Methods.—Methods of analysis of water, sewage, and sludge approved by a Joint Committee of the American Public Health Association. American Water Works Association, and Federation of Sewage Works Associations.

Stator.—The stationary member of an electric generator or motor.

Sterilization.—The destruction of all living organisms, ordinarily through the agency of heat or of some chemical.

T

Tank.—A circular or rectangular vessel.

    Detritus.—A detention chamber larger than a grit chamber, usually with provision for removing the sediment without interrupting the flow of sewage. A settling tank of short detention period designed, primarily, to remove heavy settleable solids.

    Final Settling.—A tank through which the effluent from a trickling filter, or aeration or contact aeration tank flows for the purpose of removing the settleable solids.

    Flocculating.—A tank used for the formation of floc by the agitation of liquids.

    Imhoff.—A deep two-storied sewage tank originally patented by Karl Imhoff. consisting of an upper or continuous flow sedimentation chamber and a lower or sludge-digestion chamber. The floor of the upper chamber slopes steeply to trapped slots, through which solids may slide into the lower chamber. The lower chamber receives no fresh sewage directly, but is provided with gas vents and with means for drawing digested sludge from near the bottom.

    Primary Settling.—The first settling tank through which sewage is passed in a treatment works.

    Secondary.—A tank following a trickling filter or activated sludge aeration chamber.

    Sedimentation.—A tank or basin. in which water, sewage, or other liquid containing settleable solids, is retained for a sufficient time, and in which the velocity of flow is sufficiently low, to remove by gravity a part of the suspended matter. Usually, in sewage treatment, the detention period is short enough to avoid anaerobic decomposition. Also termed Settling or Subsidence Tank.

    Septic.—A single-story settling tank in which the settled sludge is in immediate contact with the sewage flowing through the tank, while the organic solids are decomposed by anaerobic bacterial action.

    Sludge-Digestion--See Digester.

Thickener, Sludge.—A type of sedimentation tank in which the sludge is permitted to settle, usually equipped with scrapers traveling along the bottom of the tank which push the settled sludge to a sump, from which it is removed by gravity or by pumping.

Treatment.—Any definite process for modifying the state of matter.

    Preliminary.—The conditioning of an industrial waste at its source prior 'to discharge, to remove or to neutralize substances injurious to sewers and treatment processes or to effect a partial reduction in load on the treatment process. In the treatment process, unit operations which prepare the liquor for subsequent major operations.

Primary.—The first major (sometimes the only) treatment in a sewage treatment works, usually sedimentation. The removal of a high percentage of suspended matter but little or no colloidal and dissolved matter.

Secondary.—The treatment of sewage by biological methods after primary treatment by sedimentation.

Sewage.—Any artificial process to which sewage is subjected in order to remove or alter its objectional constituents and thus to render it less offensive or dangerous.

Trap, Flame.—A device containing a fine metal gauze placed in a gas pipe, which prevents a flame from traveling back in the pipe and causing an explosion. See Arrester, Flame.

V

Venturi Meter.—A meter for measuring flow of water or other fluid through closed conduits or pipes, consisting of a Venturi tube and one of several proprietary forms of flow registering devices. The device was developed as a measuring device and patented by Clemens Herschel.

W

Waste Stabilization Pond.—Any pond, natural or artificial, receiving raw or partially treated sewage or waste, in which stabilization occurs due to sunlight, air, and microorganisms.

Water, Potable.—Water which does not contain objectionable pollution, contamination, minerals, or infection, and is considered satisfactory for domestic consumption.

Weir.—A dam with an edge or notch, sometimes arranged for measuring liquid flow.

    Effluent—A weir at the outflow end of a sedimentation basin or other hydraulic structure.

    Influent—A weir at the inflow end of a sedimentation basin.

    Rectangular.—A weir whose notch is rectangular in shape.

    Triangular.—A weir whose notch is triangular in shape, usually used to measure very small flows. Also called a V-notch.

    Peripheral.—The outlet weir in a circular settling tank, extending around the inside of its circumference and over which the effluent discharges.

    Rate.—See Loading, Weir.

Z

Zooglea.—A jelly-like matrix developed by bacteria, associated with growths in oxidizing beds.